D0215585

THE CREATIVE CONNECTION

Oversize
HF
5825
.W533
1982

THE CREATIVE CONNECTION

ADVERTISING COPYWRITING AND IDEA VISUALIZATION

DR. ARTHUR A. WINTERS

Professor and Chairman
Advertising and Communications
Fashion Institute of Technology
State University of New York

PROF. SHIRLEY F. MILTON

Advertising and Communications
Fashion Institute of Technology
State University of New York

VISUALIZED BY
JOSEPH GIANO

FAIRCHILD PUBLICATIONS

NEW YORK

DEDICATION

To the creative connection of advertisers and their advertising agencies whose work is featured in this book. Their advertisements were selected for students of copywriting and idea visualization as examples of effective communication.

Copyright © 1982 by Fairchild Publications
Division of Capital Cities Media, Inc.

All rights reserved. No part of this book may be reproduced in any form without permission in writing from the publisher, except by a reviewer who wishes to quote passages in connection with a review written for inclusion in a magazine or newspaper.

Standard Book Number: 87005-316-7

Library of Congress Catalog Card Number: 81-70523

Printed in the United States of America

CONTENTS

SOUTHERN UTAH STATE COLLEGE LIBRARY

SOUTHERN UTAH STATE COLLEGE LIBRARY

7. BROADCAST COPYWRITING FOR RADIO AND TELEVISION ———— 81

8. ADVERTISING COPY FOR OTHER MEDIA ———— 101

PREFACE

It is a common cliché to say we are bombarded by advertising when we mean we are the targets of advertising *copy* and *visuals* (art and graphics that speak "nonverbally"). Some may argue this point, but it can be said that copy is the "mind" of advertising, and visualization is its "heart and soul."

The "creative connection" is our design of a process to create more effective communication through a combination of verbal and visual thinking. This approach does not continue the tiresome verbal-versus-visual argument, but explores the value of verbal/visual synthesis.

A way that advertising and communications practitioners do this is by *thumbnailing* and *first roughs,* techniques that communicate verbal and visual concepts to each other, *and* their clients. The words and impressions we hear from the radio in the morning, the commercials that we see and hear from the TV set, the advertisements that "show and tell" in newspapers and magazines, the verbal and visual messages we receive in direct mail, the slogans and faces on billboards, the information and graphics on the package or can of food we buy—the impact of all of these comes to us through words and symbols which are working together to send the same message.

What is advertising? What is copy? What is a visual? Can we learn to become copywriters? Can we learn to use our visual perceptions to add impact to our words? *How* do we do it? These are a few of the questions that this book hopes to answer, in some practical measure, in the pages that follow. We will use "VIZTHINKS" (rough graphics in the form of thumbnails, first roughs, and storyboards) throughout the book to provide the copywriter with exercises to develop visual skills.

The opening pages will cover a discussion of advertising's function in the distribution of goods and services; in brief, its role in marketing and merchandising. Thereafter, we will explore, in detail, the task of the copywriter who must visualize and of the visualizer who should be able to come up with words that work with his graphics. The importance of the copywriter who has the ability to think visually in the initiation of advertising concepts, as well as in the handling of day-to-day copy assignments, will be examined thoroughly. The importance of the visualizer who can suggest a concept or approach will be a part of the vizthinks minicourse included in our discussion of idea visualization.

Other aspects of advertising, however, have been included with much less detail—"in the round" so to speak. Each, however, has been treated from the "copywriter-as-visualizer" point-of-view and as they may become part of the responsibility of the copywriter. Some of these phases are: client contact; market research; some media planning and selection; and certain layout, art, and production problems. Actual costs of advertising are not included, since advertising accounting almost never falls into the creative connection. On the other hand, awareness of the costs of media and advertising production—as they may become part of the copywriter's responsibility in a planning phase—can be a valuable asset. This book does, therefore, discuss briefly the kinds of costs that a copywriter/visualizer must think of in campaign planning, or in the stipulation of one kind of advertising medium and media production over another.

It is recommended that constant reference be made to analyses of advertising copy and visuals as they appear daily on television, radio, in newspapers, and at regular intervals in magazines. All of this advertising makes a vital "work manual" which brings to life the guidelines and recommendations of this book.

Copywriting is an exciting profession! Copywriters who do more than just put words together can use visual thinking to make the creative connection necessary to attain more dynamic copy concepts. The copy concept relies on the verbal/visual connection. It is to be hoped that many of the vizthinks, thumbnails, first roughs, and storyboards in this book will give rise to lively discussion.

Copywriting is also a highly controversial, fluid, changing profession, changing in style of expression, in appearance. One rule remains firm: Effective copywriting and copy concepts must sell or influence the sale of products or services or ideas.

In a profession where there is more art than science, no set of rules can guarantee success in writing copy that sells. Thus, the real aim of this book is the writing of more effective copy by making the creative connection between the verbal and the visual.

One note here about our writing style: Milton (female) and Winters (male) have had many collaborations as practitioners, teachers, and writers. We have no personal problems with the use of "he" and "she." We have agreed to interchange these pronouns throughout in order to avoid any accusations of sexism.

New York, 1982   Shirley F. Milton

                                                 Arthur A. Winters

ACKNOWLEDGMENTS

The authors wish to acknowledge indebtedness to our colleagues in the Advertising and Communications Department of the Fashion Institute of Technology and business clients who, over the years, contributed to our experience, and to the authors of many excellent texts in advertising, copy, and communications. A personal acknowledgment is due our students who allowed *us* to learn what it is to "teach" copywriting and idea visualization, and who understood our motives finally when they came to know the "blue-pencil" value of a tough, demanding, and supportive editor.

A special debt of gratitude is owed to Paul Pinson, whose vision and talent produced a "Copywriters' Art Course" in the pages of *Advertising Age* (circa 1956). His series on visual thinking has been used by the authors as an inspiration for this book and a tool through their many years of teaching copywriting and idea visualization. Through its remarkable reporting, the pages of *Advertising Age* have rendered invaluable service not only to the advertiser and communicator, but to the teacher and student as well.

The authors also wish to acknowledge the talents and efforts needed for the publication of this book: Angelo J. Virgona, editor; Walter Lindell, production manager; and Elaine Golt Gongora, book designer.

1
WHAT IS THE CREATIVE CONNECTION?

The "creative connection" is a blending of verbal and visual thinking needed for advertising copy and graphic idea visualization. The creative group in the marketing/merchandising/advertising team are those who can come up with sound ideas that contain unique selling propositions (USP's).[1] In this application of idea visualization, there must be one overriding principle: No matter what copy has to be written—and a later chapter will discuss advertising objectives of many kinds—the visual must convey to the "see-er" the same idea, the same concept that was in the mind of the copywriter.

It would not be wrong to say that despite the power of words, and not detracting from that power, the essence of the writer's message must be crystallized in the visual. The picture must convey the words, and the words produce a picture.

THE "MIND, HEART AND SOUL" OF ADVERTISING

There always ought to be a single "big idea" behind any campaign or any single advertisement in a campaign. A recent television commercial for Pampers disposable diapers wanted to make the main selling point that they keep the baby *dry*. Dry, dry, dry—the word is repeated. But how is the *idea of dryness* conveyed? Water is poured onto both a quilted Pampers and an unquilted Pampers. Blotters are then placed on both diapers, and babies are placed on the blotters. When the babies are lifted off the blotters, the blotter on the quilted Pampers is twice as dry. An important selling point is the quilted nature of the product. This was shown by a sewing machine foot which at one and the same time spells out and puffily quilts the letters "Q-U-I-L-T-E-D" right into the diaper material before the viewer's eyes! (See Figure 1-8 on page 11.)

Thus, the visual *shows* the main idea and its most important components. "Show" is better than "tell"; but the two together are best.

THE MESSAGE IS "SHOW AND TELL"

A powerful visualization, which conveys to the viewer or reader exactly what the advertiser had in mind, can even change its product appeals and create a *new* target audience! Famous in advertising history (and just again, early in 1979, called the "best campaign of the year") is the visual expression of the decision made years ago by the marketers of Marlboro Cigarettes to initiate a new he-man image for the brand. First, the agency used the visual signature of a military insignia tattooed on a rugged, masculine hand holding a Marlboro. This said exactly what the company and agency wanted: Marlboro cigarettes appeal to a masculine figure,

[1]Rosser Reeves, *Reality in Advertising* (New York: Alfred A. Knopf, Inc., 1961). Reeves named specific product difference the "unique selling proposition," the USP.

Warning: The Surgeon General Has Determined That Cigarette Smoking Is Dangerous to Your Health.

Figure 1-1. This is a different Marlboro customer—he is now associated with a popular part of American history—the cowboy. "Marlboro Country" is what many Americans, male *and* female would like to think epitomizes the beauty and "flavor" of our nation. Do you think that the associations of pure, clean, fresh, wide-open spaces are effective ones for a cigarette?

and that type of man will want to smoke a Marlboro. The old positioning and image for Marlboro had been as a woman's cigarette. The tattoo was, at the time, wholly a "macho" symbol—certainly with no *conscious* appeal for women. Who remembers the words? The visual and the brand name carried the total message.

When that message was firmly established, Marlboro moved into the campaign they still use: first, in television commercials (before

Come to Marlboro Country.

Marlboro Lights, Longhorn 100's, and famous Marlboro Red—you get a lot to like.

the ban[2]) and, now, in print. Show 'em and tell 'em—Marlboro Country! So strong was the impact, that people who were and are anticigarette smoking, nevertheless were reported to be looking at the commercials and then at the print advertisements for the beauty of the Western Rockies and the appropriateness of the action that takes place. The strength of the visual, originally meant for television, had proved equally strong in print. (See Figure 1-1.)

[2]Cigarette advertising on television was banned by an Act of Congress in 1971.

Figure 1-2. There is no doubt what the Rock of Gibraltar signifies. Some of our readers may be younger than Prudential's many years of using the popular cliché, "solid as the Rock of Gibraltar." This is the way Prudential Insurance has used a simile to say how "solid" their company is and how dependable their service. This visual symbol is so frequently associated with Prudential that for many the Rock is better known for this corporate connection than for its role in history.

One more example: For more generations than our readers may recall, one insurance company has established its identity through a visual that projected its inner concept of itself to the potential customer, Count the words it takes to say, "steady, solid, strong, reliable, dependable." It takes only one visual: "The Rock," clearly identifiable as the Rock of Gibraltar. It is no longer necessary to define it at all. Prudential Insurance Company simply provides the visual of the Rock. Rely on it! (See Figure 1-2.)

Let us be clear exactly what we are talking about in all of these examples. We are not talking about the way the illustrator drew the Prudential rock, nor how deftly the Marlboro tattoo was centered on a hand, nor how the hand was photographed, nor how the Marlboro man was placed against the Rockies and photographed. We are simply talking about an *idea* someone successfully visualized—to use a blotter for the dryness of a disposable diaper, a tattoo for rugged strength, the Rock of Gibraltar for reliability. A competent photographer can go out and, with sufficient direction, photograph the adorable baby, but the copywriter/idea visualizer must find the visual symbols that work with the words in order to communicate the message.

Beginning with a strong central idea, a campaign can convey any kind of message that product modification, time, or specific medium may dictate. The strength and continuity will lie in the creative connection of the verbal and the visual.

ADVERTISING AS A CATALYST TO MARKETING

In today's complex economy, the problems of research, development, and production are often easier to solve than the problems of promotion, distribution, and of ultimate consumption. The movement of produced goods from the factories and warehouses to the people who will use them represents just one side of the picture. What is needed is consumer demand, a desire to buy the goods that roll off the production lines. It is the job of advertising to stimulate that desire, to call the attention of consumers to a given product, to make them say, "We want *that!*"

In the largest possible sense, it is advertising that paves the way for personal selling or salesmanship. Advertising is mass communication (or nonpersonal selling) that can reach the greatest numbers of people with news about the product at the lowest possible cost. It is advertising's job to create the market for a product. It is advertising's job to "presell" products and help produce sales at the point-of-sale. The marketing process (see Figure 1-3) depends upon advertising and promotion for its dynamic energy.

THE MARKETING PROCESS

MARKET RESEARCH AND PRODUCT DEVELOPMENT

PRODUCTION

DISTRIBUTION
AT POINT-OF-SALE

THE CONSUMER

Figure 1-3. The *marketing process* is an overview of the marketing research, product research, design and development, production, pricing, distribution, and advertising and promotional activities involved in moving goods and services from primary producer to secondary manufacturer to ultimate consumer. The marketing process describes the integration of all these activities.

Figure 1-4. Brand names or trademarks (if they are registered as such) can be pictorially represented either symbolically (as in a logotype or "logo") or literally. Their importance for corporate and product identification is obvious. The brand name distinguishes a product from its competitors, often including verbal and/or visual connotations of main appeals and major selling points.

The group on the left represents a careful analysis of the nature of customer response. A highly recognized and accepted brand name and logo are considered part of a company's assets.

5

It is also advertising's job, in conjunction with the performance of the product itself, to implant a firm impression of a brand name on the customer, so that he or she asks for that product *by name* again and again. This is called *creating brand awareness,* and it eases the road for highly profitable repeat sales. In Figure 1-4, you see just a few of the great names advertising has helped you to know.

There are any number of specific roles that advertising plays and any number of goals it can achieve. The advertising functions required by the marketing process are served by copy and visuals which are effective enough to elicit response and action from customers on all market levels.

HOW DO YOU DEFINE ADVERTISING?

There are as many definitions of advertising as there have been writers of books on advertising and associations devoted to the practice of advertising. The American Marketing Association uses the definition of its own Committee, which it produced in 1948 and still considers valid in 1981.[3] It defines advertising as ". . . any paid form of nonpersonal presentation of ideas, goods, or services by an identified sponsor," to which we would add: for the purpose of influencing or inducing sales or active acceptance. Thus, advertising can be defined as any paid form of nonpersonal presentation of ideas, goods, or services placed in public media by an identified sponsor for the purpose of influencing or inducing sales or active acceptance.

THE IMPORTANCE OF COPY IN ADVERTISING

Within the definition just given, then, advertising copy can be understood as not only the verbal part, but the core of the selling message within any advertisement.

About a generation ago, there was a saying that every actor wanted "to play Hamlet." Today, we can amend that to "everyone in the advertising business thinks he can write copy." From the president of the agency to the junior account executive, everyone thinks he can write a better slogan, a better jingle, or a catchier headline than the professional copywriter.

Fortunately, copy is far more than a quick phrase. It has to do more than attract the eye or ear. It has to interest the mind, make it believe, and lead it to action. It has to sell—or presell.

This then, is the importance of the copy in the advertisement. It holds and conveys the selling message. Visuals work with copy to reinforce and contribute to the message, but it is the copy (or copy concept that results in visuals) that carries the major responsibility.

[3]AMA, *Journal of Marketing,* Vol. XIII, No. 2 (1948), p. 205.

Figure 1-5. The components of copy can be called the "blueprint" or plan of an advertisement. The headline is the stimulator, the attention-getter, the interest-arouser, the presenter of news, the promiser of benefits and satisfactions. The generation of desire and belief—the convincing—is done by the body copy. The body copy is responsible for closing the sale and persuading the customer to action.

When the objective of an advertisement is to sell a product or an idea, the body copy amplifies the headline with appeals and factual selling points, using various approaches that present "reasons to buy." When the objective is brand recognition, the headline, subheadline, slogan, and logo are the components of copy; body copy may or may not be present.

Consequently, it is the copywriter who is largely responsible for the pulling power of the advertisement.

A copywriter is a combination of journalist, novelist, and salesperson. Copywriters use their reportorial skill to research information and their creative writing skill to add excitement and appeal. Their purpose is to evoke response from the audience for the advertiser. As salesmen, they design selling messages that move products and/or create impressions.

It is the copywriter, as a general rule, who sets the theme of the advertisement, who has the task of examining buying motives, appeals, and approaches (all to be discussed later); and who has the responsibility for making choices among them. It is the copywriter, generally, who is the best trained to suggest the kind of graphic visualization that will effectively carry the message of the advertisement. Even in the case of ads with little or *no* words—there is a copy *idea* whose message can be graphically visualized. The copywriter, therefore, is usually the key figure in the creation of an advertisement or an advertising campaign.

Physically, in print advertising (advertisements appearing in direct mail, in a magazine, or in a newspaper), the copy represents all the material set in type. This includes the headline, the subhead-line (or "subhead"), the body copy (or "text"), slogan, corporate signature, address line, registration, or trademarks, and the like. Figure 1-5 indicates the components of copy in a print ad. Notice the parts of copy that are included in the body copy.

In a radio commercial, the copy represents the entire script. In a television commercial, the copy is the entire audio message that accompanies the video message. In addition, it is the copywriter's task, in both radio and TV, to indicate the sound effects, the background music needed, and for television, to indicate the action wanted as well. Figures 1-6 and 1-7 illustrate a typical *radio script* and a *television storyboard*. Figure 1-8 is a reproduction of a photo storyboard taken from the completed television commercial.

```
RADIO COPY    DANCER-FITZGERALD-SAMPLE, INC.


         CLIENT:  L'EGGS                          TYPE:  :60


         PRODUCT  SHEER ENERGY          SHOW & DATE:

     TRAFFIC NO.                             SUBJECT:  "SHEERNESS"


     DATE TYPED:


     _____


       SINGERS:

       Every day you
       walk, run and bend and stand and stoop and stretch,
       your legs don't get much chance to rest,

       your legs do a lotta nice things for you,
       woncha do something nice for your legs.

       Sheer Energy
       the pantyhose that massages your legs all day
       Sheer Energy
       the pantyhose that refreshes each step of the way.

       WOMAN:

       Sheer Energy does a whole lot more for your legs than refresh em.

       It makes them look beautiful, too.  That's because Sheer Energy's made

       with a sheer, smooth yarn.  So your legs can look as good as they feel.

       Do something nice for your legs.  Give 'em Sheer Energy Pantyhose.

       Now you can get 'em in queensize.

       SINGERS:

       Your legs do a lotta nice things for you,
       woncha do something nice for your legs.

       Sheer Energy!


     CLIENT'S O.K. _____ DATE _____
```

Figure 1-6. *The radio commercial script:* The script indicates the entire audio message, voices, sound effects, music. Radio copy should employ a relaxed conversational style that is representative of the language used by the target audience — with its typical contractions, conversational tempos, and phrasings. The opening should be an "interrupter"— using attention-compelling, "lend-me-your-ears" words. The closing should be emphatic with a call to action and with the product name repeated.

Figure 1-7. *The television commercial storyboard:* The storyboard is designed to dramatize the full effect of the sight and sounds of a television commercial. It is pretty difficult to present the full impact of exciting camera work, perfect casting, and a brilliant sound track. However, it is the job of these series of visuals and the copy that they accompany to visualize what could be a great commercial — with all of the drama that its characters, settings, dialogue, voiceovers, music, and sound effects combine to offer.

1. (MUSIC UP & UNDER)

2. THE STORE NAME'S CHRISTMAS BOOK OF IDEAS

3. HAS AN EXCITING SELECTION OF BEAUTIFUL TOPS FOR GIFT GIVING

4. SENSUOUS, SOFT POLYESTER BLOUSES WITH MATCHING SCARVES

5. GIVE HER THE LUXURIOUS LOOK OF SILK...

6. ...ONLY 19 AND 20 DOLLARS.

7. OR FIND A STYLISH WRAP-AROUND SWEATER...

8. ...TO KEEP HER SNUG THIS WINTER JUST 33 DOLLARS.

9. AND SPORTY PULLOVER SWEATERS...

10. ...FOR 16 and 19 DOLLARS.

11. FROM YOUR EXCITING SELECTION OF BEAUTIFUL TOPS FOR GIFT GIVING --

12. IN OUR CHRISTMAS BOOK OF IDEAS AT STORE NAME.

Figure 1-8. *The photo storyboard:* This is a black-and-white reproduction of the 30-second television commercial for Pampers, which visualized its important "quilted" selling point.

B&B

BENTON & BOWLES
909 THIRD AVENUE
NEW YORK, N.Y.
(212) 758-6200

Client: **PROCTER & GAMBLE CO.**
Product: **PAMPERS PE**
Length: **30 SECONDS (PGPM 9193)**
Title: **"DOLLHOUSE III REV./FP/CC"**

1. EXPERIENCED WOMAN: Now this doll house is an antique. INEXPERIENCED WOMAN: How can you tell?

2. EXPERIENCED WOMAN: No Pampers!

3. INEXPERIENCED WOMAN: Pampers? I was thinking of trying a newer brand.

4. EXPERIENCED WOMAN: Why? Dryness is what quilted Pampers are all about.

5. Pampers Susan wore, when she was born, were good. But these quilted Pampers stay twice as dry.

6. INEXPERIENCED WOMAN: Twice as dry?

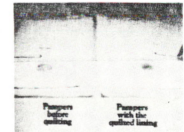

7. EXPERIENCED WOMAN: Sure. Wet both and wait.

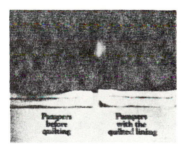

8. Quilted Pampers stay

9. twice as dry. And drier's gotta

10. feel better. INEXPERIENCED WOMAN: Sure does. EXPERIENCED WOMAN: And that advice is on the house. (LAUGHTER)

11. ANNCR: (VO) Quilted Pampers stay twice as dry

12. as before.

Twice as dry.

© 1980, Procter & Gamble. Reproduced with permission.

WHAT IS A COPYWRITER?

How does a clever headline or paragraph turn into a hard-selling message that moves goods off shelves, clears jeans off the racks, or fills up one airplane after another? Does it sound like magic? It is magic in a sense, and has never failed to fascinate those who have made it their business, profession, and livelihood.

Copywriters work hard to create this magic: a handful of words to motivate masses of people to respond. When copywriters are truly effective and have reached the top levels of their field, they are very well paid—and they earn every dollar.

EDUCATION AND EXPERIENCE

For one thing, their education, which may stretch back into freshman English and sophomore Psychology, never stops—not for a minute. They have a love for and a knack with words and language. Their training, which may likewise go back to school summers with door-to-door selling, or over-the-counter selling, or earning money at the checkout counter, never ends. They are always "in the marketplace," always listening, testing, curious about what is new, "people-watching" to see what is accepted or rejected. The research aspect of the creative connection never stops.

They are always critical of products or performance, measuring promise against actual use, and critical, too, of themselves. There is no new art form, no new entertainment, no new gadget that is unimportant to a good copywriter.

Copywriters like products; they like people; they like words. They study people in their reactions to new ideas as well as to new products and to new means of communication.

A copywriter is a combination of a hard-headed entrepreneur looking at her own product and at the competition's, and of a magician weaving a selling spell around a commodity. The copywriter, in a sense, is selling with her typewriter. But, selling with copy is more challenging than personal selling at the point-of-sale. Getting action from an unseen audience of thousands to millions is not the same as the two-way communication between a salesperson and a customer.

Thus, the job of the copywriter is to create a fundamentally sound selling idea, then to write the words (whether for newspaper, magazine, catalog, radio, television, or box label) that will communicate the selling idea to the potential customer in terms that will motivate her to buy.

There are four main areas where copywriters can be found:

1. In an advertising agency
2. In the advertising department of a retail organization

(department store, central buying office, chain headquarters, mail order firm, etc.).

3. In the advertising department of a producer of primary materials or finished products (textile firm, electronics manufacturer, book publisher, etc.).

4. In the promotion department of an organization disseminating ideas as opposed to products (as a trade association, a foundation, a publication, a television station, a political party, etc.).

The background necessary for various copywriting jobs varies as widely as the jobs themselves, but certainly must include some of the attributes already touched on: an interest and facility in handling words, an ear for the speech of today, an intense interest in people, a deep understanding of basic motivation, and finally, some experience in selling.

COPYWRITING DIFFERS FROM REPORTING AND "CREATIVE" FORMS

When we talk of *advertising copy,* we are using a term that immediately separates this kind of writing from that necessary for reporting or for the writing of narrative or any "creative" form. Advertising copy or copywriting has a very specific and strong purpose: to present concepts about an idea, service, a product, or an institution which first of all will win *acceptance for the concept.* The concept may be about a political idea or about an auto repair service or about a product such as panty hose made of a fabric that utilizes a new synthetic fiber. After the concept has been accepted by the reader or listener, then copy goes on to promote and finally to sell. At times, copy has been called "salesmanship in print," and in the best sense of the phrase, it is an apt description.

In reporting, the writing seeks to inform. The more objective the reporting, the more certainly information becomes the goal. In creative writing, there can be some argument. Is it not correct to say that the objective of creative writing is largely self-expression, to put into words one's emotions, impressions, and feelings?

The style of writing for each of these differs. Reporting requires straightforward recital of facts in an order that places the most important of these first. Creative writing calls for not one style, but any style that satisfies the inner need to communicate ideas and emotions.

The style of writing advertising copy, whatever approach is taken, must be quick and to the point and must state clearly what benefits the subject of the copy can offer. It should not trail off into a vacuum, but rather should close with some kind of "call for

*Du Pont certification mark for fabrics meeting its standards. Du Pont makes fibers, not fabrics or fashions.

Qiana* excites

Miss Dior's P.M. pj. So luxurious you'd never suspect it's practical.

Fashion of *Qiana** fabric shown available at Garfinckels and other fine stores.

DU PONT
REG. U.S. PAT. & TM OFF

action." Here is one type of writing where clarity and simplicity are paramount.

Most successful copywriters prefer to use full sentences, but it is possible to write good copy where parts of the sentences may be eliminated while the total sense can still be understood. The dash (—) and three dot (. . .) systems are "horrors" of style to some, but they can be used, and used well, if the sense calls for an extension of thought. In other words, style for a copywriter is extremely flexible, so long as basic rules for good sentence structure, correct phrasing, and accurate punctuation are followed.

KINDS OF ADVERTISING COPY

Based upon the market level[4] of the advertiser, copy uses levels of selling or promotion for three important classifications and three subgroups. The three major classifications are:

1. *National advertising*—wherein the primary producer or secondary manufacturer advertises to the *ultimate consumer*. (In this case, "producer" refers to industrial products or raw materials. "Manufacturer" refers to finished products.) This may include Du Pont's advertising for "Qiana" in *Vogue* (see Figure 2-1), Chevrolet's advertising in publications like *Newsweek*, in newspapers, and on television; or it may include a designer-manufacturer like Calvin Klein advertising in *The New York Times Magazine*, or on network television.

2. *Retail advertising*—wherein a local retail store, whatever its type or size, advertises to its own customer, again the ultimate consumer. Retail advertising is found most frequently in local newspapers, on radio and local television stations; but it may also crop up in campaigns in nationally distributed publications, like Lord & Taylor's and Saks Fifth Avenue's advertisements in *Glamour* or *Vogue*, Neiman Marcus' advertisements in *The New Yorker*, or Sears' advertisements in *Family Circle*, as well as on network television. (See Figure 2-2.)

3. *Trade advertising*—covers the advertising of products by the producer to other producers or to the manufacturer, and by the manufacturer to the retailer. (Some practitioners use "industrial" to describe advertising from the producer of raw materials or equipment to the manufacturer, as in [a] on page 22.) Advertising of this kind will be found in trade papers (business publications) in every field of industry. (See Figure 2-3.)

[4]Market level: Producers of industrial products or raw materials are *primary* resources; manufacturers of finished products are *secondary* resources; distributors of merchandise are *dealers* or *retailers*.

focus America: **Charleston**

We welcome you to a celebration
of this nostalgic and enchanted city.
Time, tradition and civilization—
pure Charleston, pure Lord & Taylor

Our exclusive
Gloria Sachs gingham silks
embrace the
Charleston mood we're in.

Blouse 150.00 Skirt 220.00
Cummerbund 40.00 Pale pink, 4 to 12.
Designer Sportswear, Third Floor,
Lord & Taylor, Fifth Avenue

The Charleston palmetto
symbolizes the special feeling
of this magical city, where
palmetto trees abound
amid beautiful historic architecture.

VOGUE, April, 1981

Figure 2-2. Lord & Taylor's advertising to the consumer emphasizes the American designer as a strong statement of their fashion philosophy and authority as a retailer with national prominence. This ad is part of a series in a campaign whose theme is "focus America"— in this case, the city of Charleston, South Carolina. The Gloria Sachs designs "embrace the mood" of Charleston and are presented with many store-wide special events, which also feature merchandise from other departments. The merchandise featured in these events has been developed to dramatize the "special feeling of this magical city."

THE SELF-MADE WOMAN.
SHE'S LIVING BETTER ALL THE TIME.

A new generation of women is leading the way to the future. And America is following.

Because today's woman is not satisfied with yesterday's solutions to today's challenges.

She's asking the tough questions. And SELF is answering them. Because there's nothing superficial about today's new woman or her favorite magazine. So each month. SELF gives her the in-depth information she wants on health, beauty, making money and making big decisions. And it is this unique editorial content that has made SELF the leading authority on today's life and lifestyles, finance and fashion, food and fun.

The SELF-made woman. She's getting better and living better every day. Making more and spending more on everything from lipsticks to luxury vacations. And she's buying SELF. The magazine that's making it because she is.

SELF: The first word in Self-Improvement for over 3,000,000 women.

© 1981 The Condé Nast Publications, Inc.
A Member of The Condé Nast Package.

Figure 2-3. The magazine of Condé Nast Publications for "the SELF-made woman" is the subject of this trade advertisement from *Marketing Communications* (a magazine whose audience is the marketing/advertising/promotion practitioner). The copy is directed to the "advertising trade," specifically the target group of media planners and buyers.

What do you think is the ad's appeal to this special audience of media professionals? How do its copy and visualization differ from national and retail advertising to the consumer?

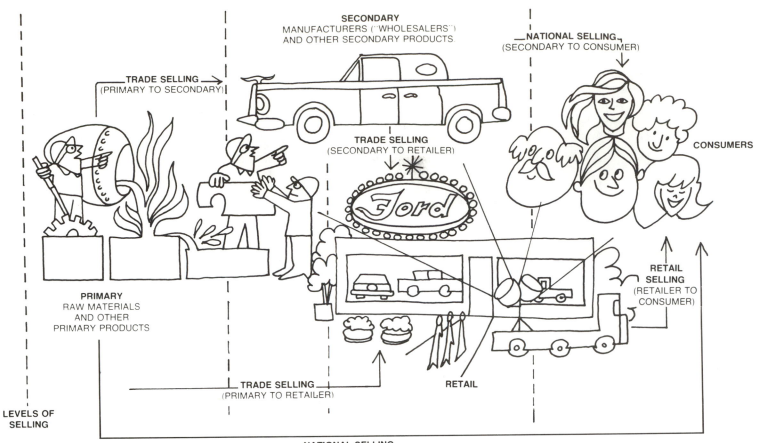

THE MARKET LEVELS AND THE LEVELS OF SELLING

SECONDARY
MANUFACTURERS ("WHOLESALERS")
AND OTHER SECONDARY PRODUCTS

NATIONAL SELLING
(SECONDARY TO CONSUMER)

TRADE SELLING
(PRIMARY TO SECONDARY)

TRADE SELLING
(SECONDARY TO RETAILER)

CONSUMERS

PRIMARY
RAW MATERIALS
AND OTHER
PRIMARY PRODUCTS

RETAIL
SELLING
(RETAILER TO
CONSUMER)

LEVELS OF
SELLING

TRADE SELLING
(PRIMARY TO RETAILER)

RETAIL

NATIONAL SELLING
(PRIMARY TO CONSUMER)

Figure 2-4. *The market levels and the levels of selling:* This *pictogram* is a visualization of the market levels, *primary, secondary,* and *retail,* which are the vertical components of an industry. Marketing relies on selling to audiences among these levels *and* to the ultimate consumer. The levels of selling, *national, trade,* and *retail,* describe the marketing communications (advertising and promotion) that occur between the sender of a promotional message and the receiver.

Refer to the arrows, which indicate the levels of selling, and to the chart (Figure 2-5), which presents the same process in a different kind of graphic visualization.

Which audience would you say gets the most "attention"? The trade? The consumer?

Sender	Receiver	Level of Selling
Producer-Manufacturer	Consumer	National
Same As Above	"Each Other" Retailer/ Retail Buyer	Trade
Retailer	Consumer	Retail

Figure 2-5. The market levels and the levels of selling.

When is a small copier a big mistake?

Now don't misunderstand.

We have nothing against small copiers. We happen to make some of the best in the business.

It's just that small copiers are built for small work loads. Overwork them and you'll get gray, streaked copies, too many breakdowns, and too many visits from the repairman.

But there's a bigger small copier built to answer the demands of a growing business.

The Minolta EP520.

It takes options like a document-feeder and sorter to handle work overloads. Or you can get a counter to keep track of the copies you've made.

Minolta's exclusive micro-toning system assures you rich contrasts and crisp, clear copies. Edge to edge, and corner to corner. On any kind of paper up to 11"x17".

It even has a special self-diagnostic system that tells you when it needs service. And what kind of service it needs.

So, if you've underestimated the capacity of your copier, get the Minolta EP520.

A big business can afford to make a few mistakes. A small business can't.

To avoid mistakes, call toll-free 800-526-5256. In N.J., call 201-797-7808. For your authorized Minolta dealer, look for our trademark in the Yellow Pages. ©1981 Minolta Corporation

The EP 520. Your Next Copier.

MINOLTA

Figure 2-6. This ad from Minolta was run in *Fortune* magazine. Its audience is obviously the executives (or purchasing agents) who buy such equipment for their own use in the operation of their businesses. The harried individual in the photograph may be the art director's visualization of a purchasing agent. How do the copy appeals, selling points, and approach in this compare to the appeals in trade advertising? In national and retail advertising?

Bentyl®

(dicyclomine hydrochloride USP)
Capsules, Tablets, Syrup, Injection
AVAILABLE ONLY ON PRESCRIPTION
Brief Summary

INDICATIONS
Based on a review of this drug by the National Academy of Sciences—National Research Council and/or other information, FDA has classified the following indications as "probably" effective:
For the treatment of functional bowel/irritable bowel syndrome (irritable colon, spastic colon, mucous colitis) and acute enterocolitis.
THESE FUNCTIONAL DISORDERS ARE OFTEN RELIEVED BY VARYING COMBINATIONS OF SEDATIVE, REASSURANCE, PHYSICIAN INTEREST, AMELIORATION OF ENVIRONMENTAL FACTORS.
For use in the treatment of infant colic (syrup).
Final classification of the less-than-effective indications requires further investigation.

CONTRAINDICATIONS: Obstructive uropathy (for example, bladder neck obstruction due to prostatic hypertrophy); obstructive disease of the gastrointestinal tract (as in achalasia, pyloroduodenal stenosis); paralytic ileus, intestinal atony of the elderly or debilitated patient; unstable cardiovascular status in acute hemorrhage; severe ulcerative colitis; toxic megacolon complicating ulcerative colitis; myasthenia gravis.

WARNINGS: In the presence of a high environmental temperature, heat prostration can occur with drug use (fever and heat stroke due to decreased sweating). Diarrhea may be an early symptom of incomplete intestinal obstruction, especially in patients with ileostomy or colostomy. In this instance treatment with this drug would be inappropriate and possibly harmful. Bentyl may produce drowsiness or blurred vision. In this event, the patient should be warned not to engage in activities requiring mental alertness such as operating a motor vehicle or other machinery or perform hazardous work while taking this drug. There are rare reports of infants, 6 weeks of age and under, administered dicyclomine hydrochloride syrup, who have evidenced respiratory symptoms (breathing difficulty, shortness of breath, breathlessness, respiratory collapse, apnea), as well as seizures, syncope, asphyxia, pulse rate fluctuations, muscular hypotonia, and coma. The above symptoms have occurred within minutes of ingestion and lasted 20 to 30 minutes. The timing and nature of the reactions suggest that they were a consequence of local irritation and/or aspiration rather than a direct pharmacologic effect. No known deaths or permanent adverse effects have been reported. Bentyl syrup should be used with caution in this age group.

PRECAUTIONS: Although studies have failed to demonstrate adverse effects of dicyclomine hydrochloride in glaucoma or in patients with prostatic hypertrophy, it should be prescribed with caution in patients known to have or suspected of having glaucoma or prostatic hypertrophy.
Use with caution in patients with:
Autonomic neuropathy. Hepatic or renal disease. Ulcerative colitis. Large doses may suppress intestinal motility to the point of producing a paralytic ileus and the use of this drug may precipitate or aggravate the serious complication of toxic megacolon.
Hyperthyroidism, coronary heart disease, congestive heart failure, cardiac arrhythmias, and hypertension.
Hiatal hernia associated with reflux esophagitis since anticholinergic drugs may aggravate this condition.
Do not rely on the use of the drug in the presence of complication of biliary tract disease. Investigate any tachycardia before giving anticholinergic (atropine-like) drugs since they may increase the heart rate. With overdosage, a curare-like action may occur.

ADVERSE REACTIONS: Anticholinergics/antispasmodics produce certain effects which may be physiologic or toxic depending upon the individual patient's response. The physician must delineate these. Adverse reactions may include xerostomia; urinary hesitancy and retention; blurred vision and tachycardia; palpitations; mydriasis; cycloplegia; increased ocular tension; loss of taste; headache; nervousness; drowsiness; weakness; dizziness; insomnia; nausea; vomiting; impotence; suppression of lactation; constipation; bloated feeling; severe allergic reaction or drug idiosyncrasies including anaphylaxis; urticaria and other dermal manifestations; some degree of mental confusion and/or excitement, especially in elderly persons; and decreased sweating. With the injectable form there may be a temporary sensation of lightheadedness and occasionally local irritation.

DOSAGE AND ADMINISTRATION: Dosage must be adjusted to individual patient's needs.
Usual Dosage
Bentyl 10 mg. capsule and syrup: *Adults:* 1 or 2 capsules or teaspoonfuls syrup three or four times daily. *Children:* 1 capsule or teaspoonful syrup three or four times daily. *Infants:* ½ teaspoonful syrup three or four times daily. (Dilute with equal volume of water.)
Bentyl 20 mg.: *Adults:* 1 tablet three or four times daily.
Bentyl Injection: *Adults:* 2 ml. (20 mg.) every four to six hours intramuscularly only.
NOT FOR INTRAVENOUS USE.

MANAGEMENT OF OVERDOSE: The signs and symptoms of overdose are headache, nausea, vomiting, blurred vision, dilated pupils, hot, dry skin, dizziness, dryness of the mouth, difficulty in swallowing, CNS stimulation. Treatment should consist of gastric lavage, emetics, and activated charcoal. Barbiturates may be used either orally or intramuscularly for sedation but they should not be used if Bentyl with Phenobarbital has been ingested. If indicated, parenteral cholinergic agents such as Urecholine® (bethanecol chloride USP) should be used.
Product Information as of July, 1980

Injectable dosage forms manufactured by
CONNAUGHT LABORATORIES, INC.
Swiftwater, Pennsylvania 18370 or
TAYLOR PHARMACAL COMPANY
Decatur, Illinois 62525 for
MERRELL-NATIONAL LABORATORIES
Division of Richardson-Merrell Inc.
Cincinnati, Ohio 45215, U.S.A.

Merrell   1-6707 (Y175C) MNQ-443R

Figure 2-7. Would you say that the copywriter and art director "teamed-up" in this professional ad to give their target audience — the physician — sympathy pains for the patient? It would certainly seem from this idea visualization that the concept of pain and distress is well communicated.

This kind of advertising is typical of professional journals. Notice that the dramatic presentation of what Merrell's "Bentyl" will help to control must be accompanied by the legally "prescribed" and technically specified *mandatories* listed in detail on the left side of the advertisement.

When painful spasm is the presenting symptom in the functional bowel/irritable bowel syndrome*...

Bentyl®
(dicyclomine hydrochloride USP)

10 mg. capsules, 20 mg. tablets,
10 mg./5 ml. syrup, 10 mg./ml. injection

helps control abnormal motor activity with minimal anticholinergic side effects†

*This drug has been classified "probably" effective in treating functional bowel/irritable bowel syndrome.
†See Warnings, Precautions and Adverse Reactions.
See adjacent page for prescribing information.

Merrell

Try leaving on a flight of fancy.

It's one thing to sit around and dream of faraway places. But when you decide to go, you've got to come up with a ticket. Wishing won't make it so. Saving will get you there.

One of the easiest, safest ways to save is to buy U.S. Savings Bonds through the Payroll Savings Plan. A little is taken out of each paycheck automatically. And the Bonds will eventually grow into a first-class ticket to anywhere.

Nothing is too far. Tahiti, London, Paris, Rome. Even a trip around the world. Or just a long vacation on a Caribbean island. Anywhere.

So go ahead, take a flight of fancy. Then start buying Bonds so you can take a fancy flight.

Take stock in America.

UNITED STATES SAVINGS BONDS

When you put part of your savings into U.S. Savings Bonds you're helping to build a brighter future for your country and for yourself.

A public service of this publication and The Advertising Council

Figure 2-8. Often the messages in nonproduct or "idea" advertising are delivered by this type of public service advertisement. These are considered the noncommercial "selling" of ideas that are in the public's interest.

The tiny symbol (logo) in the lower left corner is that of the Advertising Council—a group of creative advertising agency copywriters and art directors who contribute their talent to this and many other public service campaigns. "Smoky the Bear" is another example of a public service advertising campaign which has become one of the "immortals" in this nation's attempt to save our forests from fires. Notice, too, that the space for this public service ad was contributed by the publication.

The determination of levels of selling (or promotion) is one that who is the receiver (the audience). (See Figure 2-4, page 18.) Another way to reinforce this concept is through the chart in Figure 2-5 on page 18.

The three categories above are universally accepted—and in a large sense can cover all cases. For complete classification, however, it is as well to note here that the following three subgroups are also accepted by many practitioners:

(a) *Industrial advertising*—covers the advertising of commercial products, such as machinery, packaging, heavy equipment, and various raw materials which are expected to be sold to manufacturers for their own use in the production of their marketable products or services. The purchasing agent is preeminently the target of this advertising, which, like trade advertising, is generally found in the business and industrial publications of various fields. (See Figure 2-6, page 19.)

(b) *Professional advertising*—wherein the producers of materials prescribed by professionals for their clients or patients seek to influence these professionals to recommend the given product. Thus, drug manufacturers advertise to doctors, extolling their brands of medication over a rival's; building materials manufacturers advertise to architects and engineers to promote their own products over a competitor's. The normal place for this classification of advertising is in professional magazines, such as *Internal Medicine News* of Fairchild Publications. (See Figure 2-7, pages 20–21.)

(c) *Nonproduct or "idea" advertising*—wherein a group, a political party, a union, a philanthropy, etc., seeks to influence the thinking (and in many cases to win the contributions) of some portion of the general public. (See Figure 2-8.)

It is important, when faced with a copywriting assignment, to think through and to understand the classification of copy needed in terms of the level of selling or promotion. An analysis of the classification of copy should lead the copywriter to his next serious consideration: the *objectives* of the advertiser. This will follow as we begin to discuss the planning of a strategy.

PLANNING FOR ADVERTISING COPY STRATEGY

When a copywriter receives an assignment to write a piece of copy or to plan a campaign, there is a considerable amount of thinking to be done before the written copy emerges. In the previous pages, it has been indicated that the copywriter must recognize or determine the classification of advertising first of all. That is very often apparent to him even as early as accepting the job.

There are five elements that must be considered because they are all fundamental to the kind of copy you will write. They are the *basics for strategy planning;* to alter any one of them will be to call for a change in campaign strategy. They are fundamentals that will help to build your strategy. These five basics are:

1. The reputation (market position) of the client or organization sponsoring the advertisement—the *advertiser.*
2. The *product* or *idea* to be sold. (Here we would include both the selling features of a product as well as satisfactions and benefits to the potential user.)
3. The *target audience* (or highest potential customer) who is the most logical purchaser for that product. (After an analysis has been made about the product and the audience, we will be able to formulate *copy appeals.*)
4. The *objective* to be achieved by the given advertisement.
5. The *medium* (or media) through which the communication will pass from advertiser to audience.

THE ADVERTISER—WHAT YOU NEED TO KNOW ABOUT YOUR CLIENT

If you are the copywriter, what should you know about the advertiser? If you are employed in the advertising department of a retail store or of a corporation manufacturing primary or secondary products, it is assumed that you have already absorbed some of the atmosphere of the firm. You should know its business history, its share of market and stature in its own field, and the policies it has set for itself. You should research the development and the quality of the product, its market position, and the nature of the competition. More practically, you will know the full range of its selling area, its methods of distribution, its general price lines, and customer policies. This all has to do with the *marketing structure* of the business.

If you are a copywriter in an advertising agency, writing for a client, you will have to uncover much of the information outlined in the paragraph above, before you can get on with the writing itself.

The account executive in the agency should be of help. In many agencies, a request to see the client's plant, to talk with his advertising and marketing directors will be welcomed. Wherever possible, this is the way to do it. See for yourself. Your *own* research is valuable. "Good copy is 90 percent information and 10 percent communication."

Perhaps this is as good a place as any to urge tact in all client-contacts. For example, if the plant you visit is a complex one, with highly sophisticated equipment, accept all the plant rules and follow them. Keep your eyes open, observe, ask intelligent and pertinent questions. Do not criticize what you see and hear in your client-contacts; you can do a critical analysis in your head and talk to your typewriter later. No matter how much you prefer the competitor's product, remember that the competitor did not hire you. Your client did, however, when he hired your agency.

In the thinking of a conscientious and intelligent copywriter, there is no substitute for getting right in on the scene, for seeing the products made, for talking to the plant managers, for setting up a rapport with the advertising and marketing directors. On the other hand, there is no quicker way for an agency to lose an account than to send a copywriter out on client-contact whose one idea is to prove himself an expert in the production field, or one who has an ego problem where he must out-talk or appear to out-think the client. So, handle the situation smoothly and professionally. Make the first contact a good one, and you will have tapped a deep vein of valuable information.

Some or most of the following information is important for you, as the copywriter, to have about the advertiser:
1. What is the size of the firm? Its financial structure? Stature in its industry?
2. How old is it? Is it well-established or new?
3. What is the market share of its leading product?
4. What is its reputation? Does the reputation with customers match its own image of itself?
5. If it is a new firm, what are its goals and objectives?
6. What is its distribution pattern? Does it work with wholesalers or jobbers? Does it rely on regional distributors or manufacturer's representatives?
7. What is its marketing level?
8. Who are its customers?

Suggestion: Get your information from outside objective sources as well as the client's personnel. Try to distinguish between facts and gossip. Do not be misled by company "politics."

THE PRODUCT—RESEARCH COUNTS

The copywriter is next confronted with the product or line of products to be advertised. Again, there are questions to be asked and answered. It is a good idea to recall: "There are fewer dull products than there are dull copywriters!" The copywriter's goal is to obtain stimulating information which can be used to evoke audience response.

In marketing plans, there is often a budget for marketing research. Usually, however, by the time the product is ready for advertising, various types of research have been done. It is up to the copywriter, then, to review the research, and to study the reports. Since, in addition, the term "market" is used to describe a geographical area or a population group where sales opportunities exist, research might include studies of where the market is, what its demographic profile is, and what to expect of its psychographics.

There are many things a copywriter wants to know about a given product. With a little experience, each copywriter begins to formulate his own *product profile* which is his list of things to know about the product. But, to begin with, if the client is in the primary or secondary marketing levels where the product is either the equipment, the raw material, the supplies, or the manufactured article, the copywriter can gain a lot from talking to the manufacturer, the production manager, and the sales manager.

In a department store, the retail copywriter can study the buyer's request for advertising, can talk to the buyer, can and must examine the product itself. In addition, trade publications, trade associations, and libraries supply helpful information.

Here are some of the facts you will want to ascertain:

1. What are the design and performance characteristics of a given product?

2. What does it claim to do? Does the information supplied to you make certain claims? Check them out for yourself. If a new electric coffee maker claims to have a "brew-miser" that saves coffee, try it out and see how many cups of good coffee you get per measure. If an all-weather coat tag says it is soil and stain-resistant, take it home and check it for yourself. Above all, determine if the claim is valid.

3. How does "your product" differ from others on the market? Is it as good as any others, better, not so good?

4. How is it priced? Maybe a low price justifies an omission of a feature that another product possesses. Conversely, perhaps your product has additional features that make a higher price reasonable.

5. Try to find out its USP or unique selling proposition, its essential difference and superiority, something special that you can concentrate on in your copy.
6. Is this product of proved consumer appeal?
7. Is it a new product? If so, what customer wants or needs does it fill?
8. Where is it in its marketing life-span? Is it in the pioneering, the competitive, or the retentive stage?[5]
9. Very specifically, for retail copy, where is the product on the Merchandise-Acceptance Curve? (See Figure 3-1.)
10. Again, especially on the retail level, is it priced competitively?
11. Finally, it seems almost obvious to state that a copywriter must have the product in front of him, so that as he proceeds to the next stage, he can examine the tangible "goods" in his office, at his desk.

With as many as possible of these questions answered, the copywriter will then be able to draw up a list of selling points or product features. These may be defined as the characteristics of the design of the product or of its performance which when made known to the potential customer will cause him to want to buy the product or service.

The copywriter may find half a dozen or more qualities that are assets for that particular product. You may, in fact, wish to think of these selling points as "product benefits," ways in which the product can serve the consumer. In any event, you must study and restudy your list, then rearrange it so that the most exciting selling point or benefit, the one that has the most appeal to potential customers, is set up at top of the list. More products have been sold by stressing the benefit or satisfaction than describing the feature that provides it. "Sell the sizzle—not the steak."

At most, there should not be more than three important selling points stressed in the copy. If one does stand well ahead of the others, it can be called *dominant* or *keynote*. This determination will guide the copywriter when the time comes to write the copy.

THE TARGET AUDIENCE—GET A CUSTOMER PROFILE

The next consideration in building strategy is the customer. This is frequently called *discovering your target audience*, or *market targeting*, a process by which a company decides which market *segments* from a total population (market) to serve. Sometimes, under a strong marketing director, the advertiser will have completed a sound program of marketing research on its potential customers. If you are the copywriter working on such an account,

[5]Otto Kleppner, *Advertising Procedure*, 7th ed. (Englewood Cliffs, N.J.: Prentice-Hall, Inc., 1979), p. 52. Noting the progression of a product through consumer acceptance as "the Advertising Spiral," Kleppner named the first stage *pioneering*, when a product first comes into the market. The second stage occurs when many companies are producing examples of the same product. This is the *competitive* stage. Finally, as the product loses its novelty and excitement, it moves into the *retentive* stage. Most alert producers recognize this stage as threatening, and seek to send the product back into a pioneering stage, usually with some "new" improvement, which will build a wider or a new audience.

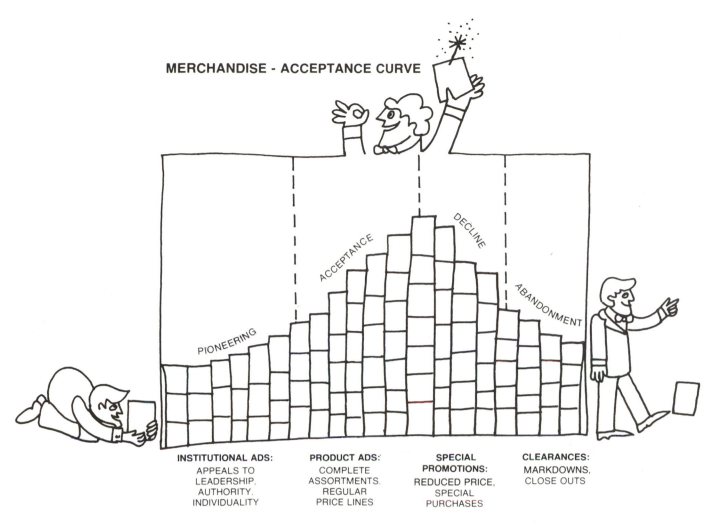

MERCHANDISE - ACCEPTANCE CURVE

PIONEERING · ACCEPTANCE · DECLINE · ABANDONMENT

INSTITUTIONAL ADS:
APPEALS TO
LEADERSHIP,
AUTHORITY,
INDIVIDUALITY

PRODUCT ADS:
COMPLETE
ASSORTMENTS,
REGULAR
PRICE LINES

**SPECIAL
PROMOTIONS:**
REDUCED PRICE,
SPECIAL
PURCHASES

CLEARANCES:
MARKDOWNS,
CLOSE OUTS

you may have an immediate source of valuable information.

The copywriter's research on the advertiser, its competition, the market, and the product should in any event lead him to know who his customer is. The closer the copywriter can come to developing an accurate *audience profile* of the customer from the advertiser's research, media research data, and his own observations and intuition, the better the results will be. An audience profile is the result of "defining" an audience as a *market segment*. The profile consists of objective and subjective characteristics of an "individual" that could represent all of the population of the segment target group. It is an attempt to describe in specific demographic and psychographic terms the background and lifestyle of a typical customer.

Even in an informal questionnaire, a good deal of demographic and psychographic information can be obtained to develop a profile. Here is a partial list of questions for which a copywriter should have answers before beginning to write:

    1. Demographics
        (*a*) Who will buy the product? This requires a breakdown
            into sex, age, residence, income level, education,
            profession, family status, religion, ethnic origins.
    2. Psychographics
        (*a*) Where do they do their buying? Department stores?
        Specialty shops? Chains? Boutiques?

Figure 3-1. The *merchandise-acceptance curve* is an attempt to visualize at any given time, for a specific product or style, the degree of acceptance (or rejection) that can be expected from its target market. Merchandise-acceptance *evaluations* are not statistical measurements, but they can help determine the type of advertising that a product warrants or requires. They can suggest appeals and approaches that are competitive and timely.

A product that has been on the market well past its competitive life might be revived if it is substantially changed or improved, or if it can be newly positioned to appeal to a new audience, or if new uses can be found for it. Thus, it can win new acceptance and thereby literally begin a new life or new pioneering phase. This cycle has been charted by Otto Kleppner as "the Advertising Spiral."

(*b*) When do they buy? Times of day? Seasons?

(*c*) How do they buy? Quantities? Assortments?

(*d*) Why do they buy? Attitudes, values, beliefs, wants, and needs?

(*e*) Brand preferences, loyalties, desired product features, "switchabilities"?

These questions might be stated differently, depending on whether the customer is at trade level (i.e., a retail buyer) or an ultimate customer. But the need for information that helps the writer to target in on an individual prospect—rather than a mass audience—is essential for all copy, whether trade, national, or retail.

Buying Motives

Motivational research is that part of marketing research which relates to the psychographic characteristics or behavior of the potential customer. It is important to understand the customer's psychological motivations in order to reach and appeal to his motives to buy and his "will to buy" mechanism. A knowledge of human behavior is essential to the competent and successful copy-writer. Here, only a brief review can be given of the material assembled by an army of psychologists, motivational researchers, and consumer behaviorists.

All human behavior is internally motivated. The interest of the copywriter, however, centers on behavior habits in the marketplace. To reach the customer to whom the selling efforts are directed, it is necessary to understand the emotions or drives, conscious or subconscious, that can induce purchase of a given product. Buying motives are the drives within the individual which influence action, determine choice, and provide the conscious reason for buying.

To write effective advertising, the copywriter must review again and again, in day-to-day assignments, the possible buying motives of the potential purchaser of the product. These possibilities must be weighed against the dominant selling point or product benefit already selected as important. Whatever selling point or product benefit can be found to build up the customer's inner image of himself will provide the most powerful appeal for the copy.

The generally accepted buying motives are fundamental in nature. They remain the same whether the potential customer is a corporation, business executive, or a consumer.

Some of the motives to buy include:

1. Desire for recognition from one's peers.

2. Desire for superiority (commonly called status or prestige).
3. Desire for good health and long life.
4. Desire for comfort.
5. Desire for appetizing food and drink.
6. Desire for security.
7. Desire to earn money.
8. Desire to save money.
9. Desire to protect one's family.
10. Desire to win approval of the opposite sex.
11. Desire to save time.
12. Desire to minimize labor.
13. Desire for amusement.

To return to a point made earlier, in addressing an advertisement to the *consumer,* it is important to try to fathom his collective mind, to try to understand (in terms of the product to be sold) what his inner goals and ambitions may be. Some of the questions that one may raise include:

1. Is he prestige-hungry?
2. Is she anxious to be the leader?
3. Is he anxious to conform to the standards of his social group, to blend into the group?
4. Is she unsure of her beauty, and anxious to be thought more beautiful, younger, more attractive?
5. Is he hoping to conceal the years and still have a "singles" life-style, still be thought of as a "swinger"?
6. Are they interested in their families, striving to provide for the youngsters, fighting for security?
7. Are they career-oriented, looking for the right springboard to the right job?

Levels of Motivation

Depending on the objectives of an advertisement and its subject matter, the copywriter concentrates on one or more of three levels of buying motives:

1. Primary (why one should buy).
2. Selective (why one should buy a specific style or brand).
3. Patronage (why one should buy from a specific store or dealer).

To appeal to some of the inner drives that the product must meet and satisfy, the copywriter must complete the mating of motivations and selling points in the copy and create a strong incentive for customers to act.

THE CONNECTION BETWEEN VERBAL AND VISUAL IN COPY STRATEGIES

Our discussion of appeals that motivate consumers to buy, might consider the most current thinking of "why do we buy?" The Association for Consumer Research has advanced the concept of "symbolic consumption." This concept advances the idea that many products are valued more for the symbolic gratification they provide than for any specific function or satisfaction they perform. These are products whose utility to the consumer is substantially influenced by their subjective meanings.

One might not "symbolically consume" a Coca-Cola, but one may symbolically consume Perrier sparkling water. Another example: A recent study at Northwestern University disclosed that certain products are bought and consumed only for special occasions—"*Weekends* were made for Michelob . . ."; pancakes are for Sunday breakfast; and tickets to the opera are for special occasions only. It is interesting to note that many advertising campaigns are designed to break these buying patterns. Among them, Michelob beer which seeks to expand the "weekend" into a "week-long weekend"; Florida orange juice with its new stress on drinking orange juice any time of day, etc.

The challenge to the advertising copywriter/idea visualizer is evident: the visualization of messages that appeal to the rapidly multiplying markets for so-called "aesthetic products." Dawn Mello, executive vice president of Bergdorf Goodman, New York, predicted at a conference in May 1980 that handknit sweaters will be a major fashion of the 1980's.[6] What does the consumer really buy when buying a *handknit* sweater?

Copy Appeals

This mating of buying motive and selling point is done by the copywriter in the selection of a copy appeal. In other words, through a knowledge of human psychology, with a conscious thinking-through, the copywriter must develop an appeal that the product will have for a potential consumer. It is somewhat like touching a small spring on a box that makes it pop open.

A copy appeal may be defined as the basic use, service, or satisfaction that the product can give and that the advertisement attempts to present to the customer as a *reason to buy*. Copy appeal represents the blending of the two concepts, selling points and buying motives, into a reason to buy which relates the product's benefits to the purchaser's needs.

The most frequently used copy appeals include:
- Acquisitiveness and the "collector instinct"

[6]Dawn Mello. Speech delivered at New York University Institute of Retail Management, May 20, 1980.

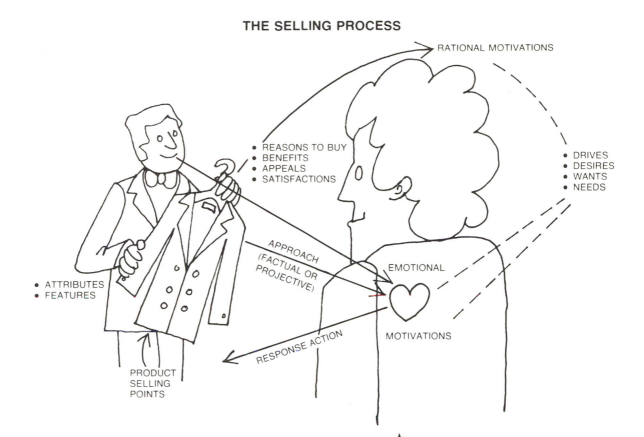

THE SELLING PROCESS

- RATIONAL MOTIVATIONS
- REASONS TO BUY
- BENEFITS
- APPEALS
- SATISFACTIONS
- DRIVES
- DESIRES
- WANTS
- NEEDS
- ATTRIBUTES
- FEATURES
- APPROACH (FACTUAL OR PROJECTIVE)
- EMOTIONAL
- RESPONSE ACTION
- MOTIVATIONS
- PRODUCT SELLING POINTS

Figure 3-2. The *selling process* describes what a copywriter must consider preparatory to writing and visualizing a message to an audience. A thorough analysis of customer motivations is necessary in order to select selling propositions and selling points that will connect with customer wants and needs.

The appeal or "reason to buy," backed by convincing selling points, should be presented by an approach (factual, narrative, or projective), which is geared to the type of response expected from the type of customers in the target group.

Rosser Reeves describes the copywriter's search for an effective selling point as the *unique selling proposition* (USP), which lifts the message (and the customer's response) to something out of the ordinary.

- Love and sex
- Egotism, status or prestige
- Health and vanity
- Curiosity
- Duty or obligation
- Hero worship
- Comfort
- Sensory reaction or pleasure
- Fear (of loss, old age, rejection, etc.)
- Happy home life.

The creative person tends to use his intuitive perceptions to project himself into the background and life-style of his customer. He develops observational skills to a high degree and becomes a constant "people-watcher" and listener. He finds it possible to set aside his own likes and dislikes in order to discover what others want and need. He develops a conscious empathy regarding his customer's wants and needs. Whatever the method the copywriter uses to develop the appeal, this effort is the key to success in advertising. (See Figure 3-2.)

As has been indicated, the sources for information about products and customers are prodigious. If no formal research is available, there are other avenues that can provide information. For example, the media will supply impressive audience profiles which

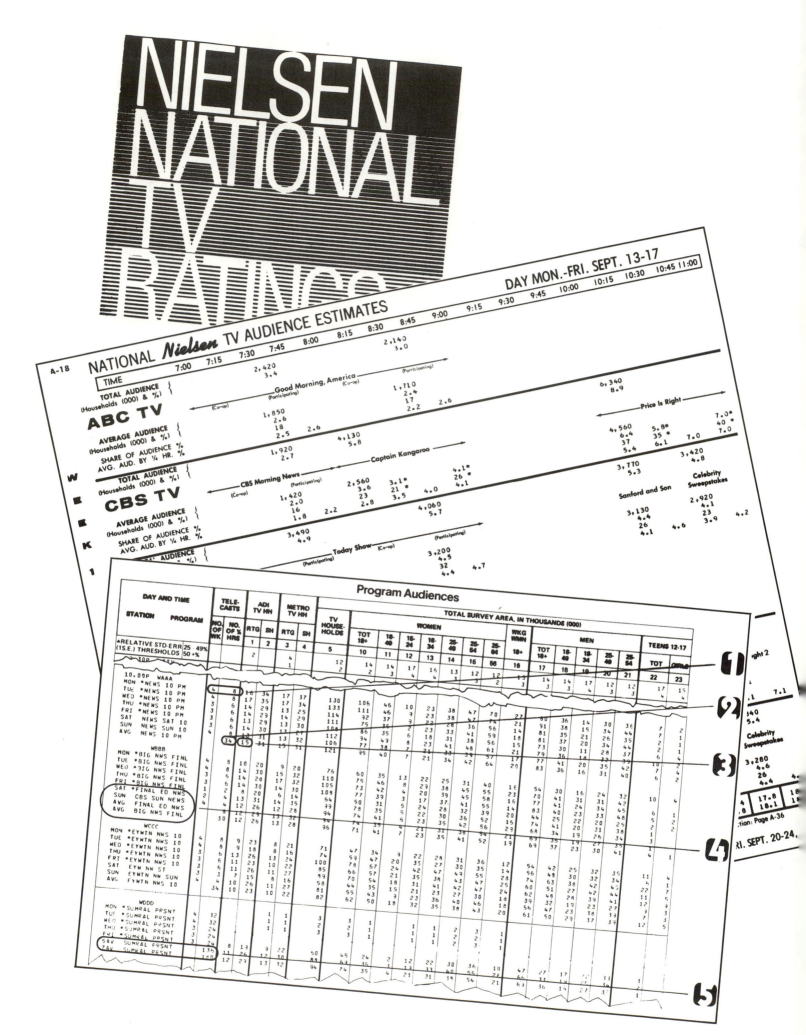

Figure 3-3. Pictured here are sample pages from research reports of some of the most prominent of the media research services. The A. C. Nielsen Company provides audience measurement for local (NSI) and national (NTI) television markets. These TV ratings include audience composition as well as audience measurement estimates for all programs throughout the programming schedule.

ARBITRON is a radio and television testing service which includes, among others, this program audience review that describes and measures audiences in selected markets. There are other services that examine audience characteristics, readership, immediate and delayed recall, viewer attention-getting and viewer impressions, copy research and testing, and the response to specific selling points.

The resourceful creative director has many established sources for obtaining valid information as well as the opportunity to initiate independent studies designed to confirm or correct preconceived notions about markets.

have to be analyzed carefully to filter out their understandable bias. There are several reliable independent media research and study firms which periodically examine and report on the media and customer response. (See Figure 3-3.)

Frequently, copywriters will get out of their offices and "hit the street" to interview customers on street corners, in the stores, shopping malls, showrooms and merchandise marts—wherever the customers do their buying. Some copywriters will develop questionnaires or oral interviews to find the reasons why customers buy or do not buy, what they would like or not like in a product, why they prefer to buy from one source or another, and what is the basic nature of their primary, selective, and patronage motivations.

PRODUCT AND INSTITUTIONAL OBJECTIVES OF COPY

A copywriter must never lose sight of the purpose of his job—to sell the product and to sell the organization behind the product. These should be his main objectives, and they must be present in each advertisement he writes. One successful advertising agency puts it this way: "It isn't creative unless it sells."

The specific copywriting job at hand, however, presents different aspects of these product and institutional objectives and permits many variations of sales immediacy.

In national advertising, the objective of the advertising is most frequently to promote the brand name. This means making the brand name so familiar to the consumer that he asks for the product by that name when he visits the retail store. This process is frequently referred to as "preselling" the consumer. A national advertisement thus can sell the product and the institution behind it. At the very time it exerts influence on the consumer, it can exert an influence on the retailer, who is glad to stock a product that exhibits the ability to do a little of his own job for him by preselling his customers.

Of course, a national advertisement also can be a "straight" institutional ad, with the objective of promoting the company as a whole or its family of branded products, without reference to any specific product. Trade advertising can have either product or institutional objectives and can blend the two in a single advertisement.

Retail advertising, at its best, always sells in all its promotions a little of the institution behind the product. Every time a product is promoted in an advertisement, even for stores that run advertisements daily, a sound advertising policy will dictate that the store be promoted as a "good place to shop."

With this explanation of how advertising can set up separate goals, its objectives may be classified as follows:

1. *Institutional* (long-term or seasonal results expected)
   (*a*) The advertisement may promote a prestige image.
   (*b*) It may emphasize a low-price policy.
   (*c*) It may present a policy of "good value" (quality at a price).
   (*d*) It may promote big assortments as a benefit to the customer.
   (*e*) It may give useful "how-to" information.
   (*f*) It may seek to sponsor a good cause for good will.

Any of the above institutional objectives could be considered in an effort to create, change, or reshape the company image as well as to maintain a currently good reputation.

2. *Product* (seasonal or immediate results expected)
   (*a*) The advertisement may promote something "new" on the market.
   (*b*) It may promote a "regular price-line" (current, seasonal merchandise).
   (*c*) It may advertise a sale, either clearance or special promotion.
   (*d*) It may wish to invite inquiries.
   (*e*) It may attempt to sell directly.
   (*f*) It may want to encourage coupon buying.

Clearly then, with all these objectives and more that will arise for specific companies and for specific products or services, the copywriter must determine the objective of the task at hand before he starts to write.

"Push-Pull"—A Marketing Concept for Advertisers

Among several marketing theories that depend strongly on advertising for implementation, the "push-pull" concept presents interesting opportunities when clearly understood.[7] At the base of this understanding must be the market level of the advertiser, for these strategies are specifically the prerogative of the producer or manufacturer in his trade or national advertising.

A manufacturer or other producer normally uses the "push" technique through heavy trade promotion. Both the actual salesman who travels the country and the mass of advertising (trade publications, brochures, catalogs, and the like) sent to his customers (*not* the consumer) provide the push that gets the merchandise on the racks and onto the counters of stores throughout the country. The

[7]E. J. McCarthy, *Basic Marketing: A Managerial Approach,* 5th ed. (Homewood, Ill.: Richard D. Irwin, Inc., 1975), pp. 315–16.

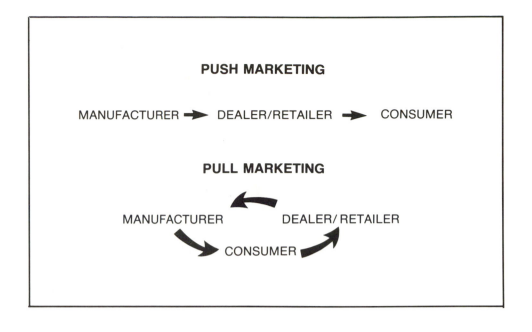

PUSH MARKETING

MANUFACTURER ➡ DEALER/RETAILER ➡ CONSUMER

PULL MARKETING

MANUFACTURER   DEALER/RETAILER

CONSUMER

Figure 3-4. Push vs. pull? The reader should now be able to determine which advertiser uses the push method, and which the pull method. For example, would a manufacturer of an *unbranded* product use the pull method? Why? Why not? It should be obvious that the decision to use either push or pull methods in marketing a product is a serious component of the advertiser's marketing strategy and market plan.

emphasis here must be on a strong profit motive. This, in turn, forges the links in the chain of selling—from manufacturer through messages to the dealer (distributor and/or retailer) and out to the consumer.

These messages may be personal (through sales representatives) or nonpersonal (through the mass of trade publications that keep the dealer-retailer informed of what exists in this area of marketing for his customers, the ultimate consumers). Thus, the producer is said to push his products through the channels of distribution until they ultimately reach the consumer.

On the other hand, the manufacturer uses national advertising addressed directly to the ultimate consumer so that the product is "pulled" through the chain of distribution. Through national advertising, the manufacturer seeks to create *consumer* demand for his product (the pull method). This national advertising is often accompanied by cents-off coupons, by distribution of samples, all designed with one objective in mind: to create or to increase an interest in the product in the mind of the final user and, thus, to create sales at retail. It would be a foolish and doomed retailer, indeed, who would ignore consumer demand. In fact, then, it is the consumer himself who pulls the product through the channels of distribution.

Very closely allied with the pull concept must be the commitment of the manufacturer to a plan for merchandising his national advertising program to his dealers and retailers. It is important that the national effort be explained and described to the middleman and retailer in strong, compelling words and pictures. They can then act on this advance notice and stock up in readiness for the consumer, who can be expected to come in and ask for the nationally advertised products.

Thus, whereas the push method can be charted in a direct line, manufacturer to dealer/retailer to consumer, the pull method is less direct, i.e., manufacturer to consumer to dealer/retailer and back to manufacturer. (See Figure 3-4.)

THE MEDIUM TO BE USED
FOR THE MESSAGE

The practice of media analysis, planning, and selection is a profession in itself. Here, it will be discussed only to the extent that a copywriter may find himself involved in media selection.

Media (plural for *medium*) represent the various channels through which the advertiser's message is brought to the public. The media may include:

- Print (newspapers, magazines, direct mail)
- Broadcast (radio, television)
- Outdoor (twenty-four-sheet posters, painted boards, spectaculars)
- Transit (subway or bus cards, station posters)
- Point-of-purchase (posters, cards, signs).

It is perhaps obvious that while creative considerations most frequently influence the concept and completion of precise copy, the medium selected will often dictate the way a copywriter plans his advertisement. In a large agency or in a large store, media planning will have been completed when a campaign is set in motion, but before the copywriter gets the individual and specific assignment. He then brings his experience to bear on the kind of copy he will write for television versus radio, for newspaper versus magazine, etc. Which station, which newspaper, which magazine will also be considerations in the selection of appeals and approaches.

He needs to know exactly what kind of readership or listenership will receive his message. To take the national magazines, for example, he must know that if his media schedule calls for *Playboy, Ms., Redbook,* and *People,* he will be dealing with four somewhat different groups of people. His media department will have given him specific details on the profile of the typical reader of each magazine. So, it will follow whenever newspapers, radio stations, or television stations appear on his schedule, he can depend on his media department and, to an extent, on his own knowledge and experience to guide him.

If the copywriter works in a "one-man" or very small advertising agency or in a small retail store, he may have to handle media selection himself. In most cases, in a small agency, the clients may be in earlier stages of their marketing development and may not be ready for a comprehensive use of media. In any case, media planning and selection call for highly specialized knowledge. He may need to know actual costs of insertions so that he can make recommendations within the client's budget.

It is useful to emphasize again that the copywriter must be aware of the differences in the various types of media, not only in their basic requirements (newspapers vs. TV, for example), but in the more subtle differences among media within a single category (e.g., in a large city, the differences in readership between the leading newspapers).

Where the copywriter needs to build his own knowledge in this area, he should be aware that there are several reliable sources of information. First, each publication and broadcast station has a local representative who will answer a telephone call with a visit to the copywriter's desk, to discuss price schedules, provide important information about his medium, and present printed rate cards and promotional material.

Second, the Standard Rate and Data Service (SRDS) publishes monthlies, covering newspapers, consumer publications, business publications, spot radio and television, network television, etc. The smallest office that handles advertising should have a set on hand brought up to date at least quarterly. These publications give basic, factual information about circulation, rates, geographical distribution, and some data about professional distribution as well. (See Figure 3-5.)

In addition to these, comparison studies of media effectiveness go on endlessly, comparing the circulation of magazines, the "reach" of radio and television stations, and the comparative *cost per thousand* (CPM). It is necessary to keep aware of these. This can be done by checking the various media associations (such as the American Newspaper Publishers Association, Television Advertising Bureau, Radio Advertising Bureau, etc.)

WRAP-UP

Enough has been said now, it is hoped, to convince the copywriter of the need to think and think hard before writing; about the five basics which will contribute to the planning of strategy: the client or organization he will write for; the product, service, or idea at hand; the profile of customers to be reached; the objective to be achieved; and the medium (or media) selected to carry the advertisement.

15. MECHANICAL MEASUREMENTS
PRINTING PROCESS: Photo Composition Direct Letterpress.
For complete, detailed production information, see SRDS Print Media Production Data.
8/9-2/7—8 cols/ea 9 picas-2 pts/7 pts betw col.
Lines to col. 300; page 2400; dbl. truck 4950.

16. SPECIAL CLASSIFICATION/RATES
Political—general rates apply.
POSITION CHARGES
(At publisher's option.) Full position 25% additional.
DAILY COMIC PAGE
25% additional sold only as a unit—35 lines on 4 col. or 70 lines on 2 col.
Alcoholic beverages, tobacco products and proprietary remedies not accepted on comic pages.

17. CLASSIFIED RATES
For complete data refer to classified rate section.

18. CIRCULATION
Established: 1873. Per copy daily .20; Sunday .50.
Net Paid—A.B.C. 3-31-79* (Newspaper Form)
PRIMARY MARKET AREA CIRCULATION

	Total	Prim. Mkt.	Outside
Morn	81,810	73,344	8,466
Sun	88,778	78,952	9,826

Max-Min rate (flat) Morn 9.73; Sun 8.97.
(*) 27 weeks.
For county-by-county and/or metropolitan area breakdowns, see SRDS Newspaper Circulation Analysis.
Submitted by Orage Quarles.

SAN CLEMENTE

Orange County—Map Location E-10
See SRDS consumer market map and data at beginning of the State.
Corporate city population (1970 govt. census) 17,063

	Households	Population
ABC city zone ('70 census)	7,811	21,213
ABC retail tr. zone ('70 census)	5,476	15,736

SUN-POST

P. O. Box 367, San Clemente, Calif. 92672.
Phone 714-492-5121.

Media Code 1 105 6635 3.00
EVENING (except Saturday and Sunday).
Not published Christmas.

1. PERSONNEL
Publisher—Stanford Manning.
Advertising Director—Brien Manning.
Editor—Warren Esterline.

2. REPRESENTATIVES and/or BRANCH OFFICES
Landon Associates, Inc.
U. S. Suburban Press, Inc.

3. COMMISSION AND CASH DISCOUNT
15% to agencies; 2%—15th following month.

4. POLICY—ALL CLASSIFICATIONS
60-day notice given of any rate revision.
Alcoholic beverage advertising accepted.
Publisher reserves right to refuse any advertising which it deems objectionable.

ADVERTISING RATES
Effective August 1, 1977.
Received August 15, 1977.

5. BLACK/WHITE RATES

Flat per line	1 page	1,500 lines	1,000 lines
.20	481.60	300.00	200.00

6. GROUP COMBINATION RATES—B/W & Color
Also sold in combination with Coastline Dispatch, extra per line .11.
Circulation Sworn 9-30-78: Total Non-Paid 13,688.
U. S. Suburban Press, Inc. Newspaper Network—see listing in National Newspapers Section.

7. COLOR RATES AND DATA
Minimum 980 lines.
Use b/w line rate plus the following applicable costs:

	b/w 1 c	b/w 2 c	b/w 3 c
Extra	85.00	170.00	255.00

Closing dates: Reservations 1 week in advance; printing material 3 days in advance. Cancellation date: 4 days in advance.

11. SPECIAL DAYS/PAGES/FEATURES
Best Food Day: Wednesday.
Church, Friday; Business and Financial, daily.

12. ROP DEPTH REQUIREMENTS
As many inches deep as columns wide. Ads over 280 lines deep, charged full column.

Figure 3-5. The Standard Rate and Data Service (SRDS) is a publication that lists rates and discounts of all major media. It is kept up-to-date with monthly issues which service the market researcher and media planner in their media analyses and planning. The excerpt illustrated indicates the listings for some of the California daily newspapers. Notice the quantity of information that SRDS provides in a minimum of space.

WRITING THE COPY: HEADLINES

Up to this point, we have been talking a great deal, not about writing, but about *thinking before writing*. It is time to move forward into the area of actual copywriting. The earlier analysis should have brought into focus several steps that will make the copywriting task smoother:

1. The selling points of the product have been set down on paper, with the dominant selling point leading the others.
2. The copy appeal should have been decided upon, based upon the dominant selling point and its benefit to an expected consumer.
3. The copywriter must now be aware of the nature of the firm she is writing for, of the potential consumer she is writing to, and where her advertisement is to appear. She should consider, too, whether the advertisement is part of a campaign or must stand alone.
4. Her next step is to determine how she will present the selling message and reach the consumer, how she will involve the consumer and create belief.

These are key steps in writing effective copy which reaches and motivates the decision to buy, which is, above all, the goal of the copy.

THE SELLING PROCESS

Advertising must persuade before it can sell, and involvement and belief are excellent means of persuasion. It is the way of activating a selling process, a mating of selling points and motivations which provides the strongest appeals.

In personal selling, we speak of the right way to "approach" the customer. So, in copywriting, we use the same word, approach, to denote the right way to get the selling message to the consumer. Again, as in personal selling, the approach must catch the customer's ATTENTION, gain her INTEREST, awaken the DESIRE to own the product, and lead her to the proper ACTION that will complete the purchase. Attention and interest are attained when the copywriter has a clear picture of the customer's motives, wants, and needs. Desire and action are activated by linking motives and selling points to create an "irresistible" appeal.

The first letters of the capitalized words above form a mnemonic or memory-word that is accepted and understood by all advertisers and sellers: A-I-D-A. This is the *selling process* in capsule form. The elements of the copy, from headline to closing should follow the four steps in the selling process in logical progression.

THE HEADLINE PROVIDES THE "A" AND "I"

In copywriting, the attention and interest of the potential customer must be caught by the headline, or the page will be turned and the possible sale lost.

(Let it be said again that the visual portion of the advertisement shares this task with the headline. At this point in the text, however, our full preoccupation will be with the headline. Later, visualization will be the subject of discussion, insofar as the copywriter should have a hand in its development and choice.)

The headline has three functions:

1. To capture *attention*.
2. To awaken the *interest* of the reader in learning more about the product.
3. To select the special readers who might have a specific interest in what you are selling.

A headline is not successful if it merely arrests the reader's eye, then only to let him go to another page. The headline's job is to arouse interest enough to lead her eye down into the body copy of the advertisement. One writer said, "The headline must force a reading of the first paragraph by those who are your prospects."

There is one major rule about writing your headline. It should flash an instant message that says: "This should interest *you!*" Some of the most effective headlines include the dominant selling point in terms of a copy appeal or of a product benefit that relates to the appeal (reason to buy).

It is therefore important to think back to your strategy, to think about the customers who are prospective buyers of your product, and to think which market segments of your target audience will be interested in the product's selling points, and which specific selling point can deliver the most powerful benefit or USP to the purchaser.

Once the dominant selling point and copy appeal have been determined, there are several grammatical forms the headline can take. It may be written as:

- A statement or part of a statement
- A question
- A command.

While some writers issue the manifesto: "Never use a command headline; never use a question," we do not agree. There are a hundred examples of effective headlines that take the form of a command or question. In fact, a question that is interesting enough is an excellent attention-getter; it involves the passing reader and rivets her interest into reading further to see what answer the advertiser provides.

I can't seem to forget you. Your Wind Song stays on my mind.

Wind Song Perfume by Prince Matchabelli

Figure 4-1. This perfume advertisement, which may be said to be all headline and no copy, exemplifies clearly how close a relationship exists between visual concepts and verbal concepts. The words are evocative of what perfume can really do—while the photographer has been able to illustrate in the deeply focused eyes the same idea. A fragrance remembered can bring the wearer to mind.

Within the grammatical distinctions listed above, there are many things a headline can do—and what a headline conveys is perhaps more important than the form in which it does it. Headlines may be classified by performance as follows:

1. NEWS or INFORMATION. Convey real news or important information about a product.
2. SELECTIVE. Select a specific audience with specific language and words.
3. CLAIM. Insist that this product has an outstanding record or performs in a certain way. When this message becomes overly blatant and boastful—and in this case, often without stated proof— the headline is given a special and unpleasant classification (HORN-BLOWING).
4. ADVICE or PROMISE. Promise a real benefit if the product is used. Conversely, under the same classification, headlines

will sometimes indicate the damage that can result, if the product is not used.

5. LOGO or SLOGAN. Stress the reputation of the company behind it.

6. MOOD-SETTING. Set a mood to create receptivity in the reader. (See Figure 4-1.)

In the six classifications above, the *message* conveyed by the headline is "the thing." Now for a word on a *seventh* and final headline classification—PROVOCATIVE. In today's highly competitive market, where every page of a publication and every ten or thirty seconds of a commercial compete with a tight-fitting neighbor for the consumer's attention, it is often necessary to startle or interrupt in order to capture attention. In some cases, it may be the primary function of a headline. Thus, any of the above six classifications may be expressed in a curious, "gimmicky," or amusing way. A play on words is often arresting, as is a tricky use of a proverb or famous character. Humor can be very effective, especially when it utilizes what is currently considered amusing or funny. This seventh headline classification, however, *provokes* the reader into probing further. Sometimes it presents a contradiction or an apparent paradox to the reader, with the explanation provided in the body copy.

This classification, the provocative headline, has been isolated deliberately and discussed separately so that the introductory paragraphs to this section can be re-emphasized. However, do not attempt both to attract attention and to satisfy *all* questions in the few words of your headline. The headline, once it has caught attention, must awaken interest and lead the selected reader on to the full selling message in the text or body copy. There are exceptions, of course: those messages where a headline and very descriptive visuals are able to tell the whole story. (See Figures 4-2 and 4-3.)

Here, in the analysis of headlines, is an opportunity for the copywriter and the visualizer to make the creative connection. Both the "copywriter as art director" and the "art director as copywriter" should practice making connections between copy and visuals. Select a product, study it and the people who ought to be interested in it, and then do thumbnail visuals with headlines to convey the product benefit. (See Figure 4-4.)

In Chapters 9, 10, and 11, this book becomes a workshop in our "VIZTHINK" process. Our objective is to turn you into a creative "doodler," who can draw/write and write/draw as an aid to thinking and to communications problem-solving.

In reviewing a headline and considering its classification, the question may well be asked: Is one type better than another? The

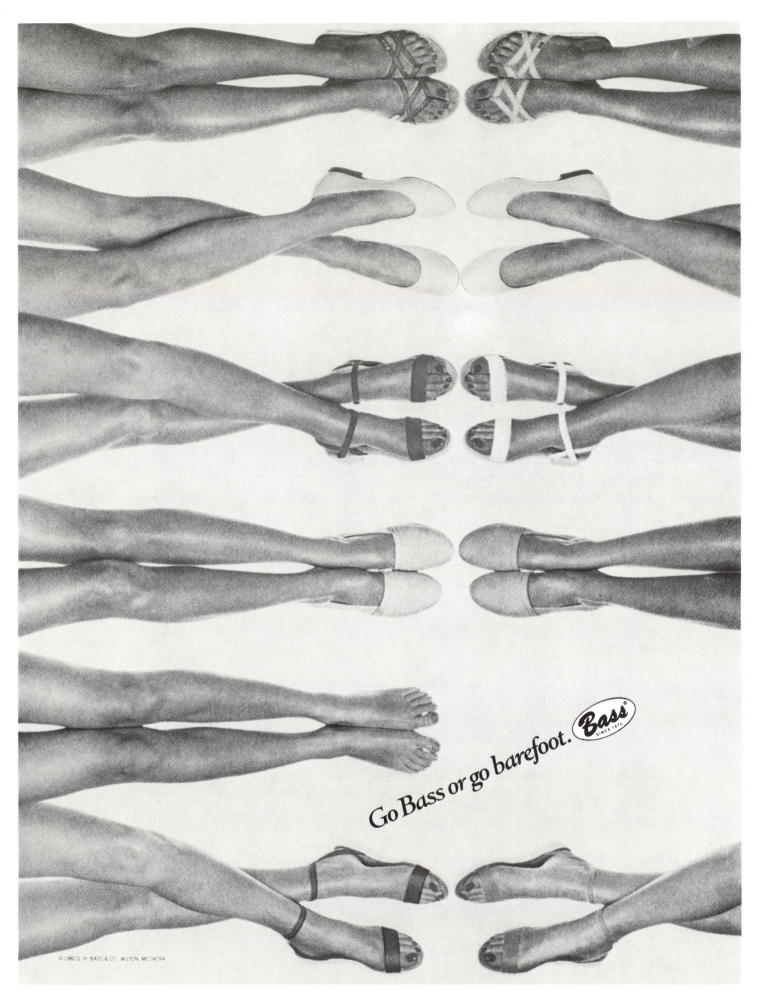

Go Bass or go barefoot. **Bass**

© 1980 G. H. BASS & CO. WILTON, ME 04294

Figure 4-3. Another advertisement where no real body copy is needed is "Have a Coke and a Smile." The two subheads and the strong illustration have clear and immediate impact on the reader, designed to attract the attention of the casual page-turner with its "slice-of-life" situation.

answer cannot be a simple yes or no. Different products, different kinds of advertising require different headlines. A sale, obviously, can be handled by the news/information headline. The potential purchasers of a perfume, on the other hand, can be arrested by a mood-setting headline. A new product or one that offers a real and perhaps tangible benefit could use the advice/promise headline.

The claim headline is a difficult one to use effectively. It must be followed by copy that proves the claim. If this sequence is not adhered to, the headline, as has been noted earlier, becomes self-serving (horn-blowing), a type in justifiably bad repute.

Now that the classifications have been discussed, it becomes clearer that any of them may be utilized in the three previously mentioned grammatical forms (statement, question, or command).

It must be obvious that in the experience of the writers of this text, a good advertisement should have a headline. Often, the

◄ Figure 4-2. This Bass advertisement tells its story with five words, a logotype, and eleven pairs of legs. The single pair of unshod feet backs up the simple words. Would you agree that body copy was not needed here?

Inside the advertisement image:

The world's best-fitting jeans.

Jeans never fit like this before. Because now every inch is accounted for!

Your exact waist size? You've got it. Exact leg length? It's yours. And imagine, the seat and thigh are proportioned so everything goes with everything else.

Put these jeans on and you'll know it's no put-on to say they're the best fitting jeans in the world.

Heavy denim and other rugged shape-holding jean fabrics that keep the fit perfect forever.

chic by
h.i.s
1411 Broadway, N.Y. 10018

Available in Canada

FOR NEAREST RETAILER
CALL TOLL-FREE 800 821 7700 EXT. 317
IN MISSOURI CALL 800 892 7655

Figure 4-5. The selling message of an advertisement is often complicated, as in health items, nonprescription pharmaceuticals, and vitamins. As we see in this example, the headline must be supported by strong, complete body copy which, itself, may need subheadlines to separate and clarify the product features and benefits.

Figure 4-4. Before you try your own "vizthink" thumbnails, take a good, long look at this jeans advertisement where the headline and the visual tell the reader that the primary product benefit is "fit." Notice the way the product benefit expressed by the copywriter in the headline has been integrated into the layout by the art director.

headline that could work best can be pulled out of the body copy. It is a current fad to write certain types of advertising without headlines. This is sometimes done, not by direction of the copywriter, but by the art director who feels she gets a tighter or more "serene look" in her layout without the boldface type of a headline. However, it is not a part of good advertising to lull one's readers into serenity, but rather to awaken them into a buying mood. As for aesthetics, an art director can visualize and typeset a good selling headline artistically.

Here is another argument for the creative connection—a dynamic visualization of copy, using art and graphics, which works with the headline or can speak and function as a headline. It is self-defeating to argue the merits and primary roles of art and copy. The purpose of this book is to encourage those who create messages to think verbally *and* visually for effective communication.

I can always tell when Mom's on a diet. There's Unicap M® on the table.

Unicap M - it fills in vitamins <u>and</u> minerals you may miss by dieting.

If you're a regular dieter — or even an occasional one — you should know this: dieting *can* reduce your intake of both vitamins *and* minerals.

Vitamins *and* minerals. They are equally important. And Unicap M has both.

10 Important Vitamins. One Unicap M tablet guarantees you 100% of the U.S. Recommended Daily Allowance for all ten vitamins.

Four Vital Minerals. One Unicap M tablet also gives you your full daily requirement of iron, iodine, copper, and zinc.

That's why Unicap M is called a *vitamin-mineral supplement* — it *supplements* your diet. And that's why it can be especially important to dieters.

Unicap M — ask your physician or pharmacist.

Unicap M®

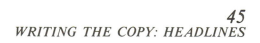

SUBHEADLINES

Subheadlines are a relatively ambiguous element in the copy structure. First, a subhead may not be called for in a given piece of copy. Second, the actual element may refer either to a fuller explanation placed above or below the actual headline, or it may refer to the small type headings that separate and break up parts of long copy. (See Figure 4-5.)

The writing of subheads follows the rules for headline writing. However, whatever form the subhead takes, its role is a subdued one, and the writing is equally subdued in comparison with that for headlines.

Subheadlines, when they appear close to the headline, should add information, explain a little more, or clarify a perhaps too-clever headline of the provocative type. Where the subheads break up copy, their very presence *visually* adds liveliness to the page.

WRAP-UP

The following is a useful checklist for headlines:

1. First and obviously, the headline should be present. There should be no omission of a headline unless the visual performs the function in a unique and highly communicative manner.
2. A headline must be arresting. It should work with the visual—either in its own typographical design or in the "picturization" of which it is a part.
3. It must draw the reader's interest into the body copy.
4. It should select the interested potential customer.
5. It should carry the main selling proposition as a benefit to the reader, thus involving her in self-interest. This may be either in the form of the major selling point or the copy appeal.
6. It may be a complete sentence, or it may be part of a sentence.
7. It should contain a verb, if at all possible. This adds drama and action.
8. If a provocative headline is used, it must be pertinent to the product. If it presents a question, the answer must lie in the subheadline or body copy and in the product's characteristics, features, and performance.

DEVELOPING THE COPY: BODY COPY, MANDATORIES AND LEGALS, COPY LANGUAGE

In considering the actual copywriting of an advertisement, it is necessary to differentiate between the basic body copy that carries the selling message and the requirements of the company and of the laws that may govern a given product or industry. Here, we will first discuss the elements of the basic body copy: approaches, development, and closing. Later, we will cover what is referred to by advertising practitioners as mandatories and legals. Finally, we will discuss the language of copywriting.

BODY COPY

It is in the writing of the body copy that the phrase *copy approach* has its full meaning. Again, to use the A-I-D-A analogy in the case of personal selling, once attention has been captured and interest stimulated, the salesperson may tell the customer of the selling points and benefits or satisfactions of the product. Or he may tell an anecdote in connection with the product or relate the product to the customer's needs as he thinks wisest.

In an advertisement, once the headline and visual have attracted attention and aroused interest, the body copy attempts further to develop the interest of the potential customer, to awaken desire to own the product, and to close with a "call to action." The copy approach is the way the copy and its appeal are presented. Copy approaches, various as they may seem, can be grouped into three categories:

1. Factual, direct, or rational approach.
2. Narrative approach.
3. Projective or emotional approach.

The Factual, Direct, or Rational Approach

Within this category we will find variations in presenting the facts about a product, service, or idea:
- Direct selling information
- Implied suggestion ("soft sell")
- Testimonial copy.

First, the style of presenting direct selling information provides the opportunity for the copywriter to state clearly and bluntly the selling points, benefits, and uses of the advertised product. Its great advantage is that it is perhaps the "shortest line between two points," between the product and the customer.

Depending on the point of view, the fact that this is often called "hard sell" copy can be an advantage or a disadvantage. We feel it should be called "rational" sell. It is certainly a copy approach often

Figure 5-2. Another type of factual → copy takes a softer approach, one called *implied suggestion*. The Hanes copy moves from the somewhat male chauvinistic headline idea (but possibly still true), to "smooth" to "sheer" to Hanes and back to the headline. Everything incorporates suggestion, but it is all basically factual.

Truth in wine labeling started with San Martín.

What does the fine print on the San Martin label tell you?

The truth. The whole truth about the wine we put inside the bottle.

You see, San Martin started

Truth in Wine Labeling. And we live up to it. On every single label, we tell you every single grape that goes into our wine. The percentage of each grape. And where it was grown.

We think these facts say a lot about the quality of San Martin wines.

And we let them speak for themselves, on our label.

San Martin Winery, San Martin, California

The Award Winning Winery

Figure 5-1. Here, in the San Martin wine advertisement, a lesser copywriter might have tried to sell "bouquet" in emotional language, but on the contrary, concept and vocabulary here unite in a strong persuasive effort which can only call forth recognition and agreement from the reader of "yes, that's so," and a consequent feeling of confidence. "Truth in wine labeling" is the headline for factual body copy which, in the end, sells persuasively with straight talk.

used in retail and national advertising. In trade, industrial, and professional advertising, it is almost universally used. This approach is admirably suited to special promotions and clearance sales. It is straightforward and states its case in clear terms. (See Figure 5-1.)

The involvement in the direct selling facts is precisely through the reader's understanding of the unique product benefit the copy presents. This must be strong, for little or no emotional play is used here.

A second variation, implied suggestion, avoids a direct recital of selling points. It stresses the benefits the product can bring to the consumer. It suggests that it might be worthwhile to give the product a try. It asks, in a way, that the potential customer become involved from a sense of fair play; no pressure is applied, just a rational presentation of possibilities. This is often referred to as a "soft sell." (See Figure 5-2.)

The third variation of the factual approach is verified testimony. This is a well-known technique in advertising copy. It gives a case history of the product in actual use by an actual user or by an

Gentlemen prefer Hanes

Sensuously smooth. Luxuriously sheer. Unmistakably Hanes.®

© 1980 Hanes Hosiery.

"**Personally, I count on Playtex Tampons.**

You just can't buy better tampon protection than Playtex."

"That's not just my opinion. Playtex did tests to prove it with women just like you and me. And there are literally millions of us who like Playtex® Tampons best. Only Playtex has that double-layered design you can count on to help prevent accidents. The smooth plastic Gentle Glide® applicator is comfortable to use. Playtex has three different absorbencies—regular, super, and super plus—so that you can always have just the amount of protection you want. Only Playtex Tampons are available with or without deodorant protection—that's your choice, too. It's true—you just can't buy better tampon protection than Playtex. Millions of us like knowing that."

"**I count on Playtex. So can you.**"

Brenda Vaccaro

© International Playtex, Inc., 1981. Playtex and Gentle Glide are registered trademarks.

Figure 5-3. Still factual copy, but of another type is *verified testimony.* This is a straightforward statement of facts about the product in a "quote" signed by Brenda Vaccaro. In brief sentences, this well-known actress tells of her use and preference for this product.

Today, by law, *a testimony must be an honest statement of real use.* Not all testimonial advertisements are as clear as this, with its quotation marks and signature which together verify that Ms. Vaccaro knows what she's talking about and has "really and truly" used Playtex Tampons.

In addition, this advertisement provides a clear example of the steps in the development of the factual approach. After the statement in the headlines, the subhead amplifies the same idea of "preference." The body copy moves on to provide proof (tests and "millions" of opinions). Additional details follow to a strong closing.

objective laboratory. It is equally useful in retail, trade, and national advertising. It can develop a strong reader involvement in the test or tests that have been performed. Federal Trade Commission (FTC) regulations require that *all* testimonials today be based on factual data which can be supported.

If Mrs. Robinson of Burbank, California has washed a pair of denim slacks 150 times and has found they are still strong and ready for more wearings and washings, then Mrs. Greene of Lincoln, Nebraska knows exactly what that means and can identify with the entire situation. A variation of this type of approach is found in Figure 5-3.

Body Copy Development for the Factual Approach

There is a logical progression in the development of the factual approach in order to create strong and effective selling copy. After the headline itself, the body copy follows in a logical sequence. In outline form, these are the components of body copy developed for the factual approach:

1. Amplification of headline in the *lead* (first sentence[s] of body copy).
2. Proof or evidence.
3. Additional details.
4. Closing.

It has been noted in Chapter 4 that the headline comes first and usually carries the most powerful appeal to catch the attention and arouse the interest of the casual reader.

In opening the body copy, the writer should amplify the headline idea, restate it, repeat it or, in some way, emphasize it. The headline carried "the punch"; it also selected the audience and awakened its interest. Now the copy lead reassures the reader he has come to the right place.

The next step is to "back up" the statement, the claim, or the promise that the headline idea set forth. In a product advertisement, this can be done by giving details of construction, the reputation of the company, the experience of other users, the popularity of the product, and so forth. In this step, the copy gives some evidence or proof that can hold the reader's interest and begin to build a desire to own the product.

The third step is to add more selling points about the product which support the main reason to buy (appeal), and possibly add additional details and "subreasons" to buy. It is in these three areas that the copy does everything it can to create a desire in the reader to own the product.

Finally the copy comes to a close. This must give the potential customer who may now have reasons to *buy,* reasons and methods for *action.* So, not only should he be led to a decision to buy, he must be given something to do: "Come down," "Phone," "Write," "Don't delay," "Fill out a coupon," etc.

Too frequently, copy that might otherwise be effective loses out at this important "last chance." Read the leading papers and magazines. Listen to the top television commercials. The most effective selling messages are those that give the reader or listener something to do. This is not hard sell; it is just good sense.

(The classifications of closings will follow this discussion of all three copy approaches. But remember: Closings are important. Ask any good salesperson!)

The Narrative Approach

The narrative approach constructs a *story* for the customer, out

"Meeting with Harry Baldwin over lunch added up to a lot of new business for my company. And a lot of calories for me.

The stuffed mushrooms were 350 calories. The vichyssoise was 275 calories. The Caesar salad was 265 calories. The veal scallopini was 675 calories.

But the TAB? Thank goodness, it was just 1 delicious calorie."

TaB. You're beautiful to me.
One calorie never tasted so good.

TAB is a registered trade-mark of The Coca-Cola Company © 1980 The Coca-Cola Company

Figure 5-4. In the narrative approach, a subclassification frequently used is "slice-of-life," which in a fictional way, seems to present a real-life situation. The body copy for the Tab advertisement would fall under this classification. Here the product features are implied as the little situation unfolds. The reader is involved through association with the "true-to-life" situation which any modern person can recognize.

of the product and its selling points. There are several ways to work out this approach:

- Descriptive or human interest story
- "Slice of life"
- Fictional testimony
- Monologue or dialogue
- Humor
- Comic strip
- Verse.

The variations lie in the way the story is told. It is important to remember that under the narrative approach, there is always a kind of miniature storytelling that soon moves on to the facts of the selling points. The selling message is conveyed as the "plot unfolds."

The story, whether descriptive (perhaps telling of the glamour of a newly carpeted room) or human interest (how a father assures his daughter's future education), is fictional. (See Figure 5-4.)

This whole approach, because it is inventive, is often called "the imaginative approach." We have reservations about this term, because it implies confining the use of the imagination to one approach. (It is hoped and expected that the copywriter will apply his imagination to everything he writes—even to copy for a clearance sale.)

The second variation, "slice of life" copy, is useful in lending a kind of reality to a story which may be dramatized as follows: Almost everyone is familiar with the "retirement" copy that is told as if by a woman who experiences the whole process of not being able to save, meeting a friendly insurance company representative who tells her what kind of policy to take, so that she is now, with her mate, enjoying their retirement years.

A third variation is used in radio and television commercials. Headache remedies frequently set forth their selling message in the form of fictional testimonials by "everyday" sort of people who might be our neighbors. Surveys indicate that this kind of copy is effective; it involves the reader or the listener. Reactions indicate that listeners and readers relate to "plain folks," simple, neighborly people who recite their experiences in so real a manner.

The monologue (one person talking) and dialogue (conversation) capture and hold interest very easily. The now "legendary" dialogue for Alka-Seltzer, between a stomach and its owner, ran for over two years, and it is still one of the best ever written. Each of these approaches, monologue and dialogue, has been used successfully even for modern bank and insurance advertising, as well as in current status designer campaigns.

Humor, comic strip, and verse forms should be used carefully and perhaps only by copywriters who have been proven successful in these forms. But, how do you achieve success in these forms if you are not permitted to start? Perhaps "not permitted" is too strong. There are people, young and untried, who have natural wit or a natural talent for easy verse. This kind of person should try his hand at humor or verse in his advertising copy. If he has talent, it will be quickly and enthusiastically recognized and welcomed. A strong teacher-editor in a classroom experience or a strong and effective copy chief in an agency can be helpful guides in this area.

Body Copy Development for the Narrative Approach

The development of narrative copy differs from that found to be effective for the factual or direct approach. (See Figure 5-5.) In outline, the body copy components are developed in steps as follows, after the headline:

    1. Predicament.

"What a big, beautiful diamond. Your fiancé must really be rich!"

Rich? No way. In fact, we didn't think we'd ever spend $1,200 on an engagement ring. We figured all the good ones would be way out of our price range, which we had originally set at $600. So of course we were nervous about going shopping for it.

Well, the jeweler put us right at ease. He let us examine several different diamonds up close. He even pointed out the subtle variations that make one diamond worth so much more than another. And then he gave us a great tip on how much we should spend on the ring. He said that today, a diamond engagement ring should be worth at least one to two months salary.

When we realized how much money a person constantly dishes out on things that just don't last, we figured we couldn't afford _not_ to go for the best.

The ring we finally chose cost us several hundred more than we had planned. But I think it was worth every penny. After all, Jack gets as big a kick out of the compliments as I do.

1/4 carat	1/3 carat	1/2 carat	3/4 carat
$600 to $1,200	$800 to $1,700	$1,500 to $3,500	$3,000 to $6,000

actual size

Prices shown are based on retail quotations and may vary. Send for the booklet "Everything You'd Love to Know...About Diamonds." Just mail $1.00 to Diamond Information Center, 3799 Jasper St., Philadelphia, PA 19124.

JEWELERS OF AMERICA, INC.

This message is presented by the Diamond Information Center in cooperation with Jewelers of America, Inc. Look for their logo for more information.

A diamond is forever.

2. Discovery of a solution.
3. Happy ending.
4. Transition to the product.
5. Closing (suggestion to the reader).

Let us review these steps in detail.

First, the narrative approach sets up a predicament, some small happening that is somewhat of a catastrophe. Examples of typical television commercial predicaments range from nervous underarm

Figure 5-5. The narrative advertisement for the engagement ring tells a story with appeal to any young person who is, or hopes to be, in love. The development first presents an emotional, intriguing headline and then develops the copy along the lines set forth. The predicament, a slightly complex problem, is revealed in the words: "We were nervous about going shopping." The discovery of the solution comes in the next paragraph: "The jeweler put us right at ease." The transition to the product, "The ring we finally chose," carries smoothly to the conclusion, wherein styles and prices are not only written about in the copy, but also illustrated.

perspiration during a job interview to a teenager who is lonely and depressed, thinking about his friends back in the town from which his family recently moved.

Second, will be the discovery of a solution to the predicament; e.g., the telephone rings in the second example given above.

Third, the happy ending carries the story itself to its pleasant conclusion. (Thus, in the same example, the teenager is reunited with his friends through the magic of Ma Bell's new, reduced long distance rates!) Sometimes, however, this step may be skipped. For instance, in the underarm deodorant commercial, how can our hero escape his fate? ("Don't let it happen to you. . . .")

The fourth step, transition to the product, should always be included, but sometimes it occurs before the happy ending. The transition to the product is perhaps the most important step next to the headline idea itself. It is at this point that the narrative changes either subtly or boldly to the "sell" copy.

In our teenager's phone call, his joy and relief from depression are apparent; it is obvious that this is a telephone company commercial. In the underarm deodorant commercial, the solution lies solely and completely in the transition to the product—and there is no happy ending for that particular unfortunate person who did not choose the brand that could overcome "nervous perspiration," and keep him dry through stress. He would not have had to worry if he had used our product. That is the implication of the copy.

Finally, and this, too, is a must, is the closing: the suggestion to the reader that he buy the advertised product.

It is well to remember that while the opening steps of the narrative approach are fictional, the transition to the product and the closing must return to a factual selling message.

The Projective or Emotional Approach

This third approach puts the reader realistically into the situation, involving him emotionally through a projected "factual" story or through a fictional story about fictional characters. This approach relies on the cutomer's association or identification with the characters in the story—as if it were happening to him. (See Figure 5-6.)

A highly successful Hertz Rent A Car campaign ("Let Hertz put you in the driver's seat") which ran some years ago has recently been revived. A more recent version of this campaign used ex-pro football star O.J. Simpson (who "flies" into the driver's seat); the original campaign actually had "you" (represented by an actor) flying through the air to take the driver's seat. It is an excellent example of projective approach. It says exactly what is meant by

the little shops
On a sultry day, your favorite companion is Calvin Klein.

What do you wear as you slowly sip your cool drink on the white-washed terrace that overlooks the sea? Calvin Klein, of course. Smoke blue linen sweater in XS, S, M, L. $120. Moroccan henna/jade stripe skirt, 4-12. $150.

Little Shops (D.170) 3rd Floor Herald Square. Macy's welcomes the American Express® Card. Or, use your Macy's charge.

macy's
New York

Figure 5-7. The magnetic quality of body copy that carries strong factual details in emotional language is clearly illustrated in the United Airlines advertisement addressed to the "two faces" of the career woman. The facts are clear: United travels to many divergent places; United has convenient schedules; United is economical; gives friendly service; has an association with the group of hotels or motels. All this is embodied in the language of serious effort and leisurely fun (and note how the inset photos carry out the duality of this advertisement).

Figure 5-6. In this Macy's advertisement for their Little Shops (where designer clothes are sold) projective body copy puts the reader into a desirable situation and into the Calvin Klein sweater and skirt. The image of oneself sipping a cool drink and sitting on a whitewashed terrace adds an extra dimension of value to the somewhat expensive Calvin Klein outfit.

this type of copy. The headline makes a claim and the copy goes on to tell how "you" (the reader or listener) can achieve the desired result.

The emotional impact of this type of approach is often felt in copy written about lingerie, perfume, cosmetics, cars, and travel. A run-through of current publications will provide many examples of this copy approach, quite factual in the reporting of selling points, but utilizing mood-evoking language and working for an emotional response. This is highly effective because it involves the potential customer both factually and emotionally and lets him rationalize his wants into needs. (See Figure 5-7.)

She travels two worlds.

She depends on one airline.

There's a world where she works, a world where she plays. And an airline that takes her to both. United.

For business, United's convenient schedules get her where she wants to go. When she wants to go.

For vacations, she depends on United to give her the most for her dollar. Because we save her money to more of this land than any other airline.

But whether she's flying for business or pleasure, she always appreciates the friendly service and attention that have made United this country's most popular airline. And the only airline she needs.

Partners in Travel with Western International Hotels.

"We think the world of each other."

Fly the friendly skies of United.
Call your Travel Agent.

"Each time we come to Bermuda, we find some marvelous little spot we never knew existed."

Harry and Jeannette Gregor on their 14th visit to Bermuda.

"The day we visited St. George's, we made a lot of new friends. They make you feel so at home here."

"It's incredible, the lushness and the beauty, less than 2 hours from the States."

Bermuda
Get away to it all!

See your Travel Agent or write Bermuda, Dept. 1121, 630 Fifth Ave., New York, N.Y. 10111 or Suite 1010, 44 School St., Boston, Mass. 02108 or 300 North State St., Chicago, Ill. 60610 or Suite 2008, 235 Peachtree St. N.E., Atlanta, Ga. 30303

← Figure 5-8. As suggested in the text, price and/or prestige do not necessarily prescribe the type of the closing to be used. Here in a "status" advertisement for Bermuda, a command closing is used: "Get away to it all!" Further instructions are less prominent, but are also in command form, i.e., "*See* your travel agent or *write* Bermuda. . ." The imperative is used here to reinforce the concept that a vacation is a "must" and some people really need to be pushed into action.

Body Copy Development for the Projective Approach

The steps or components in the development of the projective approach invariably follow those for the factual or direct approach, with some difference given to the interpretation of one or two. Generally, there will be a greater attention to details, adding mood-influencing selling points to the basic copy appeal. In addition, the proof or evidence may concern itself more with proving that the product can evoke the desired mood or emotion than with the "nuts and bolts" of construction, fabric, or the like. In other respects, the development is similar.

Closings

While several of the preceding paragraphs have touched on the closing, it is important to devote a section to this subject and to classify the various types it is possible to use, including:
- Direct or command closing
- Soft-suggestion closing
- Implied-suggestion closing.

The direct or command closing is a sentence at the end of the body copy that quite plainly tells the reader or listener to do something: to come in now, to phone now, to write, to mail the coupon, to rush right down, etc.

If your copy has been built steadily and surely, you have caught attention, aroused interest, and awakened the desire to own the product. Now, here is where the action is. Your potential customer has gone a long way with you; do not lose him now. A retail advertisement can suggest an immediate phone call or visit. A trade advertisement can remind the buyer of the respresentative's impending call at the store or invite a visit to the showroom. In industrial and professional advertising, as in national advertising, there can always be the admonition: "Next time specify Vulcan boilers." "Ask for Carrier air conditioning for year-round satisfaction."

It is important to note that Henri Bendel, one of the most exclusive specialty shops in New York City, frequently ends its very imaginative, exclusive, and expensive product copy with a command closing, such as "Hurry down!" Price has nothing to do with the ability to get action in closing the selling message. (See Figure 5-8.)

There are occasions when a softer closing is called for, perhaps when the advertisement is repeated with great frequency or when the message is a "reminder." The soft-suggestion closing is appropriate when the selling objective is not immediate, but long-term, or

Chosen #1 in
People Pleasin'

Pleasin' Dreams

Our #1 People Pleasin' Standards^{sm} give you a good night's sleep... every time.

At Holiday Inn, we really want to make you comfortable. So we give you our famous "no surprise"^{sm} standards. Standards that make it easy for you to get a good night's sleep—like all mattresses are specified "manufacturer's top-of-the-line."

And Holiday Inn hotels offer you our #1 People Pleasin' Locations^{sm}. Locations that let you be near where you want to be.

Our #1 People Pleasin' Standards and Locations^{sm} are just some of the reasons we please more travelers than anybody else.

So the next time you travel, let us be #1 in pleasing you.

Figure 5-9. In this Holiday Inn advertisement, it is appropriate to the kindly, gentle message in the slogan to use a soft suggestion closing, and so this does. "So the next time you travel, let us be number one..."

when the advertising is institutional in character. This is the kind of closing that is a gentle invitation: "The next time you're in Water Tower Place [Chicago's unique shopping mall] come to the County Seat for the largest selections of Western wear in Chicago." Also see Figure 5-9 for the Holiday Inn ad, whose soft-suggestion closing is: "So the next time you travel, let us be #1 in pleasing you."

The word "implied" means "understood, but not stated," and that is exactly what the implied-suggestion closing is. The "call to action" is implied. The copy closing may contain a statement of loss if the product is not bought or a hint at the benefit if some action is taken. (See Figure 5-10.) On the other hand, much department store advertising, as a matter of individual style, uses no apparent closing, but concludes the copy with the department and floor where the product can be found. This is, in itself, telling the customer where to find the article or how to ask for it. In department stores that advertise daily, this may be enough, for they have a loyal clientele. They can save strong closings for an immediate sale, a short-term clearance, a special purchase, or the like.

Each has its place, but the copy should have a closing. Otherwise, you have left an interested customer "standing at the counter," so to speak, and you have walked away.

An interesting and often powerful closing is the use of the well-known slogan of a company (discussed below). It adds the impact of familiarity and closes the sale by saying, "Rely on us!"

MANDATORIES AND LEGALS

The *mandatories* include the client's requirements on company signature, logo, address, and other matters that *must* be in each piece of copy. They are usually unique to each institution, its family of products, its product divisions, and its conditions of sale.

The *legals* are the legal requirements that must be inserted by the copywriter, such as the inclusion of the trademark or registration insignia. If the fabric used in a garment, for example, is covered by a registered name, that must be shown. In liquor advertising, there are certain requirements and certain prohibitions (usually set by state laws). (See Figure 5-11.)

The Company Signature

The company's signature is as important to the company as your name is to you. It is annoying to have your name forgotten or misspelled. In a company where signature stands not only for identity but for what may be called the legality of the corporate body, the correct presentation, spelling, and placement of the company or corporate name are essential in advertising.

The copywriter is responsible for the whole signature of the advertisement: the use of the corporate name in its agreed-upon form, the address, and any other legal formalities that a given business or industry may require. The copywriter is responsible, in a retail establishment, for store hours, branch locations, etc., being listed with accuracy.

Credit lines (references to the photographer or the designer of clothes, where clothes are a prop), trademarks, registration symbols, Patent Office information—all these come under the aegis of the copywriter. It is his reponsibility to know what is needed, in what form, in what spelling—and to see that it gets into the typesetting of the advertisement.

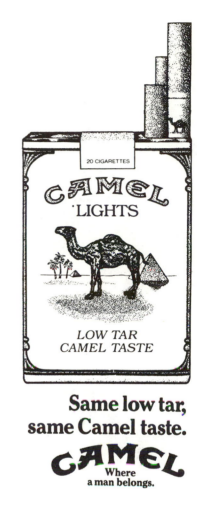

Figure 5-10. Here in the last line, "Where a man belongs," Camel implies that a "man," with all the "macho" references of that word, will find himself at home with Camel cigarettes, and further implies that a man should buy Camels. That statement is not actually made, but the implication is there, and the inference can be made by the interested reader.

DEWAR'S® PROFILE

A thirst for living...a taste for fine Scotch.

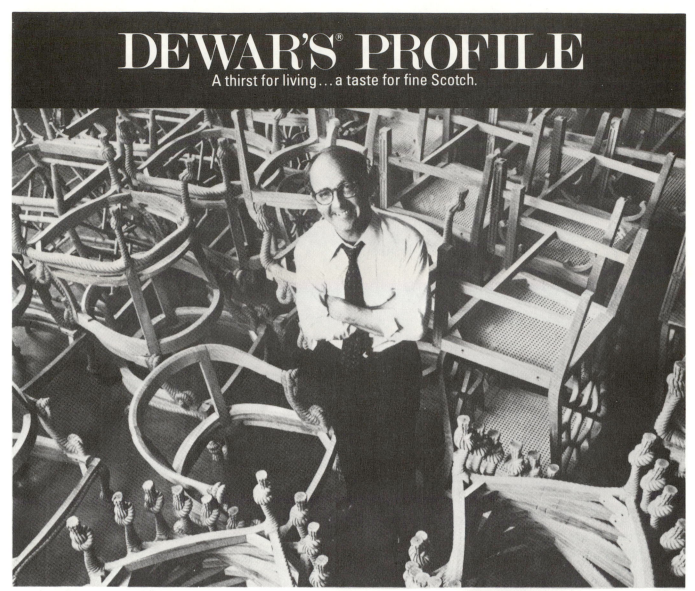

J. PHILLIPS L. JOHNSTON

BORN: Memphis, Tennessee, 1940.

HOME: High Point, North Carolina.

OCCUPATION: Maverick small-business entrepreneur.

CURRENT POSITION: President and Chief Executive Officer, Erwin-Lambeth, Inc., premier furniture manufacturers.

GROWTH POTENTIAL: Unlimited. For example, Phil started a small piano manufacturing firm when he was 26, and by his active management built it "into one of the Big 10 in the business in less than a decade."

SPARE-TIME ACCOMPLISHMENTS: Wrote and illustrated *Success in Small Business Is a Laughing Matter*, an irreverent, commonsense guide to buying and running a small business. Phil is also a master at tournament bridge and a pinball wizard.

BUSINESS PHILOSOPHY: "Whether you're a lieutenant leading a platoon in Antequitok, or manager of the jewelry department, get down with people. Practice hands-on management."

SCOTCH: Dewar's "White Label!"® "I like to drink it in unpredictable situations; for example, straight up from a Dixie® cup while a rainshower delays a round of golf or over frozen soda cubes after seven-digit pinball."

Dewar's never varies.

The Dewar Highlander

BLENDED SCOTCH WHISKY • 86.8 PROOF • © 1980 SCHENLEY IMPORTS CO., N.Y., N.Y.

Figure 5-11. *Mandatories* and *legals* are often spoken of together. While they are similar in that they *require* placement in the copy, there is a difference. Legals are required by explicit law; mandatories are required by usage, tradition, or a desire to safeguard against misuse of a name or intangible property by a competitor.

In the Dewar's Scotch advertisement, New York State laws for the advertisement of liquor require the inclusion of the corporate name and state location. That is the legal. The mandatory is the ® at the "White Label" and at the Highlander's figures, and the © at the address line of the copy; they ensure that no one loosely uses the name "White Label" or "Highlander" or copies the format of the advertisement.

Figure 5-12. The advertisement for Camel cigarettes indicates a return to the old, traditional type style for their logotype and package face rather than a more modern, perhaps colder, typeface.

Figure 5-13. Bloomingdale's, the nationally known retail store, redesigned its logotype completely on the occasion of its 100th anniversary. Note that the artist incorporated "100" permanently in the new signature, viz., 100 after the "B." The older, script logotype was thus brought "up to date."

Figure 5-14. Here is the current logotype for the company known as Minnesota Mining and Manufacturing Company. Today they advertise as 3M, and the logotype makes that clear.

Logos

Most often company signatures and brand names are visualized in individual graphic designs. When a corporate symbol is registered with the federal government, it is called a *trademark*. The symbol is accompanied by an "®" signifying it is registered. A "T.M." indicates that the registration is pending. The word *logotype* or *logo* refers to the entire legal signature of a company, whether that be a visual symbol, a name printed in a special type, or both. A recognizable logo is one of the best devices to ensure that a product, corporation, etc., are remembered.

There are several successful companies that specialize in the creation of a total corporate "look," invariably centered around a corporate symbol. Alert and respected corporations, as the years pass, keep looking at their corporate trademark. They analyze it in relation to "today." Thus, we see corporations doing any of a number of things:

1. They may stay with their corporate symbol through the decades. (See Figure 5-12.)
2. They may subtly change the symbol. While the public may not be consciously aware of a change, younger people generally are more comfortable with an updated look.
3. They may change the symbol demonstrably, to drop an old-fashioned type or to indicate growth or incorporation of new businesses. (See Figures 5-13 and 5-14.)

Slogans

A major concern of effective advertising is to make sure that the product is remembered. One of the best devices and among the most helpful is the use of a memorable slogan.

A slogan is a sentence or part of a sentence designed to aid the reader or listener to remember the essential message. An advertising slogan, of course, attempts to achieve this "remembering" on behalf of the product. The creation of a good slogan must be based upon certain characteristics that have been proven effective:

1. The slogan must be short.
2. It must be easily understood.
3. It should be appropriate to the product (or company).
4. It should be easily recognized.
5. It should be easy and pleasant to remember.

The last point is important. Like an old saying, the phrase must be fun to repeat and "come trippingly off the tongue." Lest that seem too literary, it is suggested that you attempt to identify and evaluate a few of the slogans that have been around for many years. Some examples follow:

"I could have had a V-8." (vegetable juice)

"Good to the last drop." (coffee)

"It never varies." (Scotch whiskey)

"Like no other store in the world." (retailer)

"We are driven." (automobile)

Many of the figures of speech that apply in literature and poetry may be applied to the creation of a slogan. It usually has rhythm, rhyme, alliteration, or parallelism.

All slogans share the major function of aiding memory. There are, however, certain specific tasks or functions that different slogans may perform. Among these functions are the following:

1. To describe the use of a product:
   "Go Greyhound and leave the driving to us."
2. To suggest the product's special advantage or unique benefit.
   "Pan Am, the world's most experienced airline."
3. To suggest increased use or frequency of use:
   "The one beer to have when you're having more than one." (Schaefer beer)
   "It's not just for breakfast anymore." (Florida orange juice)
4. To stress the quality of the product:
   "The quality goes in before the name goes on." (Zenith)
   "That is the Total difference." (Total cereal)
5. To associate a family of products:
   "From a company called TRW" (TRW, an industrial conglomerate)
6. To sell the company as an institution:
   "The store America shops at." (Sears)
   "Where we are all the things you are." (Saks Fifth Avenue)
7. To prevent substitution and thus to protect patent rights:
   "Kleenex,® a product of Kimberly-Clark Corporation."
   "Sanka® brand decaffeinated coffee."

A slogan is not merely a clever headline nor a sound campaign idea. It can be either one of these or neither. It must be catchy, easily remembered, and it must be repeated again and again. In the purest sense of the word, a slogan should not be called that until it almost enters our daily speech, when one person who uses it is promptly understood by another. It is this repetition that creates its effectiveness.

De la mazorca...
a la botella...
a su cocina...
Aceite Mazola

El Aceite Mazola es aceite 100% puro de maíz, de color dorado como el sol. Es ligero, y todos los platos preparados con Mazola quedan ricos y con sabor delicado, como le gustan a su familia. Para comidas saludables y sabrosas, cocine con Aceite Mazola.

Aceite Mazola es bueno... naturalmente.

ASK YOUR DOCTOR... about a total dietary program that includes MAZOLA CORN OIL

Mazola
100% PURE
CORN OIL
32 FL. OZ. (1 QT)

© 1980 Best Foods, CPC International Inc.

Finally, it is to be kept in mind that a slogan is particularly effective in implanting a single selling idea and in providing a basic overall theme for a multi-product company. (See Figure 5-15.) It can provide continuity for a campaign and thus is a powerful tool in political campaigns and causes.

Any slogan should be closely linked with the corporate symbol (logo). To "visualize slogans" implies that the slogan existed in words first, and it may have. Instances of slogans whose visuals are as famous or more famous than their words include: the Doublemint Twins, Aunt Jemima, and the Campbell Kids (where the "kids" are the visual slogan). Another is the leaning figure in the slogan for

Klopman Fabrics (division of Burlington Mills), "You can lean on Klopman." But they are few.

The word "slogan" is derived from an old Gaelic war cry meaning "To battle!" A good slogan creates memorability, for the battle here is the sale, and the battlefield is the market place. Once the words are established, the visual most often comes to the aid of the creative mind.

The kind of verbal and visual thinking used in developing both slogans and logos is very useful in special projects, such as merchandising promotions. The excitement here starts with the earliest planning, and never lets up until the close. If it has been a successful promotion, the excitement does not stop, but usually provides impetus for a swing into something else—similar but different. The opportunity for creating a merchandise or institutional theme will give your verbal and visual talents full play. Everything may revolve around that theme. Color, decorations, copy lines, advertising headlines, display posters—all must "take off" from the theme. The concept must be appropriate to the company, to the merchandise, to the objective to be accomplished, and to the timing. The sources for theme ideas in this kind of promotion lie in ethnic cultures, popular heroes, historic events, the arts and sciences, or any aspect of our lives and times.

THE LANGUAGE OF COPYWRITING

Finally, in the whole area of copywriting, the writer must be constantly concerned with the language of copywriting.

Several times before in this book, the importance of involving the reader (or viewer, listener, etc.) has been stressed. The potential customer can be involved through strong selling ideas, through an interesting story, or through his own emotions—each of which incorporates the copy approach previously discussed. In all of these approaches, language plays a large part in the nature and degree of customer involvement.

We have an easy-to-understand concept of *emotional* involvement, but the involvement of *reason* must be accepted as well. Today, with every consumer better educated, better advised, more knowledgeable, it is important for the language in advertising to be sincere, honest, and believable. Products should be described in bright, vivid words, not in limp clichés. Be specific rather than general in expressing the superiority of your product. Above all, work to create belief. *Believable copy* creates *belief.*

It is just as important in the current market, with its emphasis on youth, movement and change, to be fast-moving, to avoid the slow, dragged-out explanation. Move with the times. Use current language, but avoid slang terms that are quickly in and out of vogue. Before the advertisement is printed in a national publication or broadcast over a TV station, the current phrase that was "in " when you wrote the advertisement, may possibly be "out." Where are the slang terms of several years ago, "boss" and "tough," (meaning good, great)?

The language of advertising also should be appropriate to the product, to the medium, to the expected audience, and to the objective of the advertisement itself. Years ago, this list also would have included, "appropriate to the company." Today, with the consumer orientation of every alert business, organizations have given up their stuffy ideas of what is appropriate to their own images. Banks can now laugh at their own campaigns; insurance companies choose the "slice of life" technique to talk about life insurance. Language, too, can be lighter. We should avoid pompous, smug phrases which may send a "hidden message" more forcefully than the intended message.

Finally, the days of talking about the twelve-year-old level of American mentality are passé. Advertising talks to masses of people who have a higher level of awareness and sophistication than ever before in history. Some advertising can talk at the level of a fast-reading, interested adult. But even the university-educated person with multiple degrees is put off by over-complicated sentences and four-syllable words. For all advertising, the simple, concise language of radio and television news, of the news magazines, or of the *New York Times* is the most desirable.

In industrial or professional advertising and in some trade advertising, technical language may certainly be called for and should be used in order to provide a more complete explanation. Here, the audience is a highly specialized and knowledgeable one. Laymen's terms would not be as effective as the jargon or professional language associated with a specific group, used to being "talked to" on a technical level. Therefore, in this kind of copywriting, the technical vocabulary is the appropriate one to use.

WRAP-UP

To summarize the writing of "strong" copy, all or some of the following fifteen rules and suggestions may be applied as your own *copywriter's checklist:*

1. The copy must involve the selected audience.
2. It should communicate its objective clearly to the audience.
3. It should work with the visual—send the same message.

4. It should help provide identity for the product, brand, and/or institution.

5. It should provide continuity with other ads in its series or campaign.

6. It should generally maintain the "you" (customer) point of view.

7. Avoid saying, "We offer a 50% discount." Rather, say, "Now you can have 50% off!"

8. The copy should open with the customer benefit, i.e., the dominant selling point or copy appeal.

9. Thereafter, it should move smoothly and simply through the steps of copy development and give the less important selling points.

10. The information given should be specific. For example, the copy should not say "much stronger," but 40% stronger than. . . ."

11. The copy must make believable statements—*belief* is the key to responsive action!

12. It should support all claims with specific proof.

13. It ought to tell the reader where to buy the product. (Frequently, as the marketing and distribution picture gets more complicated, there can be confusion as to the place to buy a given product. Is it to be found at the supermarket? At the drugstore? In a department store? Or in all three?).

14. Use language that is appropriate, current, fast-moving, simple, honest, and specific.

15. Finally, make a closing statement. Ask for action, even if it is just a suggestion. Ask for action with a stronger closing if the nature of the product and the offer warrants such a message.

THE ADVERTISING CAMPAIGN

From time to time, we have made reference to the "advertising campaign." Now that the basic elements of writing copy have been investigated, it is time that more detailed attention be given to the overall picture of planning and executing a long-term program, and subsequently, an advertising campaign.

HOW ADVERTISING IS PLANNED

In national advertising for large businesses, a program of advertisements is laid out for a year. The year is sometimes calculated from January 1, as any calendar year would be. More often, however, it is a fiscal year and begins with whatever month follows the largest block of sales for that business.

For example, in the automotive industry, September and October are the important months in which the cars of the coming year are "unveiled." In this industry, then, the big advertising thrust would be throughout September and October, and the calendar year ends in December. In women's fashions, August and September are the big seasonal kick-off months. In toys, (now more than a billion dollar business), all planning is targeted at late November and December for Christmas sales.

In the retail world, too, November and December see 25 percent or more of business, in which Christmas buying is the big focal point. Here the end of January is inventory time; accordingly, February is the initial month, and other promotions are lined up for the months to come.

Planning for these programs begins six months to a year ahead. In fact, as soon as one year is launched, a wise advertising manager or agency will begin thinking of the following year's advertising. This thinking will be done on one level of his intelligence, while other levels attend to the implementation of all the current secondary promotions throughout the year, of trade campaigns, local advertising, and so forth.

While this text will not concern itself specifically with budgets, it should be noted that the setting of general marketing goals, the determination of advertising's role in their achievement, and the budget needed to accomplish what is projected, all come before the planning of an advertising campaign.

A graphic view of national advertising plans is represented below (arbitrarily using a January kick-off).

Figure 6-1. Say "hello" to the Pan Am campaign whenever you meet its advertising, whether on TV, radio, outdoor billboards or, as here, within the pages of *Fortune*.

ADVERTISING PLANS FOR 1983

January 1982:	Goals set. Budget plans approved.
January to March:	Themes discussed. Copy platform under discussion.
March to May:	Agency decisions made. Presentation written with preliminary recommendations. General client approval sought.
May to July:	Final plans presented and approved by client. Media determined. Campaigns set.
July to September:	Copy written, art and photography completed. Client approval obtained. Production of print and broadcast advertising. Sales meeting held at end of this period.
October, November:	Trade campaigns and promotions start.
December:	Final details. Local advertising set, direct mail, etc.
January 1983:	Campaigns begin.

Lost Wax:
Jet engine blades from a 6,000 year-old technique.

Long before the Pyramids, ancient craftsmen used a method called the "lost wax" process to produce bronze, silver and gold objects of astonishing detail.

Very simply, a wax carving was covered with clay and baked. The wax was melted, or "lost," leaving a perfect mold.

Only the materials have changed.

At TRW we still use this **timeless** technique to cast **computer-precise turbine engine** blades for **jet aircraft**.

Today our metal is a **complex alloy** which **can withstand engine** temperatures up to 2,500°F while spinning at 8,000 RPM.

Creating single crystals.

Our metallurgists have perfected unique new ways to control the metal's crystalline structure.

Normally metal hardens into multiple crystals as it cools. But tomorrow's new fuel-efficient jet engines demand even tougher blades.

So we perfected a process that forces the metal to reject all but one crystal as it hardens in the mold, forming finished blades from one incredibly strong single crystal of metal.

But the process still begins with a 6,000-year-old idea.

Tomorrow is taking shape at

A COMPANY CALLED
TRW

©TRW Inc., 1981

← **Figure 6-2.** The importance of the campaign lies in its part in adding strength, continuity, and memorability to each individual advertisement that appears. The TRW advertisement from *Newsweek* magazine may automatically trigger the memory and call upon the familiarity of the dynamic TV commercials while adding those factors of detail and information that print provides.

THE CAMPAIGN

An advertising campaign is a series of advertisements concerned with a product or family of products (or services), having generally the same objective, with a unifying central creative theme or idea. This may be expressed in any number of appeals or approaches, but each advertisement indicates a "family resemblance" when it is varied for different media. The "personality" of the verbal and visual elements gives a campaign identity and continuity.

For example, the Ford Motor Company maintained the same basic campaign for several years with "The Better Idea," a central theme running through season after season of advertising campaigns. From billboards to television, the unifying idea was retained with many variations, but always clearly making its impact on the public. Recently a corporate variation has been added, extolling the factory operation and the finished cars as an "incredible" product.

This, in essence, is the importance of a campaign, and the importance of a strong central idea. It provides the maximum impact on the consumer for every dollar spent. No matter what the budget, the continuity and cumulative effect provided by a unified campaign make each advertisement more memorable. In addition, a campaign forces each advertisement to contribute to the one that follows it. This continuity provides a cumulative impact which is the synergism the advertiser hopes will give him extra sales. (See Figures 6-1 and 6-2.)

For the copywriter, there is a special plus derived from the aesthetic satisfaction of having created an effective campaign. (The satisfaction is not what the client pays for, but it adds immeasurably to the excitement of the job!)

THE COPY PLATFORM

A copy platform is a written statement of creative plans that goes through two stages. First, when a presentation is made to a copy supervisor and finally to the client, as all advertising agencies must do at regular intervals, a copy platform is included at the beginning of the section on copy. The copy platform has been discussed by copy chiefs, art directors, and, sometimes, account supervisors. It is hoped that it will later be approved by the client.

Before the campaign goes into production, the copy platform *must* be approved by the client whether or not some few changes have been or will be made. Then, in its second stage, it becomes the bible for each copywriter who works on that account.

The copy platform serves its purpose well:

1. In an actual job situation, it is sometimes difficult in coming to a new task, to know what is acceptable and what the client has forbidden; what the advertising director has stipulated as a must for inclusion in the advertisement, and what may be left out. Are there any slogans? Does this advertising fall in the midst of a campaign? What is the campaign?

2. The copy platform helps to untangle the possible confusion. It is a statement of certain large concepts and a review of small details which in actual application can be as important as the big ones.

3. Finally, it sets up the mandatories and the legals. (See the previous chapter for a discussion of these terms.)

Among the large concepts mentioned in (2) above are the goals that the advertising is expected to achieve. Next, the target audience that has been selected will be described. The central campaign idea or concept, which has been worked out by the agency, is included as a statement of the prevailing theme. The copy appeals are listed, as are the selling points that are to be covered in all copy.

The details mentioned in a copy platform include any product or merchandise specifications that are required; the way in which the corporate name and product name are to be used; and any other conventions that must become a part of the finished advertisement.

PROCEDURES FOR DEVELOPING CONCEPTS FOR CAMPAIGNS AND COPY

Up to now, we have covered a reasonably deep study of the factors that combine to produce effective concepts for advertising campaigns and copy. In fact, it would seem appropriate at this point to give the student copywriter an opportunity to look back and see how it is all put together.

The following are the steps generally covered in developing concepts (central ideas) for campaigns and then writing the copy. This need not be taken as gospel; it is a guide to a reasonable procedure that can be helpful before the copywriter gains enough experience to prepare her own procedures.

Steps to Develop Campaign Concepts

1. Assemble and analyze all the facts for planning a strategy:
   (a) The company you are writing for.
   (b) The audience you are writing to.
   (c) The product you must sell.
   (d) The objectives (product and/or institutional) of the

immediate advertisement.

    (*e*) The medium you are writing for.

2. Assemble and study the *ad facts,* mechanical facts about the proposed advertisement:

    (*a*) Is this a single ad, or a part of a campaign?

    (*b*) If print, what is the size and shape of the space?

    (*c*) Black and white or color?

    (*d*) If on radio or television, what is the length of the commercial? How will it be produced? What is the time slot? (See Chapter 7.)

3. Review the product facts; use buyers' fact sheets, all research, surveys, trade publications, etc.

4. List all the product's selling points.

    (*a*) Study and number them according to strength; relist them in order.

    (*b*) Decide on a cut-off point of usable selling points (usually three or so).

5. Determine the most effective copy appeal on the basis of the selling point chosen as the most important and dominant, the one that offers the greatest consumer benefit and becomes the theme of the copy and the headline area.

6. Decide on the copy approach. (*At this point, the copywriter has developed a concept.*)

7. Decide on tentative idea visualization; do lots of vizthinks and thumbnails. (See Chapters 10 and 11.) Make notations for the guidance of the art department.

8. Outline the body copy.

9. Write the headline. (Steps 7, 8, and 9 are interchangeable; sometimes one, sometimes another comes first.)

10. Write the first draft.

11. Check all facts again. Check copy against copy checklists and copy platform given you by your own company or against any other guides you may wish to use.

12. Confer with the art department on actual layout and artwork.

13. If necessary, rewrite the body copy or details of the copy to fit the final layout exactly. Be prepared to do a *character count* if exact typographical specification is required. This is called *copyfitting*. This technique is fully described in Chapter 11.

14. Write final copy, complete in all details, ready for typesetting. (Do not rely on the typists to do your detail work for you.)

15. After the advertisement is set in type, see the proofs at every stage. You are responsible.

As suggested in Step 11 above, it is wise to review the copy against a checklist, as well as to look at it critically, before rewriting it in final form. Some of the following may be pertinent questions to ask yourself:

1. Does the copy state customer benefit(s)?
2. Will it be interesting to a prospective buyer?
3. Is it accurate?
4. Is it clear?
5. Is it specific?
6. Does it give adequate information?
7. Is it plausible and *believable?*
8. Does it call for proof? If so, is your proof impressive?
9. Can it be made more concise?
10. Does it make the reader want the product?

MARKETING COMMUNICATIONS: FUNCTIONS AND RELATIONSHIPS

In our previous discussion, we have mentioned the term *objectives* as if we were talking to "old-timers" in the business and advertising world. We may be, but the chances are that many of you are newly entering the world of marketing, merchandising, advertising and communications, or of general business.

Let us look at some of the words that are frequently used in marketing communications, and see if we can visualize the function and relationship of one to the other. Let us consider:

- Company; client; agency
- Market decisions: potential customer, geographic distribution, demographics, psychographics, market segmentation, targets
- Objectives; goals; marketing strategy; market plans
- Audience (listener or viewer or reader) as delivered by media
- Concept or central idea
- Campaign implementation.

Campaign Objectives

The company you work for or the client of your agency must accomplish certain things. These are what we call *objectives,* and when they are projected into the distant future, they are generally called *goals*.

These objectives may seem to have a very simple base: to operate a business at a profit (to make money). This is to oversimplify. What is needed is a careful examination of what a business or

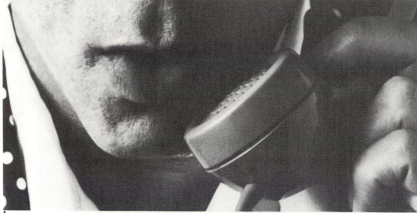

"Hello...this is Ruby Lips."

Citicorp introduces PassWord Service.℠ Suddenly all other travelers checks are old fashioned.

The luxury of ordering Citicorp Travelers Checks by phone makes PassWord Service the most convenient travelers check service in the world.

Presigned checks and your own secret password (like "Ruby Lips") make it the most secure. And it's that combination which has put Citicorp PassWord Service years ahead of any other travelers check today.

Now you'll never have to stand in line to buy a travelers check again. Just call toll-free, 24 hours a day, 365 days a year, from anywhere in the U.S., except Alaska and Hawaii. For an added convenience, we'll deliver the checks right to your home, office, or to selected Hertz Rent-A-Car counters.

© 1981, CITICORP

Signing checks is also a thing of the past. With the revolutionary process of ink-jet printing, your signature is presigned onto every check. That, plus having your own secret password, gives you security in travelers checks like you've never had before.

As for payment, you can have the checks charged to your personal bank account, MasterCard or Visa credit cards.

New PassWord Service from Citicorp Travelers Checks. Convenient, secure, and years ahead of everybody else.

Apply today by calling us toll-free at 800-645-3800. In New York State, call toll-free at 800-632-3216.

CITICORP ⊕®
PassWord Service™

Figure 6-3. Test this advertisement by asking your friends to identify the advertiser, or the advertiser's business. We are sure that the majority will never guess:"bank." But here, the creative connection of provocative headline and strong illustration work together to create an "eye-stopper" that then goes on to sell Citibank's exclusive PassWord Service.

company really needs to achieve, in very precise terms and after a great deal of precise thinking and analysis.

Some of the *specific* marketing objectives may include the following:

- To increase sales of the numbers of pieces of the product (units)
- To increase the numbers of people who will buy the product or who know the product
- To define the classifications of people who can be called natural customers for a product or a service (determining the age, the income area, etc.)
- To increase the use by those who already use the product
- To increase the prestige of a corporate name
- To combat competitive claims
- And there are many others.

Our means of attaining these objects is to create messages in words and/or symbols that carry our "need to accomplish" through

¡Llegó el momento de servir lo mejor!

<small>Añejado por 12 años, mundialmente. Whisky Escocés Blended, 86 grados prueba. General Wine & Spirits Co., N.Y.</small>

↑

Figure 6-4. The bottle shape and the label were designed to convey the prestige image for Chivas Regal's twelve-year-old blended Scotch whiskey. Throughout a campaign that has run many, many years, this package has been the visual star and the visual symbol of premium quality in Scotch whiskey.

In some advertisements, the bottle has been photographed with the label turned to the back; in others, the label has been shown alone. But the familiarity of the bottle and label has carried the Chivas Regal image and message without copy or with minimal body copy. Translate the Spanish or not—you get the message!

Figure 6-5. In this Maidenform advertisement, part of a long-running, highly recognized campaign, the advertiser understands the strength and appropriateness of the central idea to today's woman. "The Maidenform Woman, you never know where she'll turn up."

This company recognizes the value of an unchanging campaign concept, and is willing to stay with a good idea as long as the marketing picture remains much the same. This is the company that, a generation ago, initiated and stayed with possibly the first truly Freudian campaign, "I dreamt I attended the opera (. . . went to the circus, etc.) in my Maidenform bra."

a campaign with enough coverage to reach the preselected audience. Thus, in advertising, the campaign should be the focus of our efforts.

Campaign Concepts: Verbal and Visual

Our campaign concept or central idea is the result of actual mental gymnastics that result in the one best way to convey the needed message. Some of the characteristics of an effective campaign include the following:

- To carry the message quickly
- To be uncomplicated and simple
- To be easily remembered
- To be identifiable
- To be appropriate to the features of the product, service, or idea
- To be adaptable for uses in varied media
- To have pleasant associations.

**THE MAIDENFORM WOMAN.
YOU NEVER KNOW WHERE SHE'LL TURN UP.**

It's always smooth sailing in sleek, lustrous Sweet Nothings.
Elegant satin tricot with delicate scalloped lace. Sophisticated yet provocative.
Shown from left: sleepgown $20 and robe $28; demi-bra $12 and petti $11; softcup bra $7.50
and bikini $5.50. Just part of a whole collection of Sweet Nothings.
In a sea of colors.

Sweet Nothings® by Maidenform®

Prices are suggested retail. Prices higher in Canada.
Foundations and daywear made with Antron® Dupont registered trademark. Lace: Nylon. Tricot: "Antron III" Nylon, Exclusive of decoration. Photographed aboard Yacht Wuling.

Earlier, we mentioned some campaign concepts that answer all these criteria. An essential message of a product's dryness or its dependability, for example, is always conveyed by the visual and verbal ideas of the campaign. While individual advertisements (or commercials) change with different media or with different target markets to be reached, the visual and verbal *central ideas* are strong and clearly transmitted. The advertisement-to-advertisement variations simply cast a wider net around more people, but never weaken the essential unique selling benefits which are the core of the message. (See Figure 6-3, page 77.)

What may seem to be a simple task, simpler than creating a campaign concept, is the creation of a corporate symbol or trademark. But do not be misled; this is not easy. In many ways, it presents a greater challenge. Once the design is selected, a decision has been made that initially costs thousands of dollars, but may carry many millions of dollars of promotion over the years. Yet, each time it is seen, it can reinforce the identity and image that advertising campaigns have worked to build. (See Figure 6-4, page 78.)

WRAP-UP

To summarize this chapter's discussion of advertising campaigns, the following may be observed:

1. Start with a basic consumer (customer) benefit.
2. Keep the central idea simple but strong.
3. Do not be timid or fainthearted. Strike out with new, innovative ideas.
4. Subordinate techniques of advertising production, either verbal or visual, to a strong central idea. In other words, do not create the central idea around tricky type faces or grotesque camera shots.
5. Test a single idea against others.
6. Keep the central idea fresh with numerous variations.
7. Do not be swayed by "armchair" research.
8. Stick with your campaign idea so long as the marketing goals remain the same. (See Figure 6-5, page 79.)
9. Plan ahead for change.
10. Be ready to change when basic marketing conditions or new product benefits call for new goals.

BROADCAST COPYWRITING FOR RADIO AND TELEVISION

The broadcast media, radio and television, represent challenging areas for the writer. Many of the principles that have been discussed in this text of preparing copy for print media will apply equally to the preparation of copy for broadcast media. Special requirements for radio and television exist, of course, and these will be covered in separate sections.

RADIO

Radio has been around a long time, and according to the best information available, it is still growing. The Radio Advertising Bureau, the trade association to advance the use of radio as an advertising medium, has set out some statistics that can only be regarded as low given today's population explosion.

In the figures for 1980, there were said to be 456 million radios in this country. More than 80 million of us listen daily to programs coming from over 4,500 AM and 3,110 FM stations.

Car radios are a phenomenon in this field and are so important that prime time in radio is reckoned by the driving hours when people go to and from work (early morning and late afternoon to early evening).

SPECIAL CONSIDERATIONS

Radio is a personal medium, with different members of the same family listening to different radios (largely considered a personal rather than a family possession). Of course, these family members are tuned into different stations, all at the same time. Radio has the effect of "polarizing" its audiences.

This makes radio a highly selective medium, where media selection can almost pinpoint an age group, a family member, an income, an educational level.

Geographically, radio is again highly selective. A local or a national advertiser can literally cover a desired region by placing his commercials on radio stations covering the precise area that is important to him.

Marketing plans and goals figure heavily in planning any media schedule and can be particularly well-served by radio. In this medium, there are network (national) broadcasting, regional networks, and spot or local radio.

Time slots for commercial messages are bought by advertisers, and these, grouped together, are called a *buy*. Local radio schedules may be bought locally by local advertisers or sponsors. In this case, the buy is referred to as *local radio*. When time on the same local stations are bought by *national* sponsors on a pick-and-choose basis, that kind of schedule is called a *spot radio buy*. (The confusing dual use of "spot" is industry practice: A spot can be a time slot; it can also be a kind of buy.)

An advertiser may sponsor a program, may participate in a program, or buy spot announcements. Stations offer package deals, with a mixture of prime time and less desirable time, offered at a cost lower than that of a purchase of the same spots on an individual basis. Frequency discounts are offered, for number of weeks scheduled, number of commercials per week, and other considerations that involve the amount of time bought.

An advertiser can buy time at a cheaper rate if he is willing to take his chances on the timing of the spots and allow them to fall anywhere in the programming where the station can fit them. This is called *run-of-station,* always referred to by the initials *ROS*. (This is similar to the phrase used in a newspaper buy, *ROP, run-of-paper,* where the advertiser is willing to let the newspaper decide where to place his ad.)

Very often, however, the advertiser will prefer to pay a somewhat higher rate in order to gain the privilege of designating the program or features he wishes to carry his commercial or to be adjacent to certain programs. The word *adjacency* is used to cover this kind of juxtaposition as well as to the running of two commercials (competing or not) one after the other.

The advertiser will very frequently stipulate a personality program. (A *personality* in radio and TV terminology refers to a regular and familiar radio voice or television performer, such as a DJ, a news commentator, show host, or panel moderator.) The advertiser will be willing to pay a premium for a given disk jockey (DJ) to deliver his commercial, or to have the commercial occur during that program. Certain "talk programs" and panel shows have the same drawing quality as DJ's.

WRITING FOR RADIO

Radio calls for a special kind of copywriting, one that takes into full consideration the unique auditive impact of this medium. In every other form of writing for advertising, there is some place for the message to communicate with the eye of the potential consumer. This is the case in print media, television, direct mail advertising, point-of-purchase, transit, and outdoor advertising.

In the medium of radio, however, the copywriter writes for the ear alone. He has a message to deliver, a voice that will deliver it, and some sound effects, musical or otherwise to help in the impact. It implies the complete inability to illustrate the product visually. Everything is sound and imagination. Your words and sound track must do the whole job. If color is important, your description must

```
CLIENT:  Montaldo's                          LENGTH:  30 sec.

PRODUCT:  The "Two-Eighteen" Shop

AGENCY:  Emerson/Wilson, Inc.



TITLE:  "Lunch and Fashion"


_____



MONTALDO THEME

FADE MUSIC UNDER SFX OF LUNCH CONVERSATION, ANIMATED WOMEN'S VOICES, TINKLING

OF GLASSES, ETC.

                          ANNCR:

                          Nobody really has lunch at Tiffany's...But lunch at

                          Montaldo's is for real...It's for the career girl...

SFX:  LUNCH,              Every Thursday from noon 'til one-thirty.  You can enjoy
VOICES, ETC.
                          lunch for a dollar and see informal modeling.  It will

                          show you what the Two-Eighteen Shop is all about...A

                          special place where you'll find clothes that carry the

                          look of quality and fashion.  All designed and priced

MUSIC UP--                with the career girl in mind.  Enjoy.  Montaldo's lunch
DELIGHTED VOICES,
APPLAUSE.                 special every Thursday, anytime between noon and one-thirty.

                              Montaldo's Two-Eighteen Shop--Uptown
```

let the listener "see" the color. Nowhere is descriptive, dramatic language more necessary than in writing radio copy.

It is important, above all, to be clear in the meaning of the words you use. It is important to be clear, also, as to the product benefit your copy is describing to the listening audience, especially to your target audience.

It is important to capture the listener's attention a moment before you launch your most important selling line. Radio has to be an "intrusive" medium if it is to carry a selling message. Radio listening is often a matter of background, shared attention, or soothing influence. This is the reason that so many commercials open with sound effects or a musical flourish designed to attract the listener's attention.

Figure 7-1. In this radio script, the writer sets up his instructions and speakers as if writing a play. All instructions, time marks, names of actors or speakers are typed in caps. The body of the commercial is typed in upper and lower case.

These openings are the equivalent of the natural opening of a conversation. When two friends meet, there is usually a greeting before any important piece of news is announced. A "Hi there . . . Say, did you hear . . ." may not be the most formal opening for a conversation, but it is realistic. One speaker makes sure he has the other's attention before starting the important information. This is a good practice to follow in writing radio copy.

It is essential to achieve the involvement of the listener in order to get the selling message across. The words and the *sound* of the words are essential if the message is to "intrude." To achieve effective sounds for words, the director often employs unusual or strange voices with music or sound effects "under" (subdued) for emphasis. The radio copywriter "visualizes" or "soundthinks" his copy in this way, with suggestions for types of voice, music, and sound effects. (See Figure 7-1 for a typical script with "visuals of sound.")

Seasoned copywriters use a variety of devices to capture and hold the listener's attention and to invite his involvement in the radio commercial. These devices include the following:

1. Use product-in-action sound effects (like orchestrated percolator sounds for instant coffee commercials).
2. Provide a mixture of approaches, using a jingle, dialogue, straight announcements, sound effects, etc.
3. Use a "symbolic" character-voice (perhaps a foreign accent for a foreign product, for example).
4. Tie in with the station's features and programs.
5. Use celebrities whose voices are well-known.
6. After a campaign theme has been chosen, vary the musical style. A musical jingle can be arranged as a waltz for one commercial, as a polka, a march, a folk song for others.
7. Tie in with current events.
8. Permit *ad libs*. This becomes a must when the schedule includes popular personality shows, DJ's, or easily recognized announcers.
9. Try orchestrated sound effects.
10. Have the arranger provide *speed-ups* and *slow-downs*, which have humorous effects. Sometimes this can be done at the station by the sound engineer.
11. Use a popular or standard tune that is in the public domain. (This means that the rights to the use of the music have run out, and anyone may use the tune without special payment.) Besides the money-saving aspects of this device, you gain the advantage of the sentimental value that an old song always carries with it. By careful choice, you gain "instant atmosphere."

12. Instead of actors in the roles, try recorded "real life" interviews.

13. If your script calls for children's voices, insist that the casting be done with actual children. They add freshness and believability to the commercial.

14. If the script calls for an authoritative voice, ask that a celebrated commentator be used. He will always add prestige and credibility.

15. Finally, for a humorous touch, try a character switch. Call for a prize fighter with a "milquetoast" voice, for an example.

The language of the radio commercial is all-important. Consequently, the one unflagging rule to follow is this: *Read every commercial out loud,* and listen to yourself with a critical ear. (As a suggestion: The copywriter could tape the commercial he has just written and listen to it critically.)

Many figures of speech that are colorful in printed copy will not stand the "out loud" test. For example, alliteration is often used to good effect in newspaper or magazine advertising. It is usually defeating and destructive in radio (or television) commercial announcements.

As an illustration, look at the following headline:

Fresh, Flavorful, Fragrant Coffee.

In printed copy, it reads beautifully and conveys everything that is desirable in a cup of coffee. However, when read out loud, it becomes a tongue-twister.

Suffixes in "ly" can be troublesome in some word combinations, too. Too many "s" sounds result in unpleasant, hissing effects. Words should be current, rather than obscure. Sentences should be short and conversational in tone. Contractions (can't, we'll, etc.) make the copy "read" smoothly and easily and convey a friendliness that is desirable.

The actual writing of a radio script is similar to that of a play without stage directions. Copy forms are usually provided by advertising agencies and guide the new copywriter to what is wanted.

If a radio script is to be read "live" by a station announcer, punctuation becomes especially important. Indicate pauses by a double dash (--). Avoid using three dots (. . .); they do not convey an exact meaning to the announcer. Emphasis of a word or phrase or of the product name is indicated by underlining. Obviously, very few words in a thirty- or even a sixty-second commercial should be underlined. The excessive use of emphasis results in a stalemate for the announcer. Product or corporation names that are pronounced differently from their spelling or have some special kind of pronunciation should be spelled out phonetically at the bottom of the script page. Numbers and all elements of an address should be spelled the way you want them read. Do not abbreviate.

While you are reading your copy for its sound, you must read it for timing. An average of 120 words per minute is generally accepted for easy listening, with extremes of 100 words per minute as a minimum and 160 as a maximum.

BROADCAST PRODUCTION

Guidelines for the radio copywriter include the need to know the production procedure of a radio commercial and some of the costs that are involved in this and in the use of radio (and television) commercials on the air.

In copywriting for *print* media, apart from knowing whether the schedule provides for color or for black and white, and what size a given advertisement is to be, the copywriter does not need to know too much more about production costs. The art director, however, has to understand production thoroughly. Under the direction of an art director, a traffic manager and production manager are present to take the copy and set it in type, to order and to estimate costs of all forms of production. A knowledge of print production is helpful to the copywriting student, but it is not essential.

In radio and television, however, a general knowledge of how the script gets onto the air is essential, and a recognition of the costs involved is obligatory. Every word, every stage direction can cost money, and it is the copywriter's business to know what he is doing. If he calls for seventy-six trombones, he ought to know whether his firm or his client has that kind of budget. If his script calls for several voices, each one has to be figured into the budget.

TECHNICAL ASPECTS

The way radio time is bought affects the way a radio commercial may be produced and, consequently, the way it is to be written.

Radio commercials may be live or taped (prerecorded). It is obviously a mistake to pay a premium placing commercials on a DJ's program and then provide a totally transcribed (taped) commercial. In this case, a live commercial is better. On the other hand, it is a mistake to permit a live commercial to be put out over the air on ROS spots, where the advertiser retains no control over time, personality, or over the quality of announcement.

There are advantages in each type of production. The live commercial retains a vitality and personal appeal that is highly desirable. It is especially so, as has been noted, if the *time-buy* is one of a well-known radio personality who has a style and manner of delivery that has won him his popularity. In these cases, a live commercial is completely acceptable. It has the added virtue of being without any cost for production. It is also completely flexible; a change in weather can be reflected in a change of copy almost effortlessly. It may be varied almost at will; there is unlimited possibility, again because the live announcement carries no production charge.

The studio method of production, referred to as *transcribed* and abbreviated as *ET* (electrical transcription), results in a much more carefully worked out commercial. This very fact can be an advantage—for a client who wants an absolutely precise, mistake-proof delivery that comes over the air in exactly the same way, no matter how often it is repeated. (In live broadcast, there is always the possibility of human error, a slip-of-the-tongue, for example).

There are disadvantages to ET as well. No quick change can be inserted into a transcribed commercial, of course. Variety can be present only to the extent permitted by the production budget when the commercials were planned. There is a tendency to get a "canned" effect. Sometimes it intrudes oddly in the midst of a program of another mood. It is inflexible. Production charges can be expected to be high, and so, variations in a campaign may have to be limited.

Very often, a combination of live and taped announcements seems to provide a solution. The jingle (musical introduction or accompaniment) can be taped with all the studio quality and polishing that it warrants. The body of the commercial message can be taped as well, in several variations at one studio session. Then the introduction and closing (*intro* and *close*) can be inserted by the station announcer, broadcast personality, or DJ as a live announcement.

This arrangement provides the lively quality of a well-known personality whose program has been bought at a premium price. It also assures a uniform quality for the main part of the selling message.

In radio and in the audio of a television commercial, the copywriter should know that to transcribe a commercial entails the following elements:

1. Where there is music, it must be expected that there will be a payment to a commercial music library for a piece of music already in existence, or payment to an arranger for an original piece of music, and then payment for the rights to use that.
2. A studio must be engaged.

3. Musicians and/or vocalists must be hired, at union scale. The greater the number of musicians and vocalists, the higher the budget.

4. An announcer has to be hired to deliver the message, the actual spoken commercial. He, too, is a member of a union.

5. A master tape is made, and at least two tapes are provided for each station on the schedule. Commercial grade records are sometimes used, where some stations express that preference.

6. If the script calls for various speaking voices, actors and actresses are hired, again at union rate.

These factors will generally cover the recording of radio commercials and of the audio of a television commercial.

To these audio costs, television video must add directors, producers, cameramen, props, electricians, stylists (for food, fashion, home furnishings, even for industrial shots), additional actors, and so forth.

RESIDUALS

Another item that must be figured into the overall radio commercial budget (also true for television) is the talent reuse fees, called *residuals*. The musicians, announcers, vocalists, and actors are paid on a union scale under union contract agreements that stipulate how often a commercial may be replayed or reused for a given fee. Generally, the first fee pays for the recording of the commercial and thirteen weeks of use in a certain number of cities.

At the end of the stipulated period, or at the end of thirteen weeks, a new contract period is negotiated and a new fee is paid. Each variation of script and/or of musical arrangement within a campaign carries its own fee.

It should be clear then how closely allied are the task of the copywriter and the cost of the commercial. There is one bright spot in this for the copywriter and advertiser: they can look forward to having the best talent they can afford because work in broadcasting has become so lucrative it has attracted top stars of theater and films.

TELEVISION

The television industry is so big that it captures the imagination with its very size. Young copywriters are intrigued with the idea of writing for TV. Television is first and foremost a visual medium and must be so considered from the very inception of an idea. The ability to make the creative connection between visual and verbal (which includes all the possibilities of sound mixing) is a do-or-die skill for

Wells, Rich, Greene, Inc. 767 Fifth Avenue New York, N.Y. 10022

Plaza 8-4300

TELEVISION

CLIENT UNION UNDERWEAR	CODE NO. XNPR1173 DATE
PRODUCT UNDEROOS	LENGTH :30 AS RECORDED
TITLE YOU AND YOUR UNDEROOS/Girls	JOB NO. 15601-00072 TV

VIDEO	AUDIO
ANIMATED BATGIRL LEAPS IN ANIMATED SKY, CAPE FLAPPING IN THE BREEZE.	BATGIRL: Jumping Underoos! Is that another Batgirl?
ANIMATED BATGIRL JOINS LIVE GIRL IN FRONT OF PAINTED "CYCLONE" UNANIMATED BACKDROP.	GIRL: It's me and my Underoos!
LIVE GIRL JUMPS IN FRONT OF PAINTED "WEB" BACKDROP.	GIRL SINGS: You and your Underoos. CHORUS OF GIRLS SHOUT: Spiderwoman!
LIVE GIRL DANCES BY PAINTED "K-POW" BACKDROP.	GIRLS SING: Can you tell us who is who? CHORUS SHOUTS: Catwoman!
LIVE GIRL AND ANIMATED SUPERGIRL GESTURE TO EACH OTHER IN FRONT OF PAINTED "ZAP" BACKDROP.	GIRL: Is Supergirl on the left? CHORUS SHOUTS: No right!
LIVE GIRL AND ANIMATED SUPERGIRL EXCHANGE PLACES.	SUPERGIRL: Underoos look out of sight. CHORUS SHOUTS: Supergirl!
LIVE GIRL AND ANIMATED WONDERWOMAN DANCE IN FRONT OF PAINTED THOUGHT-BUBBLE BACKDROP.	GIRL SINGS: Wearing Underoos is fun.
CLOSEUP OF WONDERWOMAN AS SHE WINKS.	WONDERWOMAN: You can take it from us -- we're the ones. CHORUS SHOUTS: Wonderwoman!
5 PACKAGES POP ON IN OPTICAL SHOT WITH UNDEROOS SIGN.	GIRL SINGS: Underwear is fun to wear it's true.
PACKAGES REPLACED BY SINGING GIRLS IN UNDEROOS OUTFITS.	GIRLS SING: When it's you and your under... You and your under... You You and your Underoos!

the television copywriter. Finally, according to Marshall McLuhan, no other medium involves the consumer so completely as television[8], and this very involvement is what makes television the most powerful selling tool in the marketplace.

It is important to repeat some of the principles that have been stressed throughout these pages. The first questions that you as the copywriter must ask yourself are those mentioned in Chapter 3, "Planning for Advertising Copy Strategy," including:

 1. What is the company's image? Is it folksy, one of utility, or one of luxury?
 2. What are the specific stations on which the commercials will run? What time slots are planned? What programs will

Figure 7-2. Usually the television commercial is set up in two ways: in script form and in storyboard (see Figure 7-3). The script form calls for some very precise thinking about the *visual* on the part of the writer. Timing of action and matching action to words make the real creative connection.

[8]Marshall McLuhan, *Understanding Media: The Extensions of Man* (New York: McGraw-Hill Book Co., 1966).

our commercials precede or follow (adjacencies)? What programs has the Media Department "bought into"?

3. Who makes up the audience for which you are writing? Will it be children, teenagers, middle-aged women, men, senior citizens, tennis players, business executives, or trainees?

4. What is the product about which you are writing? What is its dominant selling point and its major benefit?

5. What is the objective of the campaign?

THE TV WRITER AND TELEVISION'S UNIQUE NEEDS

In writing a television commercial, the copywriter may well be the hub of a one-hundred-man team. The copywriter must capsule into the time-space of sixty seconds, more often thirty or even ten seconds, a little story that creates a mood, offers a "slice-of-life," conveys a selling message, and invites action. As always, the copywriter works with words. But in this medium, he is working with a whole film company as well. Producer, director, actors, artists, cameramen, union personnel, all will be responsive to what he sets down.

A television commercial is written in *script* form with vertically parallel copy. A dividing line appears on the printed form, right down the middle of the sheet. On the right, the "Audio" is typed. This obviously means everything that is to be heard and includes: announcer copy, the selling message, and desired sound effects (the latter typed in capital letters). All of these are very similar to the way the script of a play is typed, with "caps" instead of italics used for stage directions. (See Figure 7-2.)

On the left hand side of the television script in the column provided for it, the "Video" appears. These are the copywriter's instructions to the artist and director as to just what will be seen. These instructions, too, are typed in capital letters.

THE STORYBOARD

When the script has been reviewed and is generally approved, the copywriter works with the art director, who then puts the "action" (the video part) onto a *storyboard*.

The storyboard is a preprinted drawing pad with a series of panels in double series.

There are two or three types of storyboard in common use. In one style the upper panel, shaped like a small TV screen, is used by the artist to "rough-in" a succession of visual sequences which represent the video—what will be seen on the TV screen. Below each is a squared-off panel to carry what will be heard, the audio, in type beneath each scene. A second style is used when video instructions are included. It has the small TV screens running vertically down the board. The space to the left carries the *video instructions* (in capitals). The space to the right carries audio, *sound instructions* (in caps) and *speech* (in upper and lower case). (See Figure 7-3.)

The storyboard serves two purposes:

1. It permits the advertising agency to explain the planned commercial to the client in a graphic way, so that he perceives the general "drift" of the successive shots and sees each paired off with the words, the music, and/or the sound effects that will go with each shot.

2. It acts as a guide in the production studio. While not followed slavishly, it does indicate clearly to the producer and director what the agency copywriter and art director had in mind.

Since a basic television commercial is a sixty-second or thirty-second story, it follows that an effective commercial, one that projects its message into the living room, must limit itself to one message. It can sell one product benefit, and that is all that a copywriter should try to get into one commercial.

We are familiar with the complaints about television commercials being artificial, vulgar, extravagant, and repetitious. Nevertheless, television has tremendous impact on the buying habits of the listening audience—an audience that is the biggest of any medium, 97 percent of American homes. Television commercials, in fact, have gained stature as a source of entertainment in themselves; they are indeed watched.

The writer of TV commercials has an obligation to present an honest promise of a believable benefit as well as simple, useful information. He has, as well, a unique opportunity to make full use of the one selling device that television performs best—that is, to *demonstrate* his product.

TV'S TECHNICAL FACTORS

While there is a great temptation to keep away from technical language, there are some terms used in broadcasting that should be understood and some techniques that will affect the writing of a commercial. A list of these is included at the end of this chapter.

METHODS OF TELEVISION PRODUCTION

There is another technical phase that will affect the thinking as well as the writing of a commercial. These are the methods of production.

Figure 7-3. Various forms of story-board are used in the preparation of the television commercial. Either a horizontal or a vertical setup may be used to good advantage as long as there is space for the simplest kind of sketch in the miniature television screen, instructions for sound, camera instructions and, finally, the actual spoken words of the commercial.

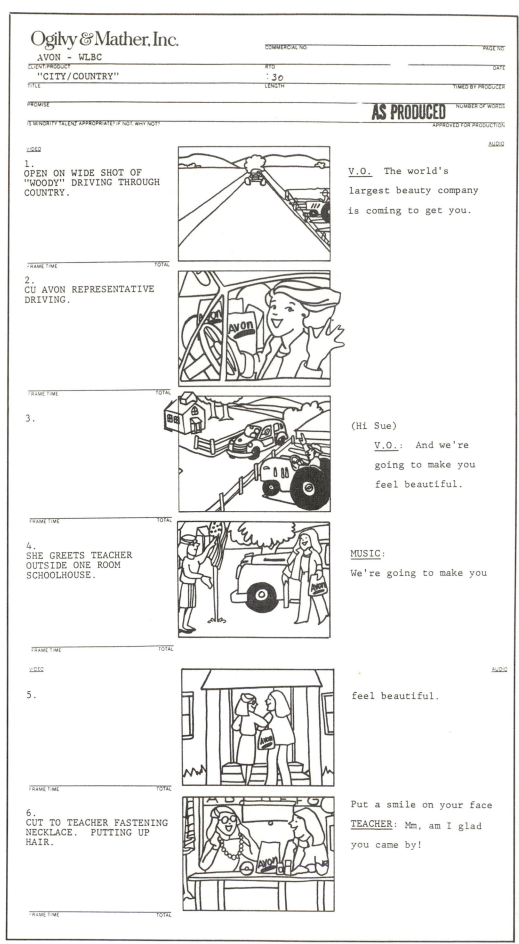

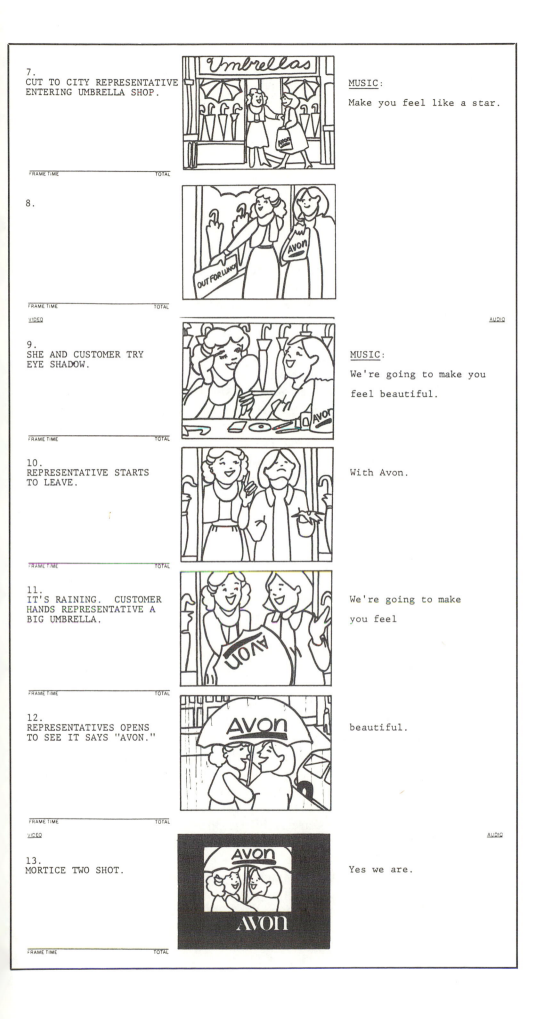

7.
CUT TO CITY REPRESENTATIVE
ENTERING UMBRELLA SHOP.

MUSIC:

Make you feel like a star.

FRAME TIME   TOTAL

8.

FRAME TIME   TOTAL

VIDEO   AUDIO

9.
SHE AND CUSTOMER TRY
EYE SHADOW.

MUSIC:

We're going to make you

feel beautiful.

FRAME TIME   TOTAL

10.
REPRESENTATIVE STARTS
TO LEAVE.

With Avon.

FRAME TIME   TOTAL

11.
IT'S RAINING. CUSTOMER
HANDS REPRESENTATIVE A
BIG UMBRELLA.

We're going to make

you feel

FRAME TIME   TOTAL

12.
REPRESENTATIVES OPENS
TO SEE IT SAYS "AVON."

beautiful.

FRAME TIME   TOTAL

VIDEO   AUDIO

13.
MORTICE TWO SHOT.

Yes we are.

FRAME TIME   TOTAL

There are three general methods of television production:

1. Live.
2. Film.
3. Videotape.

The use of one or another has a great deal to do with the expense of producing a commercial and can, in turn, limit the number of actors or the kind and place of action recommended by the copywriter.

The use of the live announcement in TV commercials is extremely limited. If used at all, it is in a smaller town locale for local broadcasts. One can imagine a live commercial shot on location for a shopping center during a special event. The spontaneous warmth of a live broadcast has its greatest effectiveness in the locality where the announcer is well-known or where the frequency of the commercials has made the announcer's voice almost a trademark for the sponsor. In a network personality show, where the celebrity delivers the selling message, it is very likely that the straight commercial has been taped previously and inserted into the program; however, a few words of lead-in or "patter" may, in fact, be live.

Filmed commercials are produced just as a motion picture is, with a producer, director, cameramen, cast of characters, casting and script directors, prop men, and electricians. Action is filmed and refilmed until it is just right; speeches can be reshot until they come over exactly as planned. The "perfectibility" of film is its greatest advantage.

Videotape, which reproduces sound and visuals electronically from live action, can be rerun immediately in order to review and approve or revise right "then and there." If a correction is called for, electronic editing permits great flexibility.

After shooting the commercial, the production footage on videotape is taken to a studio to be edited. Editing is the process of taking parts of this tape and putting them into the desired sequence. It is in the editing session that the "spot is built" and the commercial takes final shape. "Voice over" and music tracks are added. Special effects, "wipes," "fades," and "supers" can be inserted.

Modern editing studios are fully equipped with computerized electronic hardware that makes it possible to produce a spot commercial or an entire show in a fraction of the time it once took. In addition, these sophisticated machines provide superior and more varied electronic effects, including many that originally had to be done in the actual shooting session. The "squeeze zoom" allows the video editor to reposition a picture in different sizes in different sections of the screen. Split and multi-image effects, electronic "wipes" and patterns can be produced in seconds instead of hours. Computerized typesetting, no longer limited to a telegraphic typeface, enables the editor to compose and position type "supers" at will.

The important difference between editing movie film and videotape is that movie film must be physically cut and spliced. It then has to be sent to a laboratory to be made into a film composite. Videotape is physically untouched since it is cut and spliced electronically. This provides an instant editing capability that makes it possible to see the finished job as soon as the editing session is over. Copies of this final tape can be made and shipped to TV stations overnight.

NETWORK VS. SPOT OR LOCAL

Network is the term applied to national broadcasts of television or of radio programs, where local stations affiliated with an overall broadcasting company pick up the same program simultaneously or a little later in sections of the country where time changes make this desirable.

Local television or radio is just what the name indicates. It is the programming of a local station within its own geographical "coverage."

When a national advertiser buys time on local stations, it is called *spot* radio or television. Again, the name is descriptive, in that the schedules are "spotted" on stations across the country where they will do the most good to fulfill a given marketing objective.

BUYING TIME

An advertiser can sponsor a program and place his commercials within that program where they seem to the professionals to be most effective. He can be an alternate sponsor (with another advertiser) or buy *participations*. The latter is a popular, economical "buy," wherein the commercials are scheduled within the station's own programming. The weather, the news, public interest specials, a police story, a "talk show," a personality, and a situation comedy ("sitcom"), are among the programs that offer participations.

Stations offer time on varying price bases, designated as Class AA or A down to D. Class AA or A is "prime time," usually 7:30 to 11:00 P.M., so designated because surveys have shown that this is the time when most television sets are turned on. The copywriter should be familiar with the most-used options in time buying.

Time buying is handled by experts in the Media Department, but they are of concern to the copywriter because they affect the audience and the atmosphere that will surround his commercial. In the case of a "personality," there will be a well-known voice giving the selling message. This, too, can influence the writing.

TIMING COMMERCIALS

In general, a rule of thumb suggests the following for audio and video:

Audio: Allow about two words per second;
Video: Allow about five to six seconds per frame; shots can be held as long as twenty seconds, but this may be "draggy" and tiring to the viewer.

Because of the physical difference in length between a sound wave and a light wave, a given time slot does not provide the full length for the sound. A rough approximation follows:

Sixty-second spot allows for 55 to 58 seconds of sound.
Thirty-second spot allows for 27 to 28 seconds of sound.

The 10-second spot is usually an *ID* (identification spot) at the station break. With time out for the station's call letters, it usually provides for 7¼ seconds of picture and 6 seconds of sound.

Thus, it is important to write a word or two less than is apparently needed rather than to crowd the copy.

VIDEO CUES FOR TV SCRIPTS

Dolly in/Move in/Push in/Go in   Camera moving in for a closer look at subject.
Dolly out/Dolly back/Pull out/Pull back/Come out   Camera moves away from subject, creating a wider angle shot. Often used because the field of interest is broadened by the movement.
Pan   A horizontal movement of the camera on the friction head without any dolly movement. Either to left or right.
Tilt   A vertical movement of camera on the friction head without any dolly movement. Either up or down. Some directors say *pan up* or *pan down* instead of using the word *tilt*.
Truck/Travel   Usually a lateral movement of the dolly and camera. A shot that is not toward or away from the moving subject. Camera movement that parallels the scene.
Arc   A truck or curved dolly that travels a curved path or arc. Either left or right.
Follow shot   May be defined in several ways. In the true sense of the term, it means to follow by moving both dolly and camera with actor movement. It may be a shot in which the camera pulls back as the actor moves toward it, the distance between actor and camera remaining relatively constant in the movement. It may be

the reverse of this, the actor walking ahead of the camera as it follows him from behind in whatever direction he is moving. The director must be cognizant of the basic difference between a pan shot and a follow shot. In the pan shot, the dolly and camera remain in a fixed position while the cameras pan either left or right. In the follow and/or truck shot the dolly and camera both move with the actor or subject.

Zoom in   Changing a zoom lens from a wide-angle to a narrow-angle (telephoto) shot.

Zoom out   Changing a zoom lens from a narrow-angle (telephoto) shot to a wide-angle shot.

One shot (1-shot)/Single shot   A shot of an individual.

Two shot (2-Shot)   A shot of two individuals.

Three shot (3-Shot)   A shot of three individuals.

Group shot   A shot of more than three individuals.

Long shot (LS)/Establishing shot (ES)   A shot of the full figure of the person or persons, in which much of the setting is seen behind and beside them.

Extreme long shot (ELS, XLS)   A very wide shot of a large area or setting.

Full length shot (FS)   Generally a shot of a person from head to feet.

Medium shot (MS)/Close shot   Generally a shot from the waist up, unless otherwise specified.

Close-up shot (CU)   Generally a shot of the head and shoulders, unless otherwise specified.

Big close-up (BCU)/Tight close-up (TCU)   A shot of only head and face.

Extreme close-up (ECU, XCU)   A shot of a portion of the face or head. A "slice" of the face or head.

Cover shot (CS)   Usually a wide-angle shot covering a relatively large area in which action is taking place.

Combination close-up and long shot (CU-LS)   Usually a shot of two persons, one seen close to camera while other is seen in distant background.

Over-the-shoulder shot (OS)   A shot of two persons taken over the shoulder of one of them. For example, in an interview situation involving two persons, we see one person over the shoulder of the other. Quite frequently, this type of shot comes in pairs, in which case the over-the-shoulder shots are matched. For example, we see Mary over the shoulder of Jane, and when the cut is made to the other camera, we see Jane over the shoulder of Mary.

Imaginary line   In an interview situation, for example, the director may visualize an imaginary line joining two people conversing. She must be cognizant of this line so she will not make the mistake of positioning one of her cameras on the opposite side of the imaginary line. If she does position one camera on the opposite side, then the cut to that camera will reverse the direction in which the subject is looking.

Defocus   The camera is cranked all the way out of focus by rotating the optical focus control for effect, usually to end a scene.

Knee shot/Thigh shot/Waist shot/Chest shot or *Bust shot/Shoulder shot/Head shot*   Other ways to indicate shots.

AUDIO CUES

Ready audio   Standby cue to audio engineer.

Standby music, theme   Cue to audio engineer to standby with turntable going and ready to slip cue record of theme or music being used in program.

Hit theme, music/Roll theme, music   Cue to audio engineer to bring in music at full peak or volume and hold until established.

Music in full   Music is brought up to normal peak set for the introduction of program or at any other specified spot in the program.

Music under/Take music under   Volume of music is taken down under the dialogue or sound being used, usually for background purposes.

Sneak in music/Fade in music   Music is rolled with volume, either all the way down or very low. Then the volume is gradually increased until desired peak is reached. Generally used to bring music into background as a scene is progressing.

Music down and out/Fade out music   Music is taken down and faded out completely, according to speed desired.

Music up/Bring music up   Increase volume of music. For transitional purposes, at the end of a scene, and usually at the end of the program.

Sneak out music   Music is being used in background and director wants it to fade out completely. He may want it faded out slowly or rapidly according to effect he desires to convey.

Fade music and pic   At the close of the program, the music (audio) and the picture (video) are faded out simultaneously.

Open mike   Cue to audio engineer to throw switch that controls the particular mike to be used.

Mike check   Director or technical director asks audio engineer to have all mikes checked to make certain they are functioning properly before program hits the air. Usually an assistant on the studio floor does this with a "count down" technique.

Mike level   The mike is opened and the talent speaks relative to placement of mike. He speaks lines exactly as he would were he on the air. Director often wishes to hear this level check.

WRAP-UP (RADIO)

The following guidelines represent a summation of the features that combine to create effective radio commercials:

1. In writing copy for radio commercials, all the elements that lead to setting up a strategy must be considered.
2. Isolate the objective of a given commercial, and keep it in mind throughout.
3. Open with an attention-getting sound device.
4. Present an informative message that will create pleasant product associations; you want your listener to identify with and react warmly to the product.
5. Keep selling points to a minimum (generally one is enough in a thirty-second commercial).
6. Use words to create pictures; use the *sound* of words. Add to your unseen "visualization" with sound effects and music. SOUNDTHINK!
7. Repeat important words, elements, names.
8. Avoid offending your listeners with unbelievable claims or suspicious offers.
9. Persuade, do not bully the listeners.
10. Avoid tongue-twisters, difficult combinations of sounds, and meaningless adjectives.
11. Keep the dialogue believable and unforced.
12. Make your endings strong, positive, and let them suggest action.
13. Never forget you are writing for the ear/mind.
14. Read the script aloud for clarity and timing.
15. Keep the costs of production in mind.

WRAP-UP (TELEVISION)

The following guidelines represent a summation of the features that combine to create effective television commercials:

1. In writing copy for television commercials, all the elements that lead to setting up a strategy must be considered.
2. Isolate the objective of a given commercial, and keep it in mind throughout.
3. Single out one important selling point or product benefit. Make that the core of your appeal and stay with it. Even sixty seconds is too short an interval to try to make several points.
4. The video and the audio must relate to each other. Yet, the

words do not have to "mouth" exactly what is being shown on the screen. Try to have the words interpret the picture and, thus, move the action one step further.

5. Remember that television is essentially a visual medium. Think in terms of situations and rely on the video to carry more than half the weight of the message.

6. Especially in line with the current mood, the appeal to youth is full of action. Therefore, avoid static, slow-moving shots. Know what the camera can do and use it to best advantage.

7. *Time* the commercial yourself. Read it aloud. Use a tape recorder. Act it out. Use a mirror! The action takes more time than the words and must be provided for.

8. Learn the language of television production. You will need this to communicate your ideas *for the use of cameras* to effectively communicate the visualization of your copy.

9. Get to the television studio when your commercial is being produced. Seeing the actual production is extremely important, both for the commercial "in hand" and for your own growth as a copywriter.

ADVERTISING COPY FOR OTHER MEDIA

This chapter will discuss briefly four of the many channels that carry selling messages to the consumer. These are: direct mail, outdoor, transit, and point-of-purchase (POP) advertising. All of these are widely used and are handled by formal media schedules. Others, from balloons to sky-writing, are somewhat off the daily pattern and will not require additional copywriting skills to handle.

DIRECT MAIL

Direct mail advertising includes any selling message that uses the mail to reach prospective customers. It can be anything from a postcard announcing a fashion show to a six page brochure offering a set of encyclopedia.

Every business uses direct mail and frequently starts to use it before it opens its doors. Announcements are an old standby of this kind of advertising.

Two similar terms may cause confusion. *Direct advertising* uses the same materials as direct mail, but reaches the prospect by direct contact. For example, if a retail store mails an announcement of a special sale, that is direct mail advertising. When you enter the store, the identical flyer may be handed to you; then it is called direct advertising.

Mail order advertising is a method of selling (not a medium) that invites the placement of orders by mail and, in today's market, by telephone. Any medium may carry mail order: newspapers, magazines, direct mail, radio, or television. Today, even transportation advertising may offer a tear-off blank to encourage mail order.

In industrial or trade advertising, direct mail has its special functions. They include:

1. Getting orders.
2. Supplementing the efforts of the salesmen.
3. Getting inquiries for salesmen, called *leads*.
4. Following up on salesmen's calls.
5. Keeping customers and prospects posted on new products, special offerings, and interesting events.
6. Advising dealers of new merchandise, of promotional plans, and helping them sell their customers.
7. Offering services to customers (these may bring information of new services or emphasize services already in operation.)

Everywhere, retail stores make regular use of direct mail advertising. The specific uses may vary, but in general, direct mail has

SOUTHERN UTAH STATE COLLEGE LIBRARY

DISCARD FROM

been found to be particularly suitable for the following retail selling purposes:

1. To reach people in sections of the store's trading area where newspaper coverage is inadequate.
2. To address any selected group of people with common characteristics or interests: living habits, buying habits, merchandise preferences, etc.
3. To publicize single departments, especially those that offer specialized merchandise or service; to dispose of limited quantities of merchandise or merchandise of a single department.
4. To introduce new merchandise and services, such as new brands, new departments, repair service departments, and news of storewide sales events.
5. To announce private and advance sales to only a partial list of present customers. This can entice customers who patronize only one or a few departments to "check out" other departments.
6. To test customers' reactions to small quantities of new merchandise before buying and promoting in larger quantities. (This may include the distribution of advertising material provided by manufacturers.)
7. To invite cash customers and prospects to open charge accounts; to revive inactive charge accounts; and to welcome new customers.
8. To acknowledge orders or payments and to rectify grievances and complaints.

With any of these as objectives, the copywriter must fill in for herself a knowledge of the company she is writing for, of the consumers she is writing to, and the product or service she is writing about. An awareness of the medium being used, important in all advertising strategy, is *extremely* important in direct mail.

The medium of direct mail differs from others that have been discussed in two important ways: its flexibility and its accountability.

The effectiveness of direct mail depends to a large degree on the lists that are being used. In a retail store, the lists come from obvious sources: charge customers, regular "cash" customers, or those whose names have been taken down after an occasional purchase, and for prospects, those who move into the neighborhood or live in a given radial area around the store.

In trade and industry, retail buyers are generally the targets of the direct mail effort.

In an actual mail order business, which can run anywhere from the companies that sell notions and novelties to the giant Book-of-the-Month Club, Time-Life Books, etc., the lists are a much more complicated factor. Lists can be compiled by the advertiser or can be bought from brokers. These brokers advertise thousands of different lists that can be bought at a set price per thousand.

The flexibility of the medium lies in the variety of these listings: providing names by profession, by income, by club membership, by trade; geographical breakdowns; breakdowns by ownership—of cars, of homes, of boat licenses, etc. The possibilities seem endless. Flexibility, however, lies also in the way the advertiser uses the list. She may buy a list of 10,000 names, use them all at once, or use a thousand at a time. She may change her copy and send out several blocks of hundreds or thousands at a time, checking and comparing the results. Sometimes, the copy stands and the visual changes. Again, results are compared.

It is this ability to prepare different copy and to check comparative results that makes the direct mail copywriters able to check and prove out their efforts, thus providing the accountability. For the same reason, direct mail produces clear-cut results that can be tied in directly to costs. Results are based first on leads gained, then on sales made, depending upon the objective of the mailing. It is a matter, then, of simple division of results into costs in order to determine which of several variations gained the best results and thus proved most effective.

In writing copy for direct mail, the writer should observe rules that have been set forth for any copywriting. She should pay full attention to what has been described by salesmen and sales promoters as the selling process: attracting attention, arousing interest, generating a desire for the product, and inspiring customer action.

Frequently, to capture the attention of the recipient, the copywriter will create a provocative phrase or word to be printed on the envelope, to encourage the receiver to open it, at the very least.

Interest can be awakened by the headline, subheadlines, and by the illustrations and graphics where product benefits must receive heavy emphasis. In order to make a strong case for the desire to own the product, the copywriter should supply all possible specific information, details of construction, of performance, of any testimonials that may be on hand. Here, in the body of the direct mail piece, is the place to stress the quality of the product and the reliable reputation of the firm behind it. In essence, a direct mail advertisement asks the purchaser to accept a product on faith.

Inspiring customer action needs the strongest emphasis of all where a real sale is the objective of the mailing. There is almost a physical effort needed to bring a direct mail sale to a positive close. In addition to psychological priming in the closing portion of the body copy, with a strong urge to fill out the coupon, the coupon itself must be explicit in its instructions. The coupon must be strong enough to provide an incentive for the prospect to get up from an easy chair, find a pen, an envelope, a stamp, and make the real effort that filling out the information entails. Sometimes, too, she will have to enclose a check. This calls for positive persuasion at that final point of decision—all through the power of words and graphics.

There are a few simple rules for effective direct mail copywriting which deserve review:

1. Keep the writing style simple and direct. Make the graphics dynamic and eye-directing.
2. Use short sentences. In direct mail that goes to members of a specific profession or of a specific industry, technical language is appropriate and, in fact, expected.
3. Make subheads work. A four-page brochure needs the breakup that subheads provide. Each should signal a real product benefit and a fact of clear importance.
4. Place your two strongest statements in the following two dramatic places in the direct mail piece: first for the most important, and last for the second most important. In this way, you arouse attention and interest at the beginning and spur the reader to action at the end.
5. Repeat the product name frequently.
6. Give helpful information, arranged logically, as an aid to memorability. Permit the graphics to carry a large part of the logical arrangement.
7. Stress the quality and good workmanship of the product. This holds true even for a low-priced item.
8. As in all copywriting, stress the differences of your product from others available.
9. If more than one price level is included in the mailing piece, "sell up." Try to interest the prospect in the better item for "her own good," for "her own greater satisfaction."
10. Tie in to all other advertising running at the same time.

OUTDOOR; TRANSIT; POP

These three advertising media are far apart indeed in geographical placement and in function. The method of writing for these media, however, is similar. Accordingly, they are grouped in this section.

Briefly, the kind of writing needed for these media has probably already been completed by the copywriter if she prepared a total campaign. Usually the words and visual of the central campaign idea or the slogan are just enough for the reading time given to these three media.

Outdoor Advertising

Outdoor advertising, as its name implies, is the outdoor display of the advertising message. Its placement is based on the traffic that passes outdoor spots. Because this traffic is moving past the ad, it should be noted that time is an element in outdoor advertising. There is an unwritten rule that many copywriter's follow: "No more than eight words of copy on a billboard."

There are three general types:

1. *Posters* or *billboards* are the lithographed sheets that are pasted on boards and generally illuminated at night.
2. *Painted bulletins* are placed in more important traffic sites. The artwork and copy are painted directly on an appropriate surface. They are almost invariably illuminated at night.
3. *Spectaculars* particularly stand out among the various types of outdoor advertising. They are built of steel beams and sheet metals; they may use plastic; they make unusual use of flashing lights, smoke, steam—anything that will attract attention.

Transit Advertising

Transit advertising is the generic name applied to the poster advertising in terminals and stations and inside trains, subways, and buses (where they are called *car cards*). They are also found in large posters on the outside of buses.

The copy for this medium calls for a slogan, a product name, or the product's campaign idea. The same "rules" for outdoor advertising copy would apply to transit ads, which are, in effect, mini-billboards.

Since specific sections of a city can be selected in the buy (called a *showing*), it may be that more than one facet of a campaign can be emphasized in a limited variety of posters. Since it is bought on a monthly basis, seasonal copy changes can be made. These should be borne in mind if transit advertising appears on the advertising schedule.

Point-of-Purchase (POP) Advertising

Even the briefest discussion of this medium calls for an explanation of the name, point-of-purchase. The term means exactly what it says: at the place that the purchase is made—department counter, cashier's desk, bar—advertising of a specific product or brand is found as a reminder to the customer. This "advertising" is often part of a container or rack for the self-service merchandise that it describes.

In retail stores, posters and signs are very often part of display. Here, clearly, it is the poster at the entrance to a shop within shops, the card at the base of an interior display, the card in the window, that would be included in this category.

The term we have been using, point-of-purchase, should be explained further. Some people call this medium *point-of-sale* (abbreviated POS), but the association of firms involved in this kind of advertising business prefers the newer term which is used here and abbreviated POP.

The reason behind their preference is that earlier thinking about promotions was based on the seller's point of view, her products, her profit. Modern thinking is consumer-oriented, geared to the purchaser. The term point-of-purchase helps to underscore this thinking.

Here again, the copy must be simple: one idea, one product benefit, one fact. This may be where to find the item, its price, where it fits in the current fashion. The slogan, the campaign idea often are enough to remind the purchaser to choose your product.

WRAP-UP

In summary, keep these points in mind for outdoor, transit and POP copy:

1. Keep the message short so that it can be seen and absorbed by passengers in a passing car or a person walking by outdoor advertising.
2. If these media are part of a campaign (and they usually are), use the campaign headline or the central idea in the copy.
3. If visuals are used, they, too, should be easily seen by the passerby or passenger in a car. They should be dominant in the space.
4. For car cards and POP, advertising copy should be simple, short, and carry a single selling message.

IDEA VISUALIZATION: PERCEPTUAL LANGUAGE FOR COPYWRITERS

There is no point in going back to the early parts of our discussion in order to describe the kind of person who would make a good copywriter. We should have settled that question long ago, and it is expected that the copywriter has the kind of mind that is called "creative," that sees new relationships in old concepts, that visualizes innovative ways of presenting new or familiar products. This is a minimum of what can be expected.

Most people believe that they are capable of logical thinking based upon research, analysis, and evaluation. But very few will credit themselves with the ability for *creative* thinking which is a *skill* and can become a habit when it is cultivated intensively and consistently by copywriters and art directors.

MAKING THE VERBAL/VISUAL CONNECTION

An art director must be a communicator or else he is merely an arranger of elements in layout or ad design. Conversely, a copywriter must understand the language of the visual or else he is merely putting one word after another. Today's copywriter respects graphics. Today's art director respects words.

While logical thinking is vertical, procedural, and analytical, creative thinking is lateral and less structured. Creative thinking is basically a manipulation of memories or a rearrangement of fragments of memory. It uses associative patterns rather than step one, step two reasoning. It has been said that man cannot create anything absolutely new.

To test this, go a step beyond lateral thinking and try to visualize an entirely unique animal. You will find yourself taking part of one, part of another: the tail of a tiger, the mane of a lion, the ears of an elephant, etc. What if you were to say, "No, not the ears of an elephant, ears like conch shells!" You would only be proving the point that you think in terms of what you already know—and that you cannot create anything *absolutely* new. The very word "animal" requires you to think of known elements.

SOURCES OF CREATIVE IDEAS

All our inspirations are based upon memories and impressions of experiences. These experiences and impressions have at least three sources.

The first source of creative ideas is one's own personal experiences or vicarious experiences studied, read, heard about, or seen in art and/or films. Naturally creative individuals have unusual associative skills which enable them to bring a multitude of thoughts and impressions to bear upon a marketing problem, an effective product appeal, or a new approach. The writer develops the ability to turn his experience into *ideas;* this implies more than being a clever "wordsmith." The copywriter's responsibility is to *communicate.* Ideas that effect response from an audience contain a mix of visual/verbal language which is consistent with the audience's frame of reference.

The second experience source from which the writer can draw is his business and professional background. All of the copywriter's marketing information may be used as background. The greater the copywriter's grasp of professional and general business facts, the more inventive his output will prove to be. The length of time "at-the-job" also adds to inventiveness and innovative thinking—always provided, of course, that one does not "go stale."

A third source is our vast fund of abstract ideas. These are the mental patterns that two or more memories have in common. The abstractions are created when the brain recognizes the similarity. This is sometimes called a "fantasy search."

It follows, then, that a copywriter's creative output will depend to a great degree upon these supports:

- Wide education (learning experience) and its continuation
- A continued exposure to and experience of the world as well as a willingness to encourage strong impressions of these experiences to sink into the imagination
- An ability to make use of all the available techniques for getting ideas from his personal and professional life
- Willingness to let the mind wander and explore realities and fantasies, alike.

THE PROCESS OF DEVELOPING IDEAS

The verbal/visual elements of modern communication are as indivisible as words and music in a song. And some of the best songs are written by those who develop a visual sense of words with their music (for example, Cole Porter yesterday, Paul Williams today). In the final analysis, words and themes from copywriters are language fragments that can be visualized into fully integrated creative connections.

Communicating with people, either in print or in a TV commercial, requires "straight talk." It has nothing to do with "art" or "literature" other than *using* today's language. Graphics and words are merely tools for communicating. But all the tools are meaningless without an essential *idea*. Without an idea, a communicator, copywriter, artist, advertising man, display director, publicity man or special events person is unarmed. When that original idea springs out of a communicator's head and intuition, the mystical and artful blending (or even juxtaposition) of concept, image, words, and art can lead to magic (synergistically) where one plus one can indeed be three!

In a basic sense, the first step in getting an idea for a campaign is in clearly understanding the nature of the problem and the goals to be achieved. This step, defining the problem or need, is always necessary no matter what path is followed to obtain the finally accepted "idea."

The next step is to assemble and then to sift through the sources of information about the problem. From these, rough verbal and visual concepts should begin to emerge. The third step is to synthesize or to fuse these verbal/visual concepts with current experience to create new ideas. The fourth step should be the selection of the desirable solution from the copy/art idea visualizations.

Current events, immediate and past cultural events, play and film ideas, industries other than the one on which you are working—all these can supply the infusion of the unusual, the unexpected but appropriate new idea through a process that is called *creative thinking*.

GROUP METHODS OF IDEA VISUALIZATION

Sometimes, these ideas come to the copywriter alone at his desk, and indeed, this is the way it happens most often. But, group process is typical of the advertising and communications fields, and conferences are pervasive.

Brainstorming is one of the conference methods used (or one phase of the conference method). A great deal has been written about this method of obtaining new ideas. It has been criticized as cumbersome and nonproductive, but it does make an interesting group experiment for a copywriting/idea visualization class or a work team.

Brainstorming is basically the creation of a number of pertinent ideas about a subject by a group of people, observing the following few rules:

1. A short briefing of goals to be achieved is usually circulated by memo, ahead of time.
2. A secretary is on hand to take down the ideas expressed in the meeting. This requires skill, since several people often speak at once, and the secretary must be able to "sort out" the voices.
3. No negative statements are permitted. No ridiculing or downgrading of any suggestion may be expressed. Wild

Figure 9-1. "Dan River Runs Deep" is a well-known slogan and headline which is effectively reinforced by the copy and visuals in its long-running advertising campaign. This ad features cord and chambray apparel fabrics visualized by an on-location photograph that presents fashions made of Dan River cord and chambray. Notice the visual reinforcement that the river in the background gives to the headline. "Dan River Runs Deep" expresses this company's depth of assortment in apparel fabrics.

ideas are encouraged, since uninhibited, unrestrained associations are usually very productive.

4. Members of the group are encouraged to build upon one another's ideas, adding or deleting a phrase, changing a word, etc. (This must be stressed because people, young people especially, feel some embarrassment at using another's initial ideas.) Creative thinking "hitchhikes" on the creative thinking of others, and the total of associative, spontaneous contributions often produces a surprising number of ideas.

When the session is over, the notes are typed. The executive who is in charge of the session then has the responsibility of reviewing the suggestions; discarding those that are illegal, impractical, or otherwise ill-advised; amending or revising those he considers most effective; and putting them into proper form for creative use, possibly including presentation to the client.

CLASSIFICATION OF CENTRAL IDEAS FOR CAMPAIGNS

Central ideas are strong creative connections; the different types rely on dramatic relationships between art and copy.

The central ideas that finally unify campaigns fall into four classifications which are named, in the first two instances, according to the element that remains most consistently throughout all advertising in all media:

1. Verbal.
2. Visual.
3. Combination.
4. Thematic.

Verbal

This classification covers the combination of words that will form the headline and copy slant of an advertising campaign. It is to be noted that while the headline remains the same, the body copy invariably changes to suit a variety of situations.

An excellent example of this kind of central idea was the "UnCola" idea for the 7-Up soft drink campaign. It is easy to trace what marketing problems existed and what goals this campaign had to achieve. Obviously, the biggest hazard was the necessity to overcome the enormous popularity of the two most popular cola drinks. All the thirst-quenching headlines of previous campaigns had not done the job. "UnCola" was a novel phrase that described the product exactly and was based upon the popularity of the

Dan River Runs Deep™
in Boston Cord and Westport Chambray

Cool, Comfortable and Carefree . . .

Just right for casual fashions.
Insist on Boston Cord, 75% Dacron®
Polyester, 25% combed cotton and
Westport Chambray, 65% Dacron®
Polyester, 35% combed cotton. Both are
available in a full line of fashion colors.
For more information call
Pete Evans 212-554-5693.

*Reg. T.M. DuPont

**Dan River®
Apparel
Fabrics**

111 West 40th Street
New York, NY 10018

Photographer: Barry Rosenthal; Fashion Designer: John Karl; Art Director: Ed Newman

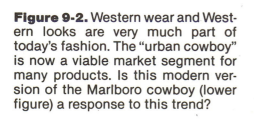

Figure 9-2. Western wear and Western looks are very much part of today's fashion. The "urban cowboy" is now a viable market segment for many products. Is this modern version of the Marlboro cowboy (lower figure) a response to this trend?

anti-heroes (*un*-heroes) of the avant garde theater. A synthesis of these factors resulted in the "UnCola."

Another example of the strong verbal as central idea is the long-running Dan River campaign that emphasizes the depth of assortment of their trend-setting apparel fabrics. This central idea is always reinforced by a visual which works with the headline "Dan River Runs Deep." (See Figure 9-1.)

Visual

This classification, as its name implies, relies heavily upon the artwork, the illustrations or photography, or the layout. Any one of these must remain constant throughout the campaign in order to supply the unity that a campaign requires.

An example of a strong visual campaign is the leaning figure that for years has been the central idea of the national advertising for Klopman Fabrics, "You can lean on Klopman." While in the current campaign the figure is now a visual slogan (a small block in the individual advertisement), for many years the leaning figure took at least three-quarters of a full page. The campaign stressed the dependability of Klopman's blends at a time when many complaints were being registered about the poor performance of other fabrics made of synthetic and natural fibers.

Combination

This classification applies to the majority of advertising ideas in which campaigns are unified by the headline (verbal) idea and the general outlines of the artwork (visual), each being given equal emphasis in advertisement after advertisement.

Here, again, the body copy as well as the specific artwork (illustration or photograph) will change in order to fit whatever the individual advertisement has to say. The general look of the campaign and the overall headline idea, however, will remain constant throughout all variations of incident or medium.

An example of a combination campaign idea is that of Marlboro cigarettes. In this campaign, which has continued for several years, "Marlboro Country" occurs constantly, both in an outright statement and its background depiction of the open spaces of the West (with a rugged, "typical" Westerner in the foreground). In their most recent campaign, there is a subtle change in order to satisfy a new marketing goal. The Marlboro man, still a Westerner, is shown as more urban and sophisticated. (See Figure 9-2.) This more subtle visualization is currently thought to be more appealing to *women* than the ultra "macho" type. The visualization of "Marlboro

Country" has also gone in this direction. It now resembles an "America, the Beautiful" travel brochure rather than John Wayne's rugged terrain.

Thematic

This final classification refers not to the verbal or the visual treatments, but to the basic inner core of the message. This remains the same no matter how the headline changes or the illustration varies. An excellent example of this kind of advertising campaign is the steady succession of ads for the major brands of beer. In recent years there have been several award-winning thematic campaigns always promoting themes that suggest human interactions, communication, and social and occupational activities, rather than the selling points of the product. "When it's time to relax—one thing stands clear—Miller Beer." This theme was built around male (macho) camaraderie, taking a break after work or play. "Weekends were made for Michelob," and Löwenbräu toasts, "Here's to good friends. . . ."

Good ideas, ideas that communicate benefits, are derived from facts, but not limited to the obvious or immediately observable. The writer should listen with an "inner ear" which hears some of the hidden messages currently in the marketplace. The writer should observe with an "inner eye" which sees with a frame of reference oriented to his customers' perceptions. What you hear and see should result in words that express ideas of interest to your audience, ideas with which they can *associate* and *identify*.

In sum, a strong central idea is absolutely essential for good advertising. It adds vitality, believability, and interest to a group of advertisements. It often adds the spark of imagination and humor that makes advertising the exciting field it is, that makes even the doubting public quote the very headlines at which they seem to be laughing. Above all, the central idea, repeated in each advertisement and in the campaign as a whole, adds memorability to the specific message in the individual advertisement.

VISUAL THINKING

Today, an unfounded discrimination between perception and thinking is still with us. Our entire educational system continues to be based on the study of words and numbers. In kindergarten, our youngest students learn by seeing and handling shapes; they invent their own shapes on paper or in clay by thinking through perceiving. But by the first or second grade of elementary school, the senses begin to lose educational status.

If you think back to your own finger painting and crayon days, you may be able to recall how naturally you used idea visualization to express your fantasies of an imagined world, pictures you saw in the eyes of your mind. For children, visualizing is a marvelous connection between their internal illusions and their external expressions. They use idea visualization as a very personal way to communicate.

What happens on the way to adulthood to inhibit our freedom to use visual perception? What happened to the "kid in us" who would scribble at the slightest suggestion? Why are adults reluctant to use their senses to obtain the perceptual information necessary to create or "think up" an idea?

ASSOCIATIVE TECHNIQUES

How many great ideas have been visualized on a paper napkin? The first gasoline pump, invented by W. L. Maxon, was visualized in a rough sketch as an elephant that could fill your tank with its trunk.

This process of association is similar to language associations (figures of speech) called *metaphors*. Visualizing a gasoline pump as an elephant with a trunk is thinking of one concept in terms of another that is similar in form or structure.

Another figure of speech that can help your associative process is the *analogy*, by which *two* concepts are compared in terms of the way in which they *operate*. As an example, think of the telephone company's campaign for its "Yellow Pages"—"Let your fingers do the walking." The visualization here is obvious and effective.

HOW TO APPROACH IDEA VISUALIZATION

At this point, you may be tempted to try to define exactly what visual thinking is.[9] If your experience is anything like ours, you will find it reasonable to consider that visual thinking is like a language whose effectiveness relies on its flexibility and willingness to experiment. The more you use visual thinking, the more you will discover new directions and innovative applications for it. Therefore, we suggest the best way to approach this method is by reading the following chapters with pencil in hand, not for note taking, but for taking a "crack" at doing your own versions of the demonstrations and exercises as they come along. This will tell you something about your visual thinking and how you can use the techniques in the examples to solve problems and create ideas.

You may occasionally be fortunate enough to come up with the approach to a writing assignment the moment you put your mind to it. An easy answer such as this could be the one that works out best,

[9]Rudolf Arnheim, *Visual Thinking* (Berkeley: University of California Press, 1969). This is an excellent book on this subject, and we recommend it to you.

although you might want to take a second look at it later on. But, what happens when instant inspiration fails? The "mind is a blank" feeling does not help get the job done.

The vizthink technique can provide that all-important first step. It will be a step in the right direction, even if all it does is get your mind off the enormity of the journey. But, chances are it will do more than that. The important thing is to maintain a level of activity and a "flow" that characteristically accompany the development of a creative idea. In vizthinking, the doodles, sketches, and symbols you put down on paper can help keep your mind trained on the problem and provide "place holders" for ideas that could be integrated with others later. You can learn to keep track of your thinking process visually, the way the pieces on a chessboard keep track of your chess strategy.

The vizthink technique, which is introduced in Chapter 10, is a translation of verbal/visual concepts into a tangible form which can be communicated to others for analysis and evaluation. It is a drawing or visual used as a tool and is a step in a conceptual process rather than part of the finished creation. It is a process rather than a result.

If you now are or plan to be involved in the creation of copy and other types of marketing communications for advertising campaigns, package designs, product designs, publicity and public relations materials, editorial features, media designs, special events, fashion shows, or displays and exhibits, idea visualization will help make your creative connection—the blending of verbal and visual thinking and skills. If you are involved in any kind of communications where "how you say it" is as important as "what you say," where style is as important as content, verbal/visual thinking will expand your "creative juices." In either case, let us begin by acknowledging that although you are not an "artist" or someone who can draw, you *can* develop your visualization skills in order to make the important creative connection.

METHODS
AND
TECHNIQUES
FOR IDEA
VISUALIZATION

Vizthinking is our way of identifying a very useful skill that is yours to use if we can help you break through your conditioned inhibitions about thinking and communicating. It is a way of making your perceptual thinking tangible in a visual form to be used for creating concepts and generating ideas. It is a way of thinking with your senses and perceptions.

Idea visualization (or vizthinking) is vital for the copywriter, journalist, publicist, advertising designer, display designer, graphic artist, or just plain doodler.

In the business of advertising, the job of providing the layout, visual, and graphics for an advertisement is that of the art director. The copywriter has, as her daily task, the job of creating the words of the advertisement and, at the height of her activity, of creating the basic *concept*.

It is in line with this conceptual part of her work that a copywriter needs to be able to think visually. Our term for thinking visually is vizthinking. More important, we have developed a series of "vizthinks," which we hope will be a virtual "layout and graphics course for copywriters."

The copywriter should be able to convey her thinking and preferences for the visualization of copy and concepts to an art director. She must do this clearly, taking full advantage of the various ways in which a product can be visualized in print, film, video tape, or in the "mind's eye" of radio.

This calls for a large degree of cooperation between the copywriter and the art director. If the proper rapport exists, the road is smooth. A great deal of tact and deft handling is called for on the copywriter's part. She must not seem to be assuming the role of art director. She must, nevertheless, get her idea across to the art department. A successful copywriter will be effective at this, as well.

Many copywriters do think visually. This does not mean that they can draw. We have demonstrated in our idea visualization classes that vizthinks are a way that copywriters can learn to "draw" thumbnails, rough layouts, and visuals that really help their writing. The ability to visualize may help the art director clearly see the central idea of the ad as conceived by the copywriter.

Vizthinking is not a drawing technique as much as it is a way of thinking with your senses. It is a tool that uses the medium of drawing, sketching, doodling, or thumbnailing to record perceptions of the mind's eye. It means that you are able to think in pictures that demonstrate some benefit, satisfaction, use, or feature of the product.

Depending upon the rapport that may exist with an art director, a copywriter who develops a skill for drawing rough layouts and visuals may also find it wise to add an extra dimension: a description of the idea in words. However, this is usually unnecessary, when a rough layout is a clear explanation of what is wanted.

The importance of idea visualization in the selling process should be stressed here. Earlier, in the discussion of headlines, the point was made that the visual shares with the headline the task of taking the early steps of the selling process, that of capturing the attention and arousing the interest of the potential consumer. It is natural, then, that the copywriter who will write the headline may also think about the visualization simultaneously. To expedite the development of this skill, it is suggested that you practice vizthinking by doodling with the vizthink examples and exercises that follow in Chapter 11.

Visualizing your product can obviously be handled effectively in many different ways. Your choice will be influenced by the product itself, current happenings, and perhaps by the policies set up by your predecessors.

In visualization, as in copywriting, identification and involvement are again the important concepts to keep in mind. Certainly, the visualization will depend to a great extent on who will be looking at your advertisement. Surveys indicate that, contrary to general opinion, men tend to look at pictures of men in ads, women at pictures of women. Naturally, this rule does not apply to the deliberately provocative, bare "midriff-plus" visualization that is intended to make everyone look at "everything." The identification of women with women, and so forth, does apply to the day-in, day-out advertising that makes up the bulk of the promotions.

The choice of visualization should, above all, be determined by the central selling message and copy appeal that you, as copywriter, have developed for the advertisement or advertising campaign. By indicating your preference and your own ideas to the art director, you can be more certain that the essential concept of your advertisements and campaign will be carried out.

RESEARCH: A SOURCE OF CONCEPTS

There never has been a better stimulus to creative thinking than solid research. Marketing research that has accurately defined a marketing problem, focused on a target group in a specific market, carefully defined the audience, and thus helped to select copy appeals and approaches can be the best foundation for the creative connection. The efforts spent on research can actually cut the time needed for verbal/visual problem-solving. Solid research may serve

to suggest alternative solutions to marketing problems, indicating additional verbal and visual approaches to a given problem.

The successful creative connection is like good orchestration in music. It works well because various instrumental elements have harmonized to produce a sound that says more than any individual instrument by itself.

TRY WORD/PICTURE ASSOCIATIONS

The creative connection is an optimum blend of visual and verbal elements which uniquely reinforce each other. The copywriter/visualizer or visualizer/copywriter must make creative decisions that choose the most effective pictures and words to deliver a message. A concept such as trust can be described by words. How would you describe it in a picture? On the other hand, which would better describe a chunk of tender lobster claw dipped in drawn butter, words or a color photograph? There are no simple answers to such questions. But, certainly, a compelling picture strongly supported by carefully composed words can evoke a greater response than the proverbial thousand words or a thousand pictures working alone.

To practice word/picture associations that can communicate your ideas quickly, clearly, and simply, try listing at least three *pictures in words* that illustrate the word "trust." (See Figure 10-1.)

Now assume that your advertisement is for a manufacturer of pharmaceuticals sold "across the counter," i.e., without a prescription. What kind of a headline would you write for an antacid tablet which would work with your visual to reinforce the concept of "trust?"

Keep in mind that the creative connection depends upon your ability to *compare* ideas. The idea visualization process will attempt to mesh ideas you know about your audience—emotions, values, attitudes, desires, and needs—with what you know about your product. This process is aided by assembling many times more

Figure 10-1. To communicate an abstract concept is a challenge for the copywriter-visualizer. These thumbnails may or may not convey the concept of "trust" to everyone in an audience. It is the job of the creative connection to find the most attention-compelling and most memorable way of visually reinforcing "trust." Now, make *your* list of "trust" concepts and do some thumbnail roughs to visualize them.

material than would be used in the ad. To compile this information, read everything produced by your client, talk to every "old timer" in the company, study the product, talk to consumers. When you have more than enough, the possibilities are enormous.

The creative connection attempts to connect "people" attributes with product characteristics and then develop a message in words and pictures which will appeal to the target audience. An essential part of the vizthink process is the consideration of the perceptual frames of reference of your target audience. The objective of the message is to evoke response from as much of the audience as possible. Perceptual psychology has given us a clue to patterns of thinking and how our mind processes visual stimuli.

IDEAS COME FROM THE LEFT AND RIGHT

Part of the excitement of working in the field of advertising is the constant updating of psychological concepts that can be put to work in our field. The analysis of consumer motivation and behavior struggles to keep up with new scientific data and with the resulting information about the way people act and react. From these new speculations, the question has arisen about the effect of the growing awareness concerning the differences between the right and the left hemispheres of the brain. What effect will this have on the planning of advertising both for copy and visuals? While the differences have been known for some time, it is only lately that the subject has been treated by skilled writers for presentation outside of the scientific world. Subsequently, some advertising research people have taken up the study in an effort to apply what is known to the creation of more effective advertising.

Carl Sagan of Cornell University is considered by many to be a leader among those scientists who can write on important scientific subjects in such a way that the rest of us can understand. Some of the information that follows is based on his writings.[10]

The left hemisphere of the brain provides reasoning and verbal skills; it processes information sequentially (step by step). The right hemisphere provides us with intuition and intuitive responses; it processes information simultaneously (all at once). For example, when we dream, the right hemisphere takes over, while the left is suppressed. The left hemisphere recognizes words; the right, signs and symbols. The left responds to a logical verbal presentation, while the right responds to color and to total patterns. However, Sagan cautions: "It is vital not to overestimate the separation of functions on either side. . . ."

Now, if we try to apply these very briefly stated propositions to the creation of advertising, we find this area of study is very new and almost not utilized at all.

[10]Carl Sagan, *The Dragons of Eden* (New York: Random House, 1977).

Thus, a challenge has developed for the current generation just coming into the advertising business to begin to think along the lines of left and right hemisphere appeals. For example, in the advertising of impulse items (those products bought on a whim or as one passes a counter), the copywriter and the visualizer would do well to present advertisements and commercials with a strong sensual appeal to the right hemisphere, such as color, quick visual changes, and emotion-laden music rather than a long statement of reasons to buy. Conversely, in presenting a product where reasoning is expected to close the sale, the appeal should be to the left hemisphere, where words and the logical sequence of thought are processed.[11]

How should a copywriter and a visualizer use this knowledge? As has been stated, a great deal of research remains to be done. But some quick and undoubtedly superficial conclusions may be drawn.

The first and most important conclusion cannot, we believe, be disputed. Here is where it is important that the copywriter and the visualizer work together. If the objective of the advertisement calls for an emotional reaction, then the artist must carry the larger burden of the appeal, with a lessened stress on words. Words "get in the way of" the intuitive action of the right hemisphere. The artist, herself, must think of the effect on her viewer (whether it be the viewer of a commercial or of a magazine page). She must think in terms of total pattern; the details and outlines of figures of any kind need not be clearly defined. She may experiment with upside-down delineation, with emphasis on negative space, on dissolves and optical devices in TV that "suppress" the ratiocination of the left hemisphere.

On the other hand, if the appeal ought to be a rational one, then the copywriter must come to the fore with a wealth of words, of exact meanings. The artist's visuals should be definite, distinct, with perhaps almost "hard" outlines. Color is of less importance in any appeal to the left hemisphere.

Music, on the contrary, calls both hemispheres into play, as would be expected from the close correlation between music and mathematics and between music and emotion. The writer for radio can, where appropriate, call upon the emotions for a reaction of the right hemisphere, while a more reasoned approach can be evoked for a reaction of the left hemisphere.

SIMILES AND METAPHORS— "IMAGES OF WIDE SCOPE"

A group of Rutgers University psychologists (The Institute for Cognitive Studies) has speculated about the nature of the creative process based on their study of the "metaphor's role at the core of

[11]By the way, right- or left-handedness does not affect the rational-intuitive properties of the left and right hemispheres to any large degree. There is evidence, however, that left-handedness in *some* cases, is accompanied by a positioning of verbal processes on the right as well as on the left.

TIME

The big blowup.

The morning was exceptionally quiet; no birds sang.

In a few seconds, Mt. St. Helens released the energy of five hundred Hiroshima bombs, and turned miles of Washington State into a sterile, gray moonscape.

For all the dramatic coverage given this awesome event day after day, the issue of TIME featuring Mt. St. Helens was bought in near-record numbers. Buyers at the newsstand chose TIME half again as many times as the next news magazine.

Although there was no way of knowing that TIME, within an hour of the blast, had teams of writers and photographers on the scene, hitching rides on the only emergency vehicles allowed into the area—and had its enviable research staff preparing a primer on vulcanology to put this latest convulsion of nature into perspective—prospective buyers assumed that TIME's coverage would be explicit, comprehensive, and unique.

Readers prefer TIME because they have come to expect the most from TIME. And this expectation has made TIME America's number one news magazine by every important benchmark. TIME is known not only for reporting all the facts with painstaking accuracy, and picturing them vividly, but also for communicating a sense of wonder—the fine and curious details (right down to the eerie silence of the birds just before the eruption) that make an event indelible.

TIME. Millions more people read it every week than any other news magazine. Because we work so hard to put more into it.

More goes into it.

© Time Inc. 1980

Figure 10-2. This *Time* magazine advertisement is a dramatic use of a metaphor. Would "The Big Volcanic Eruption" be as good a headline as "The Big Blowup"?

[12] *New York Times,* April 15, 1980, pp. C1, C4.

thought." According to this group's leader, Professor Howard E. Gruber, "metaphors have been found to be linked both with the process of discovery and with the act of organizing a body of material." Gruber cites "the use by Charles Darwin of the central metaphor of the irregularly branching tree." It was an image that clarified a great mass of evolutionary studies. It presented in graphic form (as well as a word-picture) the complex thesis that added a new dimension to the previous theory of straight-line evolution.[12]

Figures of thought are transformed by figures of speech, such as similes and metaphors, into more expressive and communicative information. These figures of speech are ways of organizing a complex or abstract thought into a recognizable message. Similes present a comparison, with the words of comparison expressed; e.g., "You're *as pretty as* a picture." Metaphors make a comparison, but drop the comparative words; e.g., "You're a picture" (See Figure 10-2.)

We know what the Prudential Insurance Company means when it claims to be as "solid as the Rock" (of Gibraltar); this is a simile. The use of the blotter for dryness (as mentioned in Chapter 1 and visualized in Pampers' TV commercial storyboard in Figure 1-8) is a metaphoric figure. The use of the simile and the metaphor to "fit an idea" is part of the process of word/picture association in idea visualization.

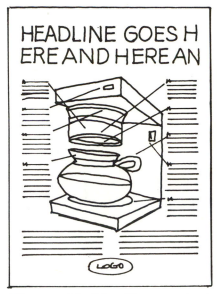

Figure 10-3A. *The product alone.* This method presents the coffee-maker's features as selling points.

Figure 10-3B. *The product in a setting.* The consumer likes to see how the product might look (and work) in its setting.

Figure 10-3C. *The product in use.* Try writing the headline for this thumbnail. Are we selling the "satisfaction" of a great cup of coffee?

The foregoing discussion has provided only a simple beginning for your own further research and application. Twenty years from the time of this writing, these studies may indeed be "old hat" and in common use. Today, they are just beginning to be pondered. They may, however, lead to more practical considerations of vizthinking, which you can put to immediate use—namely, the different ways to visualize and the uses of layout.

TWENTY WAYS TO VISUALIZE

Advertising philosopher and critic Harry Wayne McMahan refers to the Visual Image/Personality (VI/P) of advertising as a measure of the unique way used to visualize a product or service. McMahan says, "The visual image/personality is dependent on characteristics which make it distinctive and also appropriate to the product."[13]

From 1951 to 1962, a classic example of VI/P was David Ogilvy's (Ogilvy and Mather Advertising Agency) use of an aristocrat (Baron George Wrangell) wearing an eyepatch to "reinforce the high quality and fashion excellence image" of Hathaway shirts for men. At the time of this writing, "Operation Eyepatch" is a nationwide search for a new "Hathaway Man" for the 1980's.

There are many acknowledged ways to visualize the product or the concept behind the product. The following list of twenty classifications is reasonably comprehensive and would appear to cover almost every stituation. In the learning stages, the best way to make use of the list is, of course, to search out examples in actual current advertising. Please take note of the thumbnails of ads included here as examples of different ways to visualize. (See Figures 10-3A to 10-3T.)

[13]Harry Wayne McMahan, "The VI/P Factor," *Advertising Age,* July 14, 1980, pp. 50, 52.

Figure 10-3D. *Illustration of a benefit.* Practice this frequently used approach by writing "advice and promise" headlines for this method of visualization. If the visual is effective, it will reinforce the promise believably.

Figure 10-3E. *Illustration of a disadvantage of not using the product.* "We lost our travelers checks...Why didn't we get the kind that is instantly replaceable?"

Figure 10-3F. *Dramatization of the headline.* In this thumbnail, the language is so dramatic that the typography has been given great impact as an effective way to visualize the idea.

A. Illustration of the product alone (usually a line drawing in a newspaper or a photograph against a plain backdrop).

B. Illustration of a product in a setting (as in an advertisement for a chair, showing the chair in a living room).

C. Illustration of a product in use (the artwork would show a chair, for example, with someone sitting in it).

D. Illustration of a benefit from using the product (rosy-cheeked children eating a given brand of bread, with the implication that the look of health results from eating that brand of bread).

E. Illustration of the loss or disadvantage resulting from not using the advertised product. (An example of this is the now-discontinued American Express campaign for their traveler's checks—suggesting a miserable vacation if "other checks" were bought, then lost. It is interesting that strong competitive reaction turned this campaign around to a simple and much stronger positive statement of benefit.) The "loss or disadvantage" must be handled carefully to avoid total negative reaction.

F. Dramatization of the headline. (This is one of the strongest possible visualizations. When it is well done, it is so effective that there is no way to tell which came first, the idea for the headline or the idea for the illustration.)

G. Dramatization of the evidence. (A strong example is early advertising for Formica® where the claim was made that even a lit cigarette would not burn the surface; the illustration showed a smoldering cigarette lying on the table surface with no damage to the table top.)

Figure 10-3G. *Dramatization of the evidence.* Visual proof of how well something performs may be the most effective reinforcement for an advertiser's claim for a product. "Seeing is believing" still works in many campaigns.

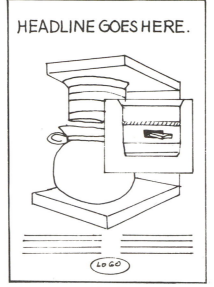

Figure 10-3H. *Dramatizing a detail.* How many products have sold over the competition because of just one highly desirable feature or characteristic? A close-up of a "detail" dramatizes its importance and increases the value of the product.

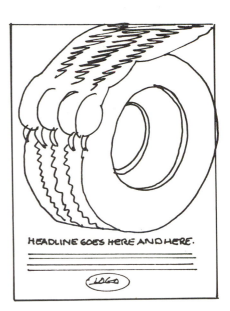

Figure 10-3I. *Comparison.* Is a big cat's grip a good comparison to the super grip of a tire's tread? This type of visual metaphor often also provides ideas for headlines, slogans, and brand names. Why are so many automobiles named after animals — mustangs, jaguars, impalas, and cougars?

Figure 10-3J. *Contrast.* The contrast of "before and after" is one of the most used visualizations of the advertiser's "advice and promise" approach. Contrast is also used to compare the appearance and performance of your product with the competition.

Figure 10-3K. *Cartoons.* In print advertising as well as film animation for television commercials, cartoons or animated figures provide an opportunity to demonstrate a product's performance with a blend of whimsy. The famous Alka Seltzer commercial, which some of you may remember, presented an animated stomach giving advice to its owner, who had made the "pepperoni pizza mistake."

Figure 10-3L. *Trade characters.* When a trade character in an advertising campaign becomes a "household word," the results can be impressive. "Morris," is a marvelous "spokescat" for 9 Lives cat food; his testimonials provide cat lovers with a true authority figure.

Figure 10-3M. *Charts and diagrams.* When the copy message includes "evidence and/or proof," the use of charts and diagrams as visuals can amplify and reinforce the verbal claim. This is especially true when groups of figures or statistics are used.

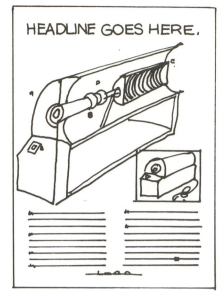

Figure 10-3N. *X-ray diagram.* This provides a "look inside" a product — sometimes real, but more often imagined.

Figure 10-3O. *Symbolism.* Merrill Lynch's performing bull is a visual metaphor which describes their optimistic view of the American economy — present and future. It works very well with their slogan which suggests their philosophy about investing their clients' money: "We're bullish on America."

Figure 10-3P. *Abstract illustration.* If a product's appeal and selling points are difficult to differentiate and convey literally, the visualization could be abstract. Performance and quality can be expressed symbolically. In this thumbnail, the product is being presented as a "masterpiece" in its field. The Wool Bureau logo, shown on the right, is an abstract graphic which attempts to represent symbolically the character and value of this natural fiber.

Figure 10-3Q. *Continuity strip.* This thumbnail illustrates one technique — almost a storyboard style — that visualizes the message in a series of "stills." The comic strip is a cartoon version of the same technique, with "balloons" for dialogue. The film strip simulates action and can be used to demonstrate the performance or utilization of the product in much the same way as a filmed television commercial.

Figure 10-3R. *Mood-setting illustration.* The range of visualization opportunities in this category is boundless. The mood-setting illustration functions as a backdrop for the product which can suggest its benefits and satisfactions better than showing the product in use. Cosmetics and fragrances are typical examples of products that lend themselves to this approach.

Figure 10-3S. *Illustration of the product in its package.* Many package-goods advertising campaigns feature what is often their key selling point — the package. The package may say it all, and it may be the "real" difference between the product and its competition. It should be noted that the most serious use of this technique is to generate *shelf recognition* by the customer for products that must compete for attention.

Figure 10-3T. *Illustration of the product's ingredients or raw materials.* A television commercial that exemplifies the technique illustrated in our thumbnail is the Progresso foods campaign: "Make it Progresso or make it yourself!" This demonstrates the advertiser's claim that it uses the same basic foods in its product that the customer might use in his or her own home cooking.

H. Dramatizing a detail (where the illustration focuses on a small area of a product or enlarges a detail).

I. Comparison (illustrating the product and another object that is similar in an essential aspect).

J. Contrast (illustrating the product and an object that differs in an essential way; for example, before-and-after pictures or the advertised brand and an inferior "Brand X").

K. Cartoons (such as the Alka-Seltzer commercial that presents a stomach complaining to its owner about the abuses of pepperoni pizza).

L. Trade characters (such as Charlie the Tuna; The Jolly Green Giant; Morris, the 9 Lives cat; and personalities, such as actor Robert Morley for British Airways).

M. Charts and diagrams. (It is well to note that this kind of illustration can be very effective in technical and trade advertising. When it is used in consumer advertising, it will often be accompanied by one or more additional illustrations of a warmer, less technical type.)

N. X-ray diagram. (The illustration portrays what a cross section would look like, were it possible to get inside the product. It is almost never real, but may be as sketchy or as realistic as circumstances call for.)

O. Symbolism (an illustration of an object that has acquired significance beyond its literal meaning, e.g., a horseshoe, a laurel wreath, the Merrill Lynch bull, the Gloria Vanderbilt swan).

P. Abstract illustration (a nonobjective visual frequently used with an advertisement for a service or an idea, or for the idea behind the product, such as the Wool Bureau's logo depicted in Figure 10-3P).

Q. Continuity strip (a series of photographs, usually small, set up like a film strip). Of course, the subject of each photograph in a continuity strip could be substantially different, one from another, which is not the case in a film strip.

R. Mood-setting illustration (usually a romanticized rendering of the product or a romantic landscape).

S. Illustration of the product in its package (important for volume, price-cutting stores, and supermarket selling where recognition of the product "on the shelf" is important).

T. Illustration of the product's ingredients or raw materials. (An excellent example of this classification was the visualization used some time ago by Campbell's for its vegetable soup, where luscious *fresh* vegetables are massed together to indicate the quality of food used to make the soup.)

THE USES OF LAYOUT—SEVEN WAYS TO GO

The creative process for visualizing starts with a layout. Layouts arrange the verbal and visual elements in an advertisement or a commercial. In print media, these would include: visuals (art work, sketches, illustrations, photography) and copy (headlines, subheadlines, body copy, logos, trademarks, signatures). For audio/visual presentations and television commercials, the layout is called a storyboard. The storyboard could be considered a "series of layouts" which represent a film or video tape *motion* picture.

The layout moves through several stages, and the first may well be *thumbnailing*. The thumbnails are produced rapidly and in quantity and represent visual thinking in a most evident yet primitive form. It is a kind of brainstorming for idea visualization, and it is most effective when the creative worker is armed with verbal concepts and ideas culled from his research. The next stage in layout is called a *rough*. Rough layouts are really not the province of the idea visualizer. Art directors develop roughs from selected thumbnails. However, a thumbnail or "first rough" is very useful. (See Chapter 11.) The purpose of this discussion is to develop your ability to get the ideas started with your own thumbnails!

Figure 10-4A. *The big picture.* Here is where a "picture" is the dominant visual in an ad. It can be accompanied by "a thousand words" or replace them—but with a closely related headline it successfully carries the message.

Figure 10-4B. *The big copy.* Almost the reverse of the big picture, this technique features the headline and copy with graphic visualizations, utilizing typography in a creative way.

Figure 10-4C. *The omnibus.* A technique that develops compartments or sections each with its own visual and verbal elements. These virtually function as separate ads within the context of the entire ad.

The rough is more refined and specific than the thumbnail in detailing graphic elements of art, typography, and color. It is invariably "correct" size. A final selection from rough layouts leads to *comprehensive layouts* (*comps*) which realistically duplicate what the completed advertisement will look like. Comps, which most dramatically portray the best of the "big ideas" which the creative team has developed, are presented to the client for approval. The accepted comp is then prepared for printing reproduction, or in the case of a storyboard, for videotape or film production.

Layout is essential to idea visualization because it enables you to say things and compose visually with space, shape, and movement. Optical illusions of dimension and distance can be created with lines and planes of perspective. Horizontal forms can widen and vertical forms can heighten people and products. The layout style affects the approach and can be used to orient the message in rational or emotional directions.

There are several basic formats and compositions of layout that can get you started. (See Figures 10-4A to 10-4G.)

    A. The *big picture* uses a dominant visual in a formal balance with headline and body copy below. It is simple and direct and can be used for almost any kind of verbal/visual concept.

    B. The *big copy* layout may have visuals, but they are supplemental to the copy. An alternative use of the big copy layout is to make the type and typographical style so dramatic and appealing that they function as the visual.

    C. The *omnibus* layout uses many visuals in spatially divided sections each with its own headline and copy. The individual spaces are separated by a variety of visual and graphic devices.

Figure 10-4D. *The mortise.* This thumbnail is a typical example of a technique that organizes visual and verbal elements into frames around each other.

Figure 10-4E. *Free-form.* The informally balanced layout of visual and verbal elements suggests unlimited opportunities for different uses of contrast, proportion, and perspective.

Figure 10-4F. *Scatter.* This technique relies on visually off-beat arrangements of art and copy to develop attention and interest. It can be used to focus attention on certain elements that need to be optically dominant.

Figure 10-4G. *Continuity strip.* This layout technique is used when a series of visuals is needed to visualize the message. Continuity may be utilized to amplify the demonstration of a product or a narrative that describes a service or idea.

D. The *mortise* layout uses either copy or visuals to form a border or frame around the other. It is formal in nature, but the verbal/visual content can create the dynamics.

E. The *free-form* layout combines copy and visuals into irregularly aligned or superimposed relationships using combinations of each to cause perspectives and interesting divisions of white space. This provides dynamic movements and gaze motion through the elements of the advertisement.

F. The *scatter* layout abounds with many different movements, and while it may seem undisciplined and brash, it is produced from an organized plan designed to present a readable message.

G. The *continuity strip* uses many more elements of headline, text, and visuals than the average type of layout. It resembles a film or comic strip and is utilized for narrative messages, demonstrations of a process, or assortments of merchandise.

11

VIZTHINK EXERCISES

T he following vizthink exercises are designed to develop your ability to do thumbnails, thumbnail/rough layouts, and storyboards, utilizing *faces, figures, groups, products,* and *places.*

They will develop your skills in *composition: balance, proportion, perspective, contrast,* and *gaze motion.* The vizthinks will also get you started on methods to *comp copy* in typographical contexts: rough lettering of headlines, *greeking* of body copy, and a simple method of visualizing copy by *copyfitting.*

FACES, FIGURES, GROUPS, PRODUCTS, PLACES

These exercises are designed to start your vizthinking. We recommend that you practice from the demonstrations with a layout pad and pencil. Start doodling!

COMPOSITION: BALANCE, PROPORTION, PERSPECTIVE, CONTRAST, AND GAZE MOTION

Now that you have practiced doodling the visual elements—faces, figures, groups, products, places—we can begin to discuss composition and layout.

The *optical center* of a layout is the balance point always vertically centered and slightly above the horizontal center of the layout around which element "weights" are placed. (See Figure 11-8, page 136.)

Balance in visualization is concerned with *visual weight.* Large elements of copy and art weigh more than small units; black is heavier than gray; certain colors have more weight than others; asymmetrical shapes outweigh symmetrical ones; even white space has weight.

A layout can be formally or informally balanced. *Formal balance* is placing of the elements symmetrically with the left side the same as the right side. *Informal balance* places the elements in balance around the optical center asymmetrically. (See Figure 11-9, page 137.)

Proportion deals with *size* relationships. Certain unequal proportions of size to size are more exciting to the eye than are regular and predictable ones. (See Figure 11-10, page 137.) The idea visualizer should experiment with different divisions of white space as well as the proportional relationships of the elements to the white space. (See Figure 11-11, page 138.)

Perspective deals with relationships that involve *distance.* It is a way of creating the illusion of moving into the distance. The visual

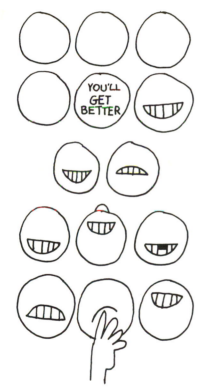

Figure 11-1. Here is how you can start your "vizthinking." If you can depict faces that *express* your copy (especially your headlines)—you are on your way. Practice doodling these "moon-heads." (Your circles do not have to be perfect.) See how even minor changes in just the mouth give you a range of expressions that seem to demand headlines.

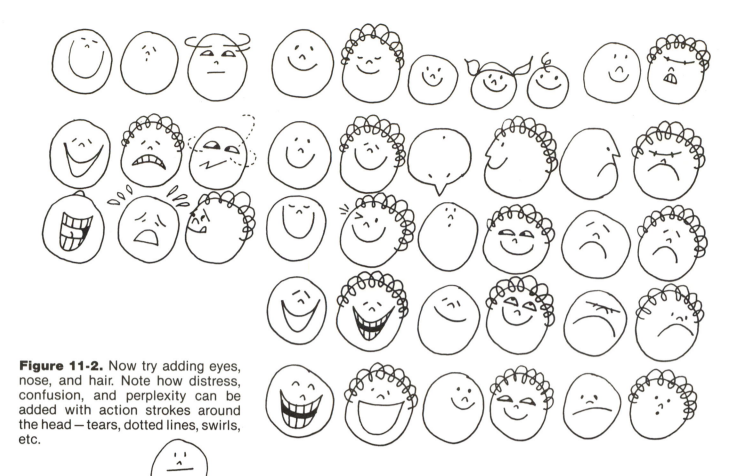

Figure 11-2. Now try adding eyes, nose, and hair. Note how distress, confusion, and perplexity can be added with action strokes around the head — tears, dotted lines, swirls, etc.

Figure 11-3. This group of moon-heads indicates the broad variety of people you can depict, indicating such differences as age, sex, occupation, hairstyle, and lifestyle!

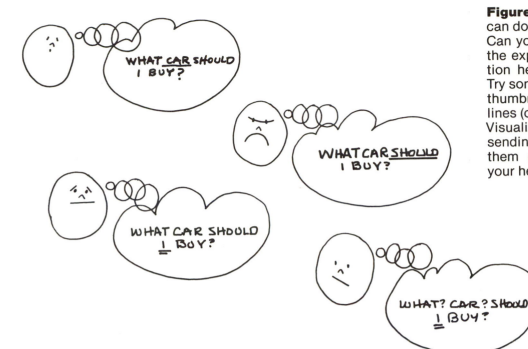

Figure 11-4. Now look at what you can do with moon-heads and words. Can you describe the emotion from the expression? Does the visualization help these simple messages? Try some of your own. Do a series of thumbnail ads with different headlines (or variations on one headline). Visualize the face or faces that are sending the messages by giving them expressions that work with your headline.

Figure 11-5. Here is how you can do *stick figures* for your faces easily. The basic stick figure is all you need to show human physical movement and action. All it takes is practice.

Cut out many samples of photographed figures from ads in magazines. Then draw your stick figure right on the form. You will soon learn the fundamental movements of standing, sitting, lounging, crouching, bending, kneeling, walking, and running. Your skill in doodling faces and figures will be invaluable in doing your own thumbnails.

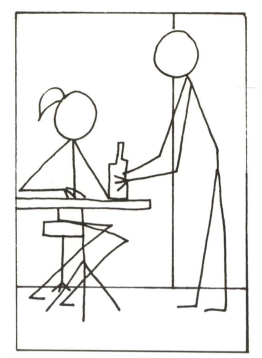

↑

Figure 11-6. Try settings with roads, mountains, trees, and houses. Put stick-figure people in them. Study these six thumbnails and then do your stuff!

Try single figures and figures in groups. Get your people to interact with each other. Demonstrate by their facial expressions and body language what they are conveying, arguing, explaining, experiencing, loving, helping, or showing.

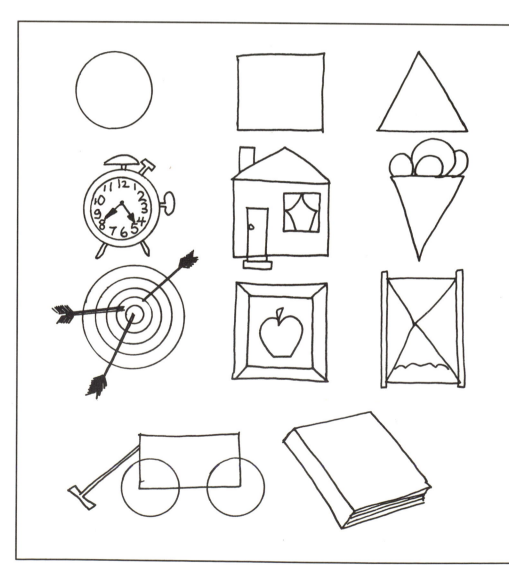

← **Figure 11-7.** The idea visualizer can visualize the product by using three basic forms that easily simulate almost any shape—the *triangle, square,* and *circle.* You can demonstrate this to yourself by tracing over photographs of products and converting them into these basic shapes and *combinations* of triangles, squares, and circles. See how easy it is to identify the products. You can forget the details; concentrate on a doodle whose look identifies your product. When you present your verbal and visual ideas this way, your co-workers will be able to "see" what you mean!

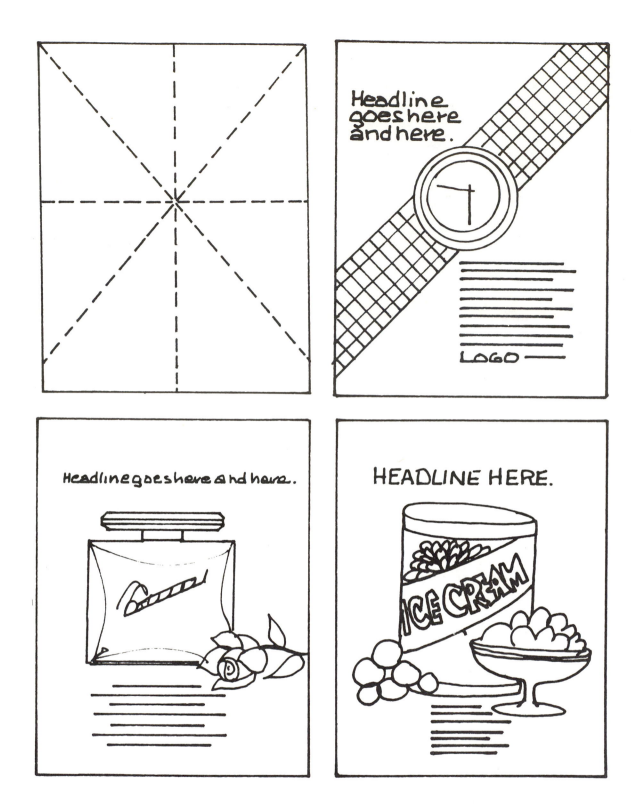

Figure 11-8. The optical center is the focal point for the arrangement of art and copy elements in an ad. Formal balance places these elements symmetrically to the left and right of the vertical dividing line. Informal balance attempts to distribute the elements into the various sectors "equally," by considering their size, shape and "visual weight."

Figure 11-9. Notice here how a simple decision between formal *(left)* and informal balance *(right)* shifts the emphasis on the elements of art, copy, and white space.

Figure 11-10. How would you write the headline in each of the thumbnails shown here? Does the difference in proportion (size relationships) change the nature of the message? Could there be a difference in the copy approach suggested by the use of different proportions between the human figure and the product in each of the two thumbnails?

Figure 11-11. The relative size of the elements in an advertisement can be an important consideration in how the copy is visualized. Look through newspapers and magazines, and notice the basic percentages of space allotted to the headline, body copy, and visual. See if you can identify patterns for certain categories of products and services. For example, which type of product would have a larger percentage of space for its visual — fashion apparel or a packaged product, such as aspirin?

Figure 11-12. The use of perspective will help you make more dynamic and more compelling thumbnails and roughs. It can put a product up front in the ad — or it can show "where a product is coming from." It can also portray the product in its setting — without the background competing for attention. Perspective in your thumbnail can tell the art director what is important. It suggests emphasis and direction for the visual message.

Figure 11-13. The variations in these three similar thumbnails indicate the visualizer's experimentation with differences in intensity, proportion, and perspective. Think of the numerous variations that are possible if we now show the product in a setting or in use.

Figure 11-14. The informally balanced advertisement provides the widest opportunity for arranging elements to lead the eye from the optical center through the parts of the message being expressed by verbal/visual combinations. The thumbnail here is a rather obvious example of how to "point-up" the name and package of a product. ➡

illusion of distance is created by making objects smaller as they move away. Shapes can be made to look three-dimensional by the use of overlapping lines and converging lines. (See Figure 11-12.)

Contrast is the factor that provides emphasis and attention to various elements of the layout by rearranging and comparing their different intensities, proportions, and perspective. Contrast enables you to provide a unit of dominant interest—an optical focal point which needs attention. (See Figure 11-13.)

Gaze motion considers the layout arrangement of copy and art elements designed to lead the eye through the message of any advertisement. Figure 11-14 illustrates some of the various patterns of gaze motion which it is possible to create. Certain motions are more dynamic and rapid, leading the eye differently and at a rate different from the more static and organized layout. The idea visualizer should decide which suits the message best.

Figure 11-15. It is just as important for the idea visualizer to be able to doodle headlines and body copy! The method illustrated is a simple way to visualize the headline in standard block letters and the body copy in solid strokes which roughly indicate the length and "weight" of the lines of type.

Figure 11-16. This technique of copy comping is the same as in Figure 11-15, except that the double-line stroking of body copy can be a more accurate representation of the height of the typography, measured in points, and the leading between lines. (See Figure 11-20.)

Figure 11-17. In this version of copy comping, both the headline and subheadline (if one has been written) are hand-lettered as they will appear. The body copy here has been rendered in a third version, which could be described as a "squiggly line" designed to represent the look of typography.

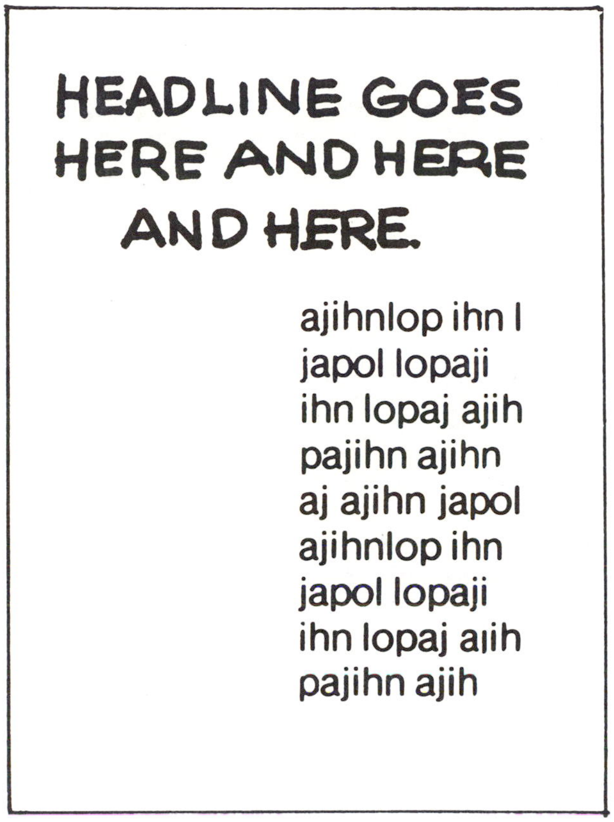

HEADLINE GOES HERE AND HERE AND HERE.

ajihnlop ihn l
japol lopaji
ihn lopaj ajih
pajihn ajihn
aj ajihn japol
ajihnlop ihn
japol lopaji
ihn lopaj ajih
pajihn ajih

Figure 11-18. "Greeking" simulates body copy with paste-ups of similar looking typography cut out from print advertisements. It is an effective way to visualize typography, when a more comprehensive rough is desired.

Pressure-sensitive acetates of "Greek" type in the most-used typefaces are available in art supply stores. These can be cut to size and pasted into position. Some versions of this "press-type" can be rubbed onto the layout. These also are available in alphabets of all sizes and typefaces for headlines and subheadlines.

"COPY COMPING": "GREEKING" AND COPYFITTING

There are several ways for the idea visualizer to *comp the copy* in layout roughs and comprehensives. The idea is to simulate the space and weight that the copy will take in the ad, as well as to provide some indication of its style and character.

Figure 11-15 illustrates a technique used for a rough. The solid strokes represent the height of the type you are trying to represent. A flat chisel-lead pencil or chisel-point felt pen can be used.

Another technique utilizes a double line with a fine point which simulates the height and size of a line of type. (See Figure 11-16.)

Headlines and subheadlines are hand-lettered to appear as they will in the actual advertisement. (See Figure 11-17.)

Greeking is a technique which looks like words, but in reality is just "Greek to most of us." It is any portion of printed copy which can be traced or pasted into position to simulate the copy that will appear in the finished ad. (See Figure 11-18.)

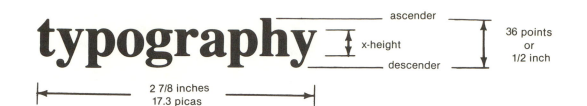

typography

ascender — x-height — descender

36 points or 1/2 inch

2 7/8 inches
17.3 picas

Figure 11-19. Notice that the point size of type (72 pts. = 1 inch) is measured from the top of an ascending letter (*h*) to the bottom of a descending letter (*y*). The *x-height* is the body of the letter. The width of the word is measured in picas (6 picas = 1 inch).

Copyfitting is a more precise way to convert typed copy to typography. It involves *character counting* of the typewritten text. The character count includes all letters and spaces. The copywriter is often constrained to write for a predesignated space in a layout, for which the number of characters has already been determined. In this case, the copywriter knows how much copy to write. In the case of the copywriter who is attempting to visualize his copy as it will appear in a certain style of type (or *typeface*), it is necessary to calculate the following:

1. The width of type is measured by *picas*. There are 6 picas per inch. The height of type is measured by *points*. There are 72 points to an inch. (See Figure 11-19.)

2. The number of *characters per line* which can be fitted into a desired width of space will be determined by the number of characters per pica of the selected typeface. For example: if a typeface measures 2 characters per pica, (or 12 to an inch in width), then a block of copy which is 4 inches wide (24 picas) will accommodate 48 characters. (See Figure 11-20.)

3. The number of *lines of copy* that will fit into a desired depth of space will be determined by the point size of the type and the amount of space between the lines, which is also expressed in points. Space between lines of type is called *leading* (pronounced led/ing, from the leaden slugs used to separate lines of metal type). (See Figure 11-20.)

To illustrate, here is a simple problem in copyfitting: How many characters of copy (characters can be converted into approximate number of words by dividing by an average number of characters per word, usually 5 or 6) should be written for a copy block that is 2 inches wide by 3 inches deep? The typeface selected is 10 pt. News Gothic Medium. It measures 2 characters per pica. It will be leaded 1 pt.

Solution:

1. Convert the dimensions of the copy block into picas wide and points deep. In this case, the copy block is *12 picas wide* (2 inches × 6 picas per inch) and *216 points deep* (3 inches × 72 pts.).

In the light of present-day events the young people who are in high school will be the men and women to solve the serious problems in a new world, problems of state and nation requiring honest and fair judgment of a momentous nature. The question arises as to what the young people are doing to prepare themselves for the problems which are sure to con-

---

10 point Times Roman

Ink-smudged hands with calloused, nimble fingers, they g ave the world the gift of knowledge. They came first into the hopelessness of the dark ages—bringing light. They yo UND THE LEARNING OF THE CENTURIES MOU LDERING IN ARCHIVES. THEY BROUGHT IT OU
1234567890$ 1234567890$

10 point Times Roman Italic

Ink-smudged hands with calloused, nimble fingers, they g ave the world the gift of knowledge. They came first into the hopelessness of the dark ages—bringing light. They yo UND THE LEARNING OF THE CENTURIES MOU LDERING IN ARCHIVES. THEY BROUGHT IT OU
ABCDEFGHIJKLMNOPQRSTUVWXYZ   1234567890$

10 point Times Roman Bold

Ink-smudged hands with calloused, nimble fingers, they g ave the world the gift of knowledge. They came first into the hopelessness of the dark ages—bringing light. They yo UND THE LEARNING OF THE CENTURIES MOU LDERING IN ARCHIVES. THEY BROUGHT IT OU
1234567890$ 1234567890$

Figure 11-20. The number of characters per line (cpl) is calculated in this sample by multiplying the characters per pica (cpp) by the number of picas in the width of the block of copy. In this case, the cpp = 2.4; the pica width is 24; so the cpl = 58.

The cpp is often given in type sample books with the type specimen. The following is an easy way to calculate cpp yourself: (a) Measure an inch of a line of copy and count the characters in 1 inch to the nearest character, counting spaces as 1 character; (b) Divide the number of characters in an inch by 6 for the number of characters per pica.

The number of lines of copy that will fit into a desired depth is calculated by dividing the point size of the type, plus the leading between lines, into the depth size of the copy block. This sample is 11 point type. This 11 pts., plus the leading of 1 pt., is divided into the depth of the copy block, which is 1 inch or 72 pts. Thus, the number of lines can be calculated by dividing 72 by 12. The number of lines = 6.

Figure 11-21. This type specimen page represents a "family" of type and all its variations—letter slant, stroke weight, and proportion. The terms used for describing type variations are *roman, italic* (slanted), *bold, semibold, condensed, expanded,* and so forth. It is possible to use several different versions, each of which maintains the original identity of the type family, in one advertisement.

---

2. The News Gothic Medium typeface at 2 characters per pica will run *24 characters per line* (since the line is 12 picas wide).

3. The number of lines is calculated by dividing the point size of the type (plus the leading) into the point depth of the space. In this case: 10 pts. + 1 pt. = 11 pts. divided into 216 = approx. 20 lines.

4. The number of characters of copy to write is calculated as follows: Number of characters per line × Number of lines, or 24 × 20 = 480 characters (or about 80 to 96 words).

Visualizing with type can be as expressive as visualizing with pictures. Typefaces are like other visual symbols. Their personality, size, and weight can help supplement the content and tone of the art and layout design. Although not a general practice, if the copywriter is permitted to specify the type, then a typographer's specimen catalog is a valuable tool. (See Figure 11-21.) All of the typefaces that a specific typographer has to offer are presented in various sizes and weights. The specimen pages enable the copywriter to select a typeface that makes the creative connection with her words.

Figure 11-22. Get your thumbnail visuals started through the use of the three basic shapes. Notice how the triangle, circle, and square are used in these thumbnails.

Try vizthinking some of these on your own, remembering the *twenty ways to visualize,* the *seven different types of layout,* and the uses of *balance, proportion, perspective, contrast,* and *gaze motion.* Do not forget to draw moon-faces with expressions and stick figures with actions. Vary the size relationships of the elements of copy, art, and white space. Do them small—in a grid—and keep doodling!

TECHNIQUES FOR DEVELOPING THUMBNAIL VISUALS

Figures 11-22 through 11-24 illustrate a few of the many techniques that even the novice can utilize to develop thumbnail visuals. We recommend that you use the vizthink exercises we have discussed to practice all of these. Follow through on a copy problem of your own, using several of the techniques in the same way as we did in the illustrations provided.

Even a thumbnail/rough can be used to sell an idea if the words are visualized graphically. The techniques of copy comping enable you to use the "personality" of the typeface to add emphasis and tone to your message.

THUMBNAILING FOR PRINT AND BROADCAST MEDIA

The caption under Figure 11-24 encourages the reader to start doing small layouts to develop idea visualization. These first rough layouts are called *thumbnails* or *first roughs.* Thumbnails can be considered the first step in translating market research and the central idea into idea visualization.

The thumbnail, used in both print layouts and television storyboards, enables the copywriter or visualizer to vizthink with a pencil. It enables him to test and compare creative options economically and rapidly in a scaled down version of the original advertisement or commercial. (See Figure 11-25.)

Figure 11-23. Note the changes in emphasis that the idea visualizer can effect by experimenting with the elements in an ad. The treatment in each of these is different — while the elements of headline, subheadline, body copy, logo, and visuals are basically the same.

Figure 11-24. In a very short time, in a relatively small space, the copywriter/idea visualizer can experiment with a variety of approaches. We have done just six thumbnails here which are merely a start in the process from thumbnail to comprehensive layout. We have deliberately kept them very simple, so you can see what the product is we are trying to sell — as well as what is obviously a weak suggestion of its main appeal.

Try to continue the "thumbnailing," but first write a headline that better expresses the satisfaction of this product by a French chef. We think you will see how making the connection between your copywriting and idea visualization will improve your creative effort.

Figure 11-25. These four thumbnails demonstrate the variety of options that the copywriter/visualizer can use to experiment with visual elements that represent copy and art.

Figure 11-26. Stock photos can be traced or pasted into position for larger thumbnails and "first rough" layouts.

We hope that your practice and experience with the vizthink exercises will convince you that vizthinking with thumbnails does not require highly developed drawing skills. It need not always be "freehand," although visual thinking with a pencil or free-flow ink pen is ideal for fast tryouts of a great variety of ideas. Remember that cut-outs of illustrations, drawings, and photographs (or tracings of these) from newspapers and magazines can be placed, collage-style, into desired positions. (See Figures 11-26 through 11-28.) These may work, but they lack the spontaneity of rapid doodling and sketching.

The thumbnail process relies on a succession of trials in composition which consider the objective of the verbal/visual message, as well as the different ways to proportion and relate visuals, typography, and white space.

The value of thumbnails is in their discipline. Thumbnailing is an orderly way to keep working on and improving on an idea. You attempt to make each thumbnail an experiment in visual thinking.

Figure 11-27. Tracing (or "swiping") is acceptable in thumbnails. They may limit your range of expression, but if cleverly combined with your doodled vizthinks, they can do the job of idea visualization almost as well. Other alternatives are stock photos (Figure 11-26) and cut-outs (Figure 11-28) carefully selected for size and shape, which can be traced or taped into a variety of positions.

Figure 11-28. Cut-outs can be pasted or taped into position for larger thumbnails and "first rough" layouts.

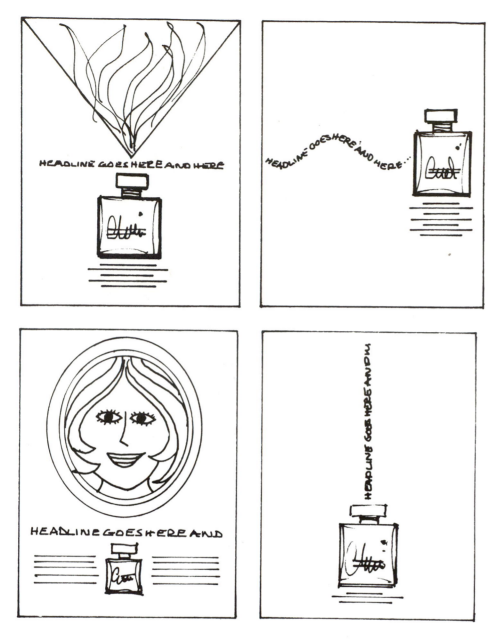

↑
Figure 11-29. These thumbnails illustrate how the level of idea visualization can progress in the vizthink process. These are more sophisticated than the previous examples, and demonstrate an attempt to add a distinct visual style to the style of the product and to the character of the message.

VIZTHINKING WITH THUMBNAILS

Figure 11-29 demonstrates the idea visualization process which thumbnailing can accomplish. Notice how the vizthinker tries various options to relate the verbal/visual components of the message in order to make a selection that seems to be the best visual communicator of the verbal message.

Figure 11-30 is an example of the thumbnail grid used to produce numerous tryouts of thumbnails which are proportionally scaled down from the original size of the advertisement. The idea visualizer can develop his own techniques for organizing the thumbnail process on paper. (Layout sheets, tissue, or bond are fine.) Thumbnails should be traced in a grid, well-spaced for notes or side sketches and for easy analysis and selection. The selected thumbnails are developed into roughs and finally into comps. (See Figures 11-31 and 11-32.)

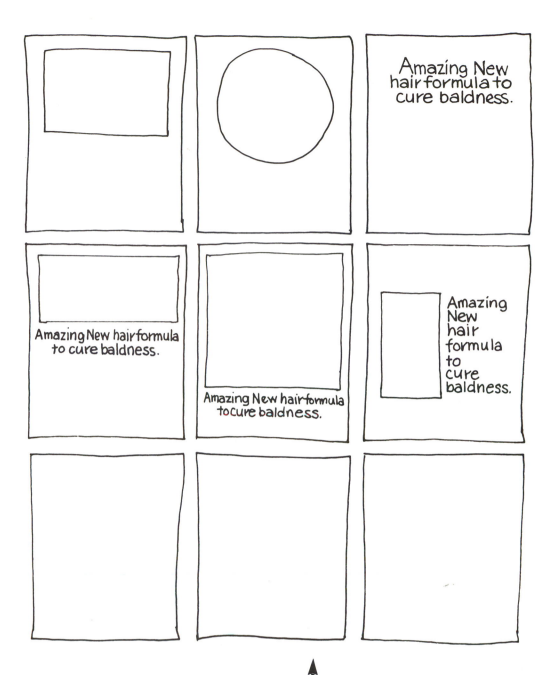

IDEA VISUALIZATION FOR RADIO AND
TELEVISION—SCRIPTS AND STORYBOARDS

In our discussion of writing for television commercials (Chapter 7), we indicated that the idea is conveyed visually by a more complex layout—storyboard—than would be used in a print advertisement.

Here, especially, it is necessary to use simple devices to convey the idea first to the art department, then in more refined form to the client and, finally, to show that the signal is "go," to the television producer-director.

As described earlier, the storyboard may supplement the television script, or supplant it. It provides a series of television screens (frames) that can accommodate thumbnail visuals which vary from rough stick figures to photographs or comprehensive drawings suitable for the client's approval. The time of the spot will usually

Figure 11-30. The thumbnail grid helps the process of idea visualization. The grid consists of a series of small rectangular spaces lined up for quick doodling, which experiments with different arrangements of art and copy elements.

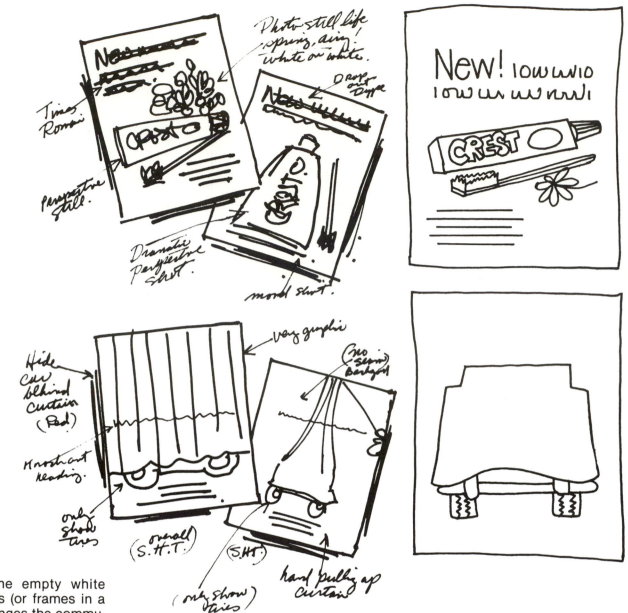

Figure 11-31. The empty white space for print ads (or frames in a story board) challenges the communicator. It should stimulate the writer/visualizer to doodle away. Do not be afraid to do many. Do not worry about wasting paper.

determine the number of frames in a storyboard. A 15-second commercial will have 3 to 6 frames; a 30-second shot, 6 to 12; a 60-second spot, 12 to 24.

The storyboard represents the clearest example of the importance, in fact the necessity, of explaining your ideas visually. Generally, television scripts are, as the term "script" implies, written down. As the writer thinks of the words that will be heard in the proposed commercial, he thinks of the situations that will be seen in the commercial. As has been described previously, the words to be heard (audio) are placed to the right of a centered vertical line, and the action to be seen (video) is placed to the left. Words to be *said* are typed in upper and lower case; audio and video instructions and descriptions are put in capitals. Depending upon the creator and

the occasion, in the creation stage, either the words or the action may come first. (See Figure 11-33.)

But absolutely first of all, there had to be the thought, the decision of what was most important. This point warrants being repeated again and again. A commercial is commonly said to sell a product or a service. Actually, it sells *an idea* about the product or the service.

With that firmly fixed in mind, perhaps it is easier to see now that sometimes one, sometimes the other (of the audio and the video) comes first. Whichever it is, the central idea must be expressed so that the final audience, the potential customer, will understand the same idea as the originator had in mind.

The copywriter must, in some way, describe what the action will

Some people need only one man. Or one woman.

Or one watch.

Omega. One classic is all one needs.

Omega Quartz Chronometer. One of the most famous watches in the world. $2,400* in 14K gold and stainless steel. Photographed on the Golden Gate Bridge, one of the world's most famous structures. For a catalogue of Omega watches for men and women, write Omega, 301 East 57th Street, New York, New York 10022.
*Manufacturer's suggested retail price.

The New York Times Magazine / May 4, 1980

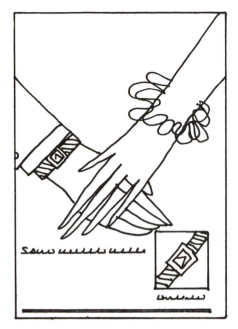

Figure 11-32. On these two pages, we have taken a finished advertisement from a campaign and imagined how it might have been created from thumbnail to rough to comprehensive layout ("comp").

An effective way for you to practice your thumbnail skills would be to try this same reverse process yourself. Clip several ads from magazines. See if you can create their basic structures in thumbnail form. Do some variations in order to practice the techniques of vizthinking you have been reading about.

TELEVISION

Wells, Rich, Greene, Inc. 767 Fifth Avenue New York, N.Y. 10022

Plaza 8-4300

CLIENT UNION UNDERWEAR	CODE NO. XNPR1173 DATE
PRODUCT UNDEROOS	LENGTH :30 AS RECORDED
TITLE YOU AND YOUR UNDEROOS/Girls	JOB NO. 15601-00072 TV

VIDEO	AUDIO
ANIMATED BATGIRL LEAPS IN ANIMATED SKY, CAPE FLAPPING IN THE BREEZE.	BATGIRL: Jumping Underoos!
	Is that another Batgirl?
ANIMATED BATGIRL JOINS LIVE GIRL IN FRONT OF PAINTED "CYCLONE" UNANIMATED BACKDROP.	GIRL: It's me and my Underoos!
LIVE GIRL JUMPS IN FRONT OF PAINTED "WEB" BACKDROP.	GIRL SINGS: You and your Underoos.
	CHORUS OF GIRLS SHOUT: Spiderwoman!
LIVE GIRL DANCES BY PAINTED "K-POW" BACKDROP.	GIRLS SING: Can you tell us who
	is who?
	CHORUS SHOUTS: Catwoman!
LIVE GIRL AND ANIMATED SUPERGIRL GESTURE TO EACH OTHER IN FRONT OF PAINTED "ZAP" BACKDROP.	GIRL: Is Supergirl on the left?
	CHORUS SHOUTS: No right!
LIVE GIRL AND ANIMATED SUPERGIRL EXCHANGE PLACES.	SUPERGIRL: Underoos look out of sight.
	CHORUS SHOUTS: Supergirl!
LIVE GIRL AND ANIMATED WONDERWOMAN DANCE IN FRONT OF PAINTED THOUGHT-BUBBLE BACKDROP.	GIRL SINGS: Wearing Underoos is fun.
CLOSEUP OF WONDERWOMAN AS SHE WINKS.	WONDERWOMAN: You can take it from
	us -- we're the ones.
	CHORUS SHOUTS: Wonderwoman!
5 PACKAGES POP ON IN OPTICAL SHOT WITH UNDEROOS SIGN.	GIRL SINGS: Underwear is fun to
	wear it's true.
PACKAGES REPLACED BY SINGING GIRLS IN UNDEROOS OUTFITS.	GIRLS SING: When it's you and your
	under... You and your under... You
	You and your Underoos!

Figure 11-33. The TV script, above, calls for animated as well as photographed narrative action. It contains numerous optical effects, sound effects, musical background, the voices of the three principal characters, and a chorus! The photo storyboard of this commercial, opposite, shows how the copywriter's TV script was visualized and produced. Notice how the copywriter has repeated the product name verbally and visually throughout.

UNDEROOS
Underwear that's Fun to Wear!

"YOU AND YOUR UNDEROOS-GIRLS"

BATGIRL: Jumping Underoos! Is that another Batgirl?

GIRL: It's me and my Underoos!

GIRL SINGS: You and your Underoos.
CHORUS OF GIRLS SHOUT: Spider-Woman!

GIRLS SING: Can you tell us who is who?
CHORUS SHOUTS: Catwoman!

GIRL: Is Supergirl on the left?
CHORUS: No right!

SUPERGIRL: Underoos look out of sight.
CHORUS SHOUTS: Supergirl!

GIRL SINGS: Wearing Underoos is fun.

WONDER WOMAN: You can take it from us -- we're the ones.
CHORUS SHOUTS: Wonder Woman!

GIRL SINGS: Underwear is fun to wear it's true.

GIRLS SING: When it's you and your
UNDER...You and your UNDER...
You and your UNDEROOS!

UNION UNDERWEAR CO.

WELLS, RICH & GREENE
CODE NO.: XNPR-1173

155
VIZTHINK EXERCISES

be. You will recall the twenty ways of visualizing with which the *writer* can try to "see" his words (Chapter 10). The art director is the first audience for the script. If he can see in his mind what the copywriter had originally in *his* mind, he can take it from there, skillfully sketching in the action on a storyboard pad, so that the script "comes alive."

STIMULATING VISUAL NARRATIONS

How does the writer come up with *visual narrations* to accompany his verbal narratives? Visual narrations include objects, places, words, colors, people, graphics, unusual perspectives and juxtapositions of various audio and visual elements. The creative connection comes to the open mind which is always collecting and cataloging visual ideas. The idea visualizer is never without a pencil, pad, or tape recorder. He is forever making notes, clipping and filing ideas from his own observations, interviews with clients, and brainstorming sessions with co-workers.

The visual metaphor is also an "image of wide scope" (Chapter 10) and can be as powerful a message-sender as its verbal partners. Visual metaphors can bring life and power especially to abstract verbal concepts. You may recall how the Prudential Life Insurance Company presents their claim of solid service in a visual metaphor, and how a long-horn Texas steer is a Merrill Lynch visual metaphor for their positive statement, "We're bullish on America."

WRAP-UP

Idea visualization for copywriters may never become second nature. But, to the degree that you begin to put your thinking "down on paper," you will realize the benefits of the visual/verbal creative connection. Keep visualizing your ideas. Language is a system that includes a large variety of audio/visual symbols. The creative communicator learns to "pull out all the stops."

ADDITIONAL APPLICATIONS FOR VIZTHINKING

There are as many applications for vizthinking as there are creative problems in communications. Here we discuss several of the most likely to occur for the copywriter and idea visualizer.

PACKAGING

When we talk of packaging, what do we mean? "The package" can convey a component of *marketing strategy* for a corporation, or it can mean the *corporate image,* or it can be the *conveyor of the product,* first into the market place, then onto the shelf, and finally into the hands of the consumer.

Frequently in this book, we have first handled the large idea and then worked down to the small. In this instance, let us travel the other way. Let us start with the product package itself and then work up to the larger usages of packaging.

The package is more than a cosmetic or an "outside wrap." It is more than a protective cover for the contents. It is, rather, the first and most immediate message about the product which can be conveyed to the potential customer. (See Figure 12-1.)

How does a package carry the message of the product?

- It can tell what the product is.
- It can convey the message of "expensive," of "high fashion," of the "utilitarian"; it can say "strong" or "fragile."
- It can tell something about the packager, the company.
- It can establish a family of products.
- When it is a multiple pack, it can suggest a convenient multiple purchase.
- If it is the currently popular "bubble pack" of see-through plastic, it provides easy, but protective covering and implies "modern," "current."

Where do package ideas come from? There are a number of "design associate" firms in all parts of the country as well as at an international level, too. Most of them will say flatly that while they are best equipped to implement ideas, the ideas themselves can come from the producer or the marketing team or the advertising agency.

In other words, the ideas need not come from a design artist alone. Nor, in fact, is it solely the arrangement of type and lines and massing of colors. Often, the basic idea develops from a marketing idea, perhaps from the need to *position* the product in a busy competitive field for a specific target audience. (See Figure 12-2.)

Case histories indicate the importance of package shape or color

Figure 12-2. In the Maxwell House ➤
advertisement, the package design was dictated by the need both to create recognition of the famous old Maxwell House reputation, "Good to the last drop," and to position the new coffee blend as strong and aromatic. "[13 ounces]...makes as many cups as one full pound." The design retains the familiar logotype with the tipped cup, but adds in larger, strong letters, "Master Blend." Again, the words and the visual work together to perform the dual task.

↑

Figure 12-1. The visual impact of a package on a shelf in a supermarket or a pharmacy is, in itself, the hardest "sell." What does the visual involve in package design?

The Revlon packaging gets its total "look" from the stock (the paper), its quality, weight, texture, and color; the size and shape; the copy blocks and the typeface and size in which they are set; and finally, the "eye-power" and the "stand-out power" of the logo selected. Here, the simple san serif, block letters of Revlon will catch the eye among any number of competitive products on the shelf. The "family" is established, companion products tend to attract the eye, too, and multiple sales are promoted.

or word emphasis. Research confirms this importance. New products need new presentations. Old products that are now "new and improved" may need new, improved packaging. Once again, it is necessary to set up marketing objectives for a given product so that the design elements of the package can express and enhance those specific objectives.

If there are corporate objectives—and there always must be—the package must work for these enlarged purposes, beyond the needs of the immediate product. The family of products within the corporation should show their relationship to each other. Typography can show the kinship of one product to another. Package shape may stay the same or change, as may package size. Even the color may change. This is frequently seen in hair shampoos, for example, which may be under one trademark, but have different color panels for different treatments. But throughout, the mood that design creates must remain. For a corporate line of products, it is *packaging that provides identity.*

In this way, the image of the corporation may well be carried by the packaging. The language of the "business of marketing" acknowledges this with the phrase "packaged goods." From cans of coffee and boxes of soap, through panty hose, jars of expensive cosmetics or inexpensive headache remedies, the great majority of the products we see on the shelves of supermarkets, drug stores, and on the shelves and counters of department stores, has strong package identification.

Finally, carrying the discussion to the largest overall concept, the package can be applied to the total marketing philosophy of a corporation. "Package," in this sense, represents the adoption by a corporation of an image or personality which it must have in the highly competitive struggle to stand out from and above its rivals.

Most active people today find themselves bombarded with hundreds of message and commercial impressions. The only ones

New Maxwell House® Master Blend.® Delicious ground coffee that can save you money!

With new Maxwell House® Master Blend® Coffee you enjoy delicious ground coffee. And you can save money, too.

New Maxwell House Master Blend tastes delicious.

Master Blend is 100% pure ground coffee that's specially roasted and ground, not concentrated or flaked.

You can save money, too.

Because we make it a special way, 13 ounces of Master Blend goes as far as 16 ounces of ordinary coffee. And you make it the same way you usually do.

Use the same number of scoops. That's how Master Blend can save you money.

New Maxwell House Master Blend Coffee comes in three grinds: *Regular, Electra-Perk,®* and *Automatic Drip Blend.* It's the delicious ground coffee that's always...."Good to the Last Drop,®" and it can save you money, too.

Mmm...smell that rich aroma! It's 100% ground coffee.

Use the same number of scoops you use with ordinary coffee.

The flavor is always "Good to the Last Drop.®"

Not available in some areas at this time.

© 1981 General Foods Corporation   GENERAL FOODS

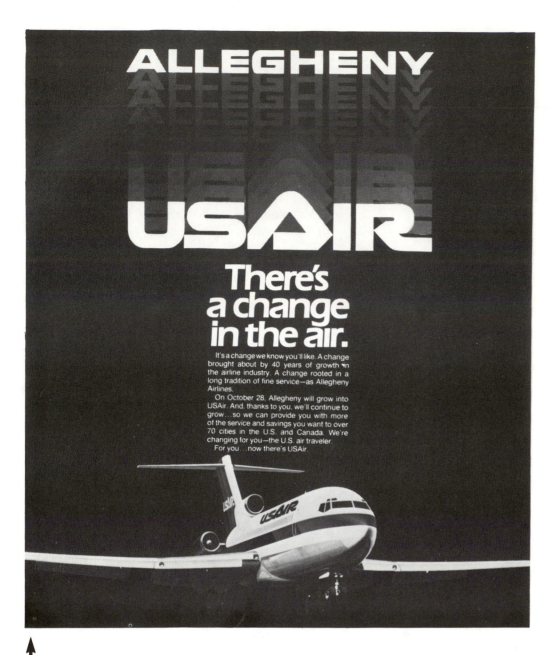

Figure 12-3. In the largest meaning of the word "packaging," the USAIR story provides a good example. Here it was necessary to create the *corporate* package to fit Allegheny Airlines' enlarged marketing concept. Therefore, USAIR, a new name to replace Allegheny, was designed to express breadth and coverage. A new typography to express a modern, uncluttered look was also developed. Finally, the logotype incorporates the entire idea.

In this national ad, the transition from the old to the new is visualized graphically—suggesting "a change in the air." There is indeed a totally new corporate image conveyed in a total corporate package.

they will remember are those that have a clear and close association to some need in their lives that day or that week—or those that "stand out in the crowd." They may remember these for a future need if some real and almost tangible vision has been given them. An excellent example is the long-lived, and ongoing symbol of the Thunderbird automobile line of the Ford Motor Company. Now something like twenty years old, it has lived through changes and new demands from engineers, the government and the consuming public; but the image of the first Thunderbird and the insignia of that car are always present and provide an aura of excitement and fine tuning to the car line, year after year, whatever the changes.

Another case in point is more recent. It covers the repositioning of Allegheny Airlines, formerly a small, regional airline, to accommodate a new larger travel pattern allotted to it by the government. The change in name to USAIR was accompanied by changes in logotype, airplane exterior design, colors, and the like, leading to new consumer acceptance of the airline as a larger, better carrier.

The airline's vice-president has been quoted as calling the change "Fantastic!" which he perceives as being accompanied by an upswing in customer recognition, customer approval, and finally, customer sales. (See Figure 12-3.)

The whole must work together with all of its parts in order to present an upgraded, more modern, and always appropriate visual.

SALES AND CLIENT PRESENTATIONS

In the hands of the idea visualizer, the early translation of words into words and pictures is achieved by the thumbnail or first rough (for print advertising) and by the TV script or rough storyboard (for television). The client is the second audience who, it is hoped, will "get the picture"—the same picture that was in the creator's mind. For example, in the case of a storyboard presentation for a television commercial, will the client get the idea? Will she see and hear what was in your mind when you wrote the script and visualized the storyboard? If she does get the same idea, the verbal/visual connection has been communicated properly and may be used to explain the idea to the third audience, the television producer. It is the responsibility of the television producer to produce a message that will effectively communicate your ideas to the *final* audience, the television viewer (and customer).

This is not an easy task. A recent study conducted for the American Association of Advertising Agencies by Professor John Jacoby, a consumer psychologist at Purdue University, concluded that more than 95 percent of viewers misunderstood some part of what they saw on television. The study revealed that 2,700 participants over the age of thirteen misunderstood at least some part of what they saw in two television spots. Each viewer was asked a total of twelve true-or-false questions about inferences and facts included in the messages. Only 3.5 percent of 2,700 tested answered all correctly.

The study is a challenge to the copywriter and visualizer to become a more effective communicator. It may indicate that complex information about products is not suitable for the medium of television. It may be that messages which are perfectly clear to copywriters, art directors, television producers and their clients, may be lost or misunderstood by the final audience. This becomes one more challenge for the creative connection to meet and overcome.

So far, the examples of the importance of visualizing the message have been explained in terms of the visual in partnership with the *written* word. But, it is very important to think in visual terms for the *oral* presentation of ideas—to friends, to co-workers, to the

Figure 12-4. In today's world, we are required to present more and more statistical data, for they touch our lives in many ways. Too often, numbers and statistics are conveyed in a meaningless jumble. Nothing clarifies them so quickly as a visual graph or chart, which can present important figures that are hard to understand in paragraphs.

Pie graphs, bar graphs, shaded charts, color and overlays all help to present clear meaning for mathematical statements, correlations, and comparisions. To give the necessary facts, diagrams, charts, and pictograms are ideal. There it is in front of one's eyes, presenting a clear statement, comparative weights, and a total, immediate impression.

"boss," to clients, and more and more, to the public at increasingly mandated public meetings. This new trend runs through community affairs, politics, and business. The spoken word almost demands the assistance of visual explanations in any numbers of ways.

The numerous kinds of audio-visual devices can easily frighten a newcomer to the speaker's platform. Each has its place, but it is too easily forgotten that one of the most crucial audio-visual devices you may ever use is yourself—your own appearance. Surely no instruction is needed here. Just be aware that you can assume any role you wish by dressing the part: a conservative businessman or woman; artistic "bohemian" type; a rising executive, and so on. In this way, you start off on the "right foot," no matter what message you want to convey. Dress the part and you have at least started providing the atmosphere you want to set for your talk.

Thereafter, as you speak, it is to be hoped that you will try to use devices to aid you in explaining and to aid your audience in understanding what you are talking about. If you want a site in your community cleared up, take a picture, enlarge it, and show what a hideous eyesore it is. If you can, go a step further and get someone to help you sketch an improvement. Complete that and use it as an overlay.

If you have something to say that involves figures, do not credit your audience with any great ability to follow your words. Use charts and graphs and "pictograms" to explain. (See Figure 12-4.) With these devices, you need only an easel and large, poster-type visuals.

But we cannot leave it at that. We said, "LARGE!" What you cannot see from the middle to the back of the room, you might as well throw in the trash basket. It is that useless! Your photograph of the site at Main and 12th Streets can be a masterpiece of photography, but it is useless if you cannot have it blown up B-I-G!

Of course, there are ways you can make small sketches big. Make use of electronic/electrical devices. An overhead projector or an opaque projector can help you. With the latter, you slide the photograph onto a mesh screen and the image is shown, blown up, on a screen or a light-colored wall. With an overhead projector, for a few cents, you make a transparency of a line drawing, such as a chart or a graph, and project that on a screen.

It is all available at little cost, but you have to do it! Provide that little budget and the extra time. It will not only make your points more explicit, but you will gain added confidence from knowing that you have only to project a chart or a graph to have the exact figures you want directly in front of you and your audience at the same time. They will be able to see what you are talking about. Both of you will understand it better.

Slides, films, and films strips are some of the more sophisticated possibilities that can be used by a speaker. But let us go back to what we have said again and again: You must have the ideas!

DIRECT MAIL

As discussed more fully earlier, in direct mail, whether it be a letter or a forty-eight-page catalog, the visual or "look" is better than half the battle. The rough ideas are worked out in "dummy" form, to convey to others what was in your mind. Just as does the dress of a man or woman, the "look" of a mailing piece says at once: quality or low price; taste or the lack of it; special selective appeal or mass appeal. Whether it be a direct mail catalog for Wisconsin cheeses or a circular from a leading museum or a Spring fashion forecast from a leading fashion shop, the visual sets the tone.

Direct mail is usually selected instead of other print media when the nature of a message and its content are too complicated and too detailed for a newspaper or magazine ad. The copywriter is asked to write copy designed to deliver a significant response—especially in *mail-order* direct mail.

Direct mail copy should be heavily based on customer benefits and satisfactions. This is why many direct mail campaigns present

Figure 12-5. Two excellent examples of small space ads are shown here in actual size. The text has suggested how these ads must fight to catch the eye. See how well these ads do just that. Oddly enough, each has about the same number of words of body copy. Each has its own way of highlighting the logo. Each should stand out on its page.

THE CREATIVE CONNECTION

special offers, free offers, and premiums. The copy is full of helpful information and stimulating ideas for the reader. The approach should be more factual than imaginative—without obvious gimmicks. The tone should be friendly and communicate on a personal level. The visuals are colorful, precise, and present a clear picture of the product.

The copy closing should be a strong request for action—to return a coupon, telephone an order, visit a showroom, or request an appointment. The response requested should be easy enough for a child to do!

OUTDOOR ADVERTISING AND POSTERS

Most billboard and poster copy has to be read in a flash. In the majority of cases, the reader is in motion—and has only time for a quick message, an impression rather than a great deal of detail. So remember the "eight-word" rule mentioned in Chapter 8. The visual has to do most of the job. Headlines are short and to the point; the layout and graphics are bold and simple. The verbal/visual connection has to be effective enough to attract attention, arouse interest, and make one very strong point!

SMALL SPACE ADVERTISING

It is amazing how much more copy you can find in some small space ads than you see in larger space ads. There is no inverse rule of proportion at work here. It might help to remember that small space ads must fight for attention; they usually have a great deal of company. The headline has a very heavy responsibility to get some attention away from the clutter of adjoining ads. The body copy has to make every word count—covering selling points and the closing as economically as possible. (See Figure 12-5.)

VISUAL MERCHANDISING (DISPLAY) AND EXHIBITS

Often an actual display (visual merchandising) can show your audience a great deal of what you are trying to say. Whatever the product or merchandise, show it!

In an exhibit or in a store, the principle is the same. use your products or merchandise in a dramatic way to make the statement you want. Whether your merchandise is Oriental rugs or lipstick, use their intrinsic shapes and colors to catch attention. One store, in its towel shop, showed every color and every size arranged against the wall to show the entire stock in a colorful, breath-taking "wall of merchandise." Imagination can be used to make your products sell themselves in shapes and forms that stop the passer-by.

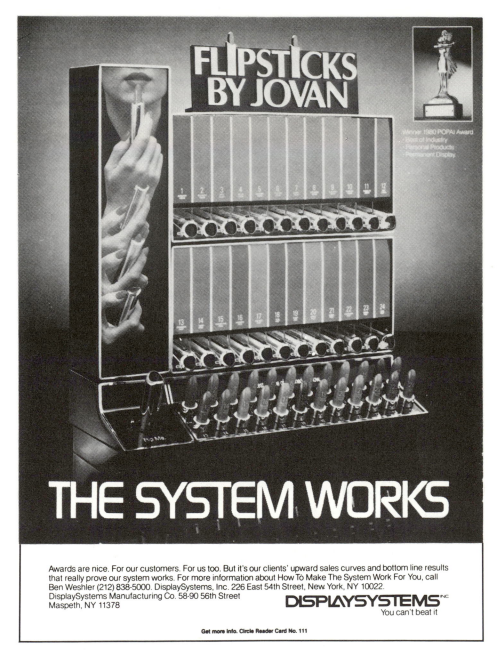

Figure 12-6. An interesting trade advertisement for a display company illustrates the impact of theatrical design. Notice how the lipstick display incorporates a mirror on the side for consumer involvement. The display rack says, "Try the lipstick right now. See how the color looks on you, now!"

Copy can be used with dramatic visualization to make displays in retail stores and showrooms—point-of-purchase displays. POP displays are often designed to stock as well as display individual packaged products. The copy should stop traffic with attention-compelling headlines and graphics. It should go on to give product and utilization information which will help customers to make "self-service" decisions. The content of the copy is often tied into a current advertising campaign featuring this merchandise. (See Figure 12-6.)

Displays for exhibits and trade shows are more sophisticated in design and structure. They may employ environmental spaces through which customers can experience, test, or sample the products displayed. Copy is written billboard and poster-style to accompany booths and enclaves where customers can read about and handle merchandise. Such exhibit displays may incorporate current technological uses of audio-visual devices—multi-image slide projection, computer retrieval systems, videotape players, and so on. Trade shows are just what the name implies. The words and pictures must dramatize and entertain in much the same way as theater!

JOURNALISM—PHOTO-STORIES

In another area of communications, that of journalism, the writer is helped immeasurably by a sense of the visual. Whether it is as a reporter catching a news story or developing a longer article, an awareness of what is visually exciting can illuminate the words. Some reporters are their own photographers. Others work with photographers. But, in every sense, the eye must seek out the central significance of a scene or a story, must often recognize it instantly, and must capture it in a single camera shot.

Since we are not addressing ourselves to professional artists or photographers here, we are saying that the "writing" reporter must catch that special instant. Sometimes it can be done with a preliminary photograph (perhaps a Polaroid-type shot) to be reset and taken later by a professional; sometimes it is accomplished by a quick nod to the photographer who accompanies the reporter.

Photojournalism, which continues to occupy a place of great popularity and professionalism, need not be rejected by one who is not a professional photographer. The writer who would like to work out an idea in that medium should have enough confidence to attempt first to visualize it completely. Let the visuals form in your head, and plan your story step by step with picture-ideas to go with the word-ideas.

Perhaps here is the place to pose the question many have when they see someone else's work: "What pictures would I have ordered

HI MOM

STUART GRAY

may
is a great month to

IMAGE BANK

SEND BALLOONS OF GOOD WISHES on **Mother's Day, Father's Day, any day.** The newest greeting card is a message on a balloon. For about $10, you can have an inflated glitzy metallic balloon in a box with a personalized message sent anywhere in the country. For an order form, write Balloons, P.O. Box 729, South Orange NJ 07079 (enclose a self-addressed, stamped envelope), or call 201-731-4495. Allow two weeks for delivery.

WATCH THE WORLD GO BY at an outdoor café. The weather's perfect for sipping drinks with a friend while checking out the street scene. Hot spots for people-watching: Boston's Faneuil Hall Market-Place; Chicago's Rush Street; Kansas City's Country Club Plaza; New York City's Columbus Avenue; Washington, D.C.'s 19th Street (between K and L).

DRESS UP YOUR WINDOWS with a blooming box of periwinkles, petunias, marigolds or zinnias. If you plant these now, their flowers will last until the first heavy frost next fall!

TRY ON A BATHING SUIT. You've still got a month to shape up before summer officially starts. If you put yourself on a 1,200-calorie diet at the beginning of the month, you could lose as many as ten pounds. Even a diet cheat could lose five!

TAKE IN A MOVIE. Catch good-looker Robert Hays (*Airplane*, TV's *Angie*) in his second film, **Take This Job and Shove It,** based on the hit country song by Johnny Paycheck. How good can a movie be that's built around a song and takes place in a brewery? See for yourself. . . . Lauren Bacall plays a glamorous actress returning to the stage who's pursued by a psychotic fan (newcomer Michael Biehn) in Robert Stigwood's **The Fan.** With Bacall's recent return to Broadway in *Woman of the Year* and the murder of John Lennon, the plot seems eerily close to real life.

PICK OUT A GOOD SUMMER READ for those long lazy beach afternoons to come. Two books you might consider: James Clavell—of *Shogun* fame—has a new novel, *Noble House*, set in Hong Kong and full of blood rivalry, financial double-dealing and high adventure (Delacorte Press, hardback, $19.95). *Tramp Steamers* is the perfect book for armchair travelers. It's the first guide to budget ocean travel and includes a directory of cargo ships and freighters that carry passengers. The next best thing to a real steamer trip could be reading about all the possibilities and exotic ports of call. *Tramp Steamers* is by Meme Black (Addison-Wesley Publishing Company, paperback, $6.95).

James Clavell NOBLE HOUSE SHOGUN

CATCH A CLASS ACT ON TV. George Balanchine choreographs a host of original puppet creatures, designed by *Sesame Street*'s Big Bird creator, Kermit Love, in the ballet *The Spellbound Child/L'Enfant Et Les Sortileges* for PBS's *Dance in America* series, May 25 at 8 P.M. It's pure fantasy as a ten-foot clock, wallpaper characters and more household objects come alive to haunt a child who's been abusing them. . . . Brace yourself for another *Dallas* cliffhanger as the TV season comes to a close. Hint: It's about J.R. again.

and used if I had been in charge?" This exercise can help to train the eye.

Again, in magazine editing, the staff writer must have a sense of what the page *spread* (a double page) should look like. The visual, here as elsewhere, is not merely a picture, but includes blocks of copy and the arrangement of the elements on the page. The sequence of elements on a page, as well as the sequence of pages as the reader will see them, are important concerns for the editor and art director of every publication. (See Figure 12-7.)

Figure 12-7. In setting up a page in a newspaper or, as here, in a magazine, the art director must constantly keep in mind the subject matter and/or theme, the materials to be presented, and the pictorial matter that will create the most impact. The page shown is very successful in putting the story across.

The authors and artists involved with this book you are now reading had the same problems constantly before them, and they have tried to make the creative connection for a lively, easily understood page.

CONCLUSION

The foregoing pages, brief indeed compared to many of the 400 and 500-page books on advertising, have, nevertheless, tried to enumerate and stress what we consider the essentials of writing effective copy. But, copywriting cannot be "taught" by textbooks or classroom lectures. Copywriting can be learned by using guidelines and procedures you have read about here, and then *writing, editing,* and *rewriting; doodling, thumbnailing,* and *revising.* The most useful thing for any copy instructor to do is to be the student's tough and demanding editor and devil's advocate.

There is no argument between strong selling copy and creative copy. It has been mentioned in the early sections of this text, and can be repeated here, that we are dealing with a consumer market that is steadily gaining in awareness, in understanding of values, in basic education. Copy must deal honestly and fairly with the consumer if it is to be effective. Advertising as a whole must be believable and responsible if it is to continue under its own code, unpoliced by government legislation. The copywriter is the focal thinker behind campaigns and promotions. If the copywriter is responsible, advertising will not need outside policing.

In accordance with this concept of setting standards within its own house, the Advertising Code, adopted by the Advertising Federation of America, is quoted below as a useful guidepost.

The nine-point code was set down as follows:

1. *Truth:* Advertising shall tell the truth, and shall reveal material facts, the concealment of which might mislead the public.

2. *Responsibility:* Advertising agencies and advertisers shall be willing to provide substantiation of claims made.

3. *Taste and Decency:* Advertising shall be free of statements, illustrations or implications that are offensive to good taste or public decency.

4. *Disparagement:* Advertising shall offer merchandise or service on its merits and refrain from attacking competitors or disparaging their products, services, or methods of doing business.

5. *Bait Advertising:* Advertising shall be bona fide and the merchandise or service offered shall be readily available for purchase at the advertised price.

6. *Guarantees and Warranties:* Advertising of guarantees and warranties shall be explicit. Advertising of any guarantee and warranty shall clearly and conspicuously disclose its nature and extent, the manner in which the guarantor or warrantor will perform, and the identity of the guarantor or warrantor.

7. *Price Claims:* Advertising shall avoid price or savings

claims which are unsupported by facts or which do not offer bona fide bargains or savings.

8. *Unprovable Claims:* Advertising shall avoid the use of exaggerated or unprovable claims.
9. *Testimonials:* Advertising containing testimonials shall be limited to those of competent witnesses who are reflecting a real and honest choice.

The creative connection in advertising, as we have discussed it, has examined the potential of messages that have words *working with* pictures. There is no doubt that the ability to create effective blends of verbal and visual communication helps get results for the copywriter and art director. However, creativity in advertising is much more than words and pictures from the creative department. It is also account management, market research, and media planning. In some of the most creative of the major advertising agencies, there is now a framework for interdepartmental communication. This is an interconnection of all of the people in the advertising process. It makes provisions for writers and art directors to understand the clients' marketing problems and objectives. It encourages them to develop their own analyses of the company, its products, its competition, and most important, its customers. When the creative team of art director and writer meets with a media planner, they work out a media plan that considers the appeals and approaches of copy and art. On the other hand, the specific selections of a media plan may affect the development of a copy and art concept.

More and more, the current practice in many of the large ad agencies is for full participation in the creative effort by the four major departments: account management, media, research, and creative. Their first step has been to get the creative team more involved with the three other functions in the advertising process. Product development and marketing strategies are now formulated with input from the creative group. After primary research and a data base is developed, creative people are involved by doing their own analyses of the market situation and product positioning. The creative team is encouraged to be critical of product and market planning—and thus be a part of the planning process.

Another aspect of an expanded network for the creative connection is to provide for direct communication between writers and/or art directors and *clients*. As in research and media, this supplements rather than replaces account management.

Does all this encourage and nourish creativity? The most successful "creatives" know that the creative process relies on an interaction of ideas between people. There is no such thing as an original, unconnected idea. The creative connection is an idea-search by the individual—the creative interconnection is an idea-search by the group.

GLOSSARY

A

Abstract: An idea or term considered apart from some material basis or object; e.g., justice, peace, goodness.

Account Executive: Member of agency staff who is the liaison between one or more clients (advertisers) and the agency. Keeps aware of advertiser's plans and needs; carries this data to agency personnel; then brings agency plans to advertiser.

Advertising: Any paid, nonpersonal message by an identified sponsor; appears in media and used to influence sales, services, or the acceptance of ideas by potential buyers.

Advertising Agency: An organization that renders advertising, promotion, and marketing services to clients.

Advertising Campaign: Series of advertising messages devoted to a single theme, concept, or idea with a definite objective.

Advertising Schedule: The plan of timing, media, amount of space, and items to be advertised for specified period.

Agate Line: Unit of measure in newspaper printed space. It is one column wide, regardless of width, and always one-fourteenth of an inch deep. (Fourteen agate lines deep to the column inch.)

Airbrush: A commercial art method of retouching by use of a fine spray of paint to produce tonal gradations and to retouch photographs.

Allocation: Percentage of appropriation assigned to activity, media, divisions, or departments.

Analogous Symbolism: Idea symbolized by an object which by its nature, function, or purpose symbolizes the idea, e.g., loneliness symbolized by a bare room.

Animatic Film: A film of storyboards with sound track attached. Used to pretest television commercials.

Animation: Movement added to static objects. Usually applied to cartoon drawings filmed for television, or to POP material or outdoor advertisements with moving parts.

Announcement: See *Commercial.*

Answer Print: The final film of a television commercial, prepared for checking and approval before release.

Appeal: Motive to which advertising is directed, designed to stimulate action by the audience. Points made in copy to meet customers' needs and objectives, and provide reasons to buy.

Approach: Manner of presentation of appeals as determined by copywriter; can be factual, imaginative, or combination of the two.

Appropriation: In sales promotion, the dollars designated for all promotional activities. It is usually a percentage of annual gross volume.

Arc: A truck or curved dolly that travels a curved path or arc, either left or right. Also see *Dolly.*

Art: An element of print advertising. Includes photography, wash illustration, or line drawings.

Ascenders: Those letters with a stroke or line going higher than the *x-height* or body of the letter—b, d, f, h, k, l, and t—and all capitals. *Descenders* are g, j, p, q, and y. Also see *x-height.*

Associative Symbolism: Idea symbolized by objects associated with it, e.g., seaside holiday symbolized by pail, spade, starfish.

Audience: People reached by an advertising medium.

Audience Composition: The demographics or kinds of people reached by advertising according to age, sex, income, home, etc. Also known as *audience profile.*

Audience Cume (Cumulative): (1) For radio and television, the total number of different people reached by a station in two or more time periods, or the net (unduplicated) audience in a specified span of time. Usually measured by the week. (2) For newspapers, the number of different people reached in a time period. Usually measured by the week.

Audience Profile: See *Audience Composition.*

Audio: Sound or pertaining to sound. In television, the transmission or reception of sound as opposed to the picture portion, or video. Compare with *Video.*

B

Balance: The placement of elements in an advertisement so that they complement each other in terms of size and weight.

Balance, Formal: Used in advertising layout and in display when a dominant point of interest is desired with subordinate elements to develop equal attention power.

Balance, Informal: Used in advertising layout and in display, whereby attention is gained by dynamic balance in arrangement of elements. Difference in attention power caused by shape, color or arrangement, often with dissimilar units.

Balloons: A visualizing device surrounding words coming from the mouth of the person pictured. Borrowed from the comics.

BCU: See *Big Close-up.*

Benday: A process for adding tone in line drawings, etc., by applying patterns of dots, stipples or the like from a transparent film onto a negative before a printing plate is made.

bf: See *Boldface.*

Big Close-up (BCU): A camera shot of only the head and face. Also called *tight close-up (TCU).*

Big Copy: A layout in which the visuals are subordinate to the copy and its typography.

Big Picture: A layout in which the visuals are dominant. Usually in *formal balance* with headline and body copy below the picture.

Billboard: (1) Popular name for an outdoor sign. Term not now generally used in the outdoor advertising industry. (2) The radio or television presentation of the name of a program sponsor and a slogan, plus performers, producer, director, and other credits. Used at the start or close of a program, usually eight seconds long.

Black and White (B/W): Printing on white paper with black ink (or vice versa). No color is used. Also known as *monotone*.

Bleed: Printed matter that runs over the edges of an outdoor board or of a page, leaving no margin.

Blister Pack: A packaging term. A preformed bubble of plastic holding merchandise to a card. Used for small items. Also called *bubble card*.

Blowup: Photo enlargement of written, printed, or pictorial materials; e.g., enlargement of a publication advertisement to be used as a poster or transmitted through television.

Body Copy: Main text of advertisement, in contrast to headlines and logotype.

Body Type: Commonly used for reading matter, as distinguished from display type used in the headlines of advertisements. Usually type 14 points in size, or smaller.

Boldface (bf): A heavy line type. **This sentence is set in boldface.**

Box Head: See *Head*.

Brainstorming: A technique for "prodding" creativity in which ideas and suggestions are expressed by members of a group; no critical evaluation or negative responses are permitted. The prime consideration is generation of ideas, no matter how unusual or impractical they may seem at first.

Brand, Brand Name: The name used to identify a specific product. It is a variety of trademark. Used to achieve customer recognition and brand preference. Also see *Trademark*.

Bring Music Up: See *Music Up*.

Broadside: Promotion piece of one large sheet of paper, usually printed on one side. As the paper is unfolded, so is the message.

Brochure: A multi-page printed information piece or pamphlet about a product or service, usually larger than a *folder*, less elaborate than a *catalog*.

Bubble Card: See *Blister Pack*.

Buy: A media purchase of time or space for an advertisement or campaign. Used more in broadcast than in print advertising. Also see *Local Buy; Network Buy; Spot Buy*.

B/W: See *Black and White*.

C

Calendered Paper: Paper with a smooth, burnished surface, attained by passing the paper between heavy rolls called *calenders*.

Calligraphy: Hand-lettering.

Call Letters: The combination of letters assigned by the Federal Communications Commission (FCC) to a broadcasting station. They serve as its official designation and establish its identity.

Camera Light: Pilot light on TV cameras indicating which camera is on the air.

Camera Lucida: A device used in making layouts, enabling art to be optically reflected from an original to the layout, enlarged or reduced as needed. Also referred to as a *lucy*.

Campaign: A coordinated series of advertising messages revolving around one central selling theme, appearing over an extended period of time.

Caps: In typography, capital or uppercase letters in contrast to small or lowercase letters.

Caption: (1) Headline of an advertisement. (2) Descriptive matter accompanying an illustration or a publicity photograph.

Car Card: Poster-like designed card, usually placed in buses or subways. Common sizes are 11-inches high and 28-inches, 42-inches, or 56-inches long. The 11-inch height is standard for such cards.

Casting Off: See *Copy Fitting*.

Catalog: A comprehensive brochure that usually contains visuals and descriptions of products and services. Information is detailed enough for the reader to make mail-order buying decisions.

Center Head: See *Head*.

Center Spread: (1) In print advertising, an advertisement printed across the two facing middle pages of a publication bound through the center. Otherwise called *double spread*. Also see *Spread*. (2) In outdoor advertising, two adjacent panels using coordinated copy.

Certification Mark: A name or design used upon, or in connection with, the products or services of persons other than the owner of the mark, to certify origin, material, mode of manufacture, quality, accuracy, or other characteristics of such goods or services; e.g., Seal of the Underwriters Laboratories; Sanforized; Teflon II.

Chain Break: Times during or between network programs when a broadcasting station identifies itself (two seconds) and gives a commercial announcement (eight seconds). The announcements are referred to as *chain breaks* or *ID's* (for identification).

Channel: A band of radio frequencies assigned to a given radio or TV station or to other broadcasting purposes.

Character Count: See *Copy Fitting*.

Checking Copy: A copy of a publication sent to an advertiser or agency, to show that the advertisement appeared as specified.

Circular: An advertisement printed on a sheet or folder.

Close Shot: See *Medium Shot (MS)*.

Close-up Shot (CU): Generally a camera shot of the head and shoulders, unless otherwise specified. *ECU* is *extreme close-up* or *extra close-up*. *MCU* is *medium close-up*.

Closing Date: The final date on which advertising must be delivered to a medium if it is to appear in a specific issue or time slot.

Coarse-Screen Halftone: A comparatively low, or coarse, screen, usually 60, 65 or 85 lines to the inch; makes the picture suitable for printing on coarse paper, such as newsprint. Also see *Halftone*.

Coated Paper: Paper having a surface coating which produces a smooth, hard finish, suitable for the reproduction of fine halftones. Surface varies from eggshell to glossy. Also known as *coated stock*.

Coined Word: An original and arbitrary combination of syllables forming a word. Extensively used for trademarks, as Acrilan, Gro-Pup, Zerone. (Opposite of "dictionary word.")

Cold Type: Type set by electronic or photographic process, not using molten metal. Used in *lithographic (offset) printing* and often now in *letterpress*. Also see *Photocomposition*.

Collage: An artistic combination of elements from different categories pasted over a surface to form a single picture. Materials as varied as sea shells, fabric, paper shavings, fish net, wire, string, etc., give meaning to a collage.

Collective Mark: An identification used by the members of a cooperative, an association, collective group, or organization, including marks used to indicate membership in a union, an association, or other organization; e.g., Sunkist.

Color: Sold in printing, art, photography, television. As opposed to black/white, more expensive and more involved in production; more realistic. Proven to have greater selling impact. Also see *Four-color Process; Spot Color.*

Color Proof: Combined impressions from separate color plates.

Color Separation: In full-color advertisements, either a black-and-white negative of one primary color in the full-color original or the process of breaking down full-color copy into its primary-color components.

Column Inch: Space one-column wide and one-inch deep (regardless of the width of the column). A measuring unit in newspaper advertising. Also see *Line; Linage.*

Combination Close-up and Long Shot (CU-LS): Usually a shot of two persons, one seen close to camera while other is seen in distant background.

Combination Plate: A *halftone* and *line cut* in one engraving.

Come Out: See *Dolly Out.*

Comic Strip: A series of cartoon or caricature drawings.

Commercial: Advertising message on radio or television. Also known as a *spot* or *announcement.* Often abused by announcer in a program who introduces the message as "a *word* from the sponsor."

Commercial Program: A sponsored program from which broadcasting stations derive revenue on the basis of the time consumed in broadcasting it.

Communications: The process of sending and receiving messages. In marketing, these messages must go in both directions as a mutual process.

Comp: See *Comprehensive.*

Comparison: Illustrating a product and another object that is similar in an essential aspect (e.g., a waxed floor and the surface of a mirror).

Completion: See *Editing.*

Composite Print (TV): A 35mm or 16mm film print of a TV commercial, complete with both sound and picture.

Composition: Assembling and arranging copy in type for printing. Also called *typography* or *typesetting.*

Comprehensive: After the *rough layout,* a layout more accurate in size, color scheme and other necessary details, to show, as closely as possible, how the final ad will look. For presentation only; never for reproduction. Also called a *comp.*

Computerized Composition: The use of a stand-alone or built-in computer in phototypesetting (or, rarely, line-casting) equipment for the purpose of justifying and hyphenating, storing (as for telephone directories, price and parts lists, etc.) and typographically manipulating copy after it has been keyboarded, but before it is set into type.

Concept: The "big idea" behind a campaign or an advertising strategy, often incorporated in a headline or slogan. The basic message that needs verbal and visual interpretation in an advertisement.

Concrete: Concerned with actual instances or realities rather than abstractions—e.g., "good" is abstract, "saint" is concrete.

Consumer: Ultimate user of a product.

Consumer Behavior: The study of how and why people make their purchase decisions.

Consumer Research: Study of the kinds of people who may use or purchase a product or service to be marketed and advertised.

Consumer Segments: Groups of people who have similar demographic characteristics.

Continuity: (1) Script for radio, television, or film production; or the script for the spoken words which gives a continuous flow to a station's programming. (2) Length of time a given media schedule will run. (3) Regularity with which messages appear in media. (4) In advertising campaigns, repetition of same theme or format.

Continuity Department: In television, determines whether or not a commercial is up to the broadcast standards of the station.

Continuous Tone: A photographic image that has not been screened, and contains gradient tones from black to white.

Contrast: (1) A factor that provides emphasis and attention to layout elements by comparing different intensities, proportions, and perspective. (2) Illustrating a product and an objective that differs in an essential way (e.g., a "before-and-after" visual).

Copy: Broadly, all elements, both verbal and visual, which will be included in the finished advertisement. In a narrow sense, the verbal elements only, or the material to be set by a typesetter or photocompositor.

Copy Approach: The method of presenting appeals in the text of an advertisement. Chief forms: factual approach, emotional approach.

Copy Block: The main body of words, or the textual matter, of an advertisement.

Copy Casting: See *Copy Fitting.*

Copy Chief: Head of a copy group in an agency or advertising department.

Copy Comping: A technique for representing headlines and body copy in a layout through the use of solid lines, double lines, or paste-ups of type clipped from tear sheets. Also see *Greeking.*

Copy Fitting: Counting the number of characters or words in a piece of copy in order to determine how much space it will require if set in a specified typeface and size. The same procedure is used to determine the amount of copy needed to fill a fixed amount of space. Also called *copy casting, "casting off," or character counting.*

Copy Outline: See *Copy Platform.*

Copy Plan: See *Copy Platform.*

Copy Platform: Statement of basic idea for a campaign or an advertisement with selling points in descending order of importance. Advertising policy in handling any elements, as instructions to agency or to copywriters. Also called *copy plan, copy policy,* or *copy outline.*

Copy Policy: See *Copy Platform.*

Copyright: Legal protection afforded an original artistic or intellectual effort. Application blanks for registry are procurable from the Copyright Office, Library of Congress, Washington, D.C. 20559. Copyright notice must appear on advertisements for this protection.

Copy Strategy: Entire plan for effective advertising with statement of objectives of an advertisement, usually applied to a campaign or series of advertisements.

Copywriter: A person who creates the words and concepts in advertisements, and often the idea to be visualized as well.

Corporate Advertising: See *Institutional Advertising.*

Cost Per Thousand: See *CPM.*

Cover: The front of a publication is known as the *first cover;* the inside of the front cover is the *second cover;* the inside of the back cover is the *third cover;* the outside of the back cover is the *fourth cover.* Extra rates are charged for cover positions.

Cover Shot (CS): Usually a wide-angle camera shot covering a relatively large area in which action is taking place.

Cover Stock: A paper made of heavy, strong fiber, used for folders and booklet covers. Some cover stocks run into the low weights of paper known as *book paper,* but most cover stocks are heavier. Basic size, 20 x 26 inches.

CPM (Cost Per Thousand): Used in comparing media cost. Can mean cost per thousand readers or viewers or prospects. Must be specified.

Crash Finish: A surface design on paper, simulating the appearance of rough cloth.

Creative Connection: The creative mixing and blending of verbal and visual "language" to produce effective communication for advertising messages.

Creative Strategy: The words and images used to convey an advertiser's message or appeal to a target market. In general there are three basic strategies: to emphasize product features and consumer benefits; to emphasize the product's or company's image; and to attempt to position the product in the minds of the target market.

Cropping: Trimming part of an illustration for various purposes: to enable the illustration to fit into a certain space, to call attention to detail, to serve as a "shocker" technique, e.g., cutting off the top of a person's head.

CS: See *Cover Shot.*

CU: See *Close-up Shot.*

Cume: See *Audience Cume.*

Customer Profile: Statement of demographic characteristics of people considered to be prospects for a given product(s) or of people who shop in a given area.

Cut: (1) A trade term for a printed illustration, or for the photoengravings used to reproduce it. Also see *Photoengraving; Plate.* (2) To delete portions of copy or program material to fit space or time period. (3) In broadcasting, an abrupt stop in a program or an instant switch from one television picture to another without fading.

Cut-in Head: See *Head.*

Cut-line: See *Legend.*

D

Dailies: All film shot, developed and printed, from which scenes are selected for editing into the completed TV commercial. The term may also apply to videotape shooting. Also known as *rushes.*

Deadline: The date when an advertisement, campaign, or program must be ready for implementation. The time limit for the creation and production of advertising and promotion components.

Dead Matter: See *Matter.*

Dealer Imprint: Name and address of the dealer, printed or pasted on an advertisement of a national advertiser. In the planning of direct mail, space is frequently left for the dealer imprint.

Decalcomania: A transparent, gelatinous film bearing an advertisement, which may be gummed onto the dealer's window. Also known as *transparency.*

Defocus: An optical effect in which camera's focus control is adjusted so that picture is deliberately out of focus, usually used to end a scene.

Demographics: Vital statistics of a population segment. Based on objective information: sex, age, education, religion, race,

family size, location, type of home, income, etc. Also see *Psychographics.*

Descenders: See *Ascenders.*

Die-cut: An odd-shaped paper or cardboard for a direct-mail piece or for display purposes, cut with a special knife-edge die.

Diorama: (1) In point-of-purchase advertising, these are elaborate displays of a scenic nature, almost always three-dimensional and illuminated. (2) In TV, a miniature set, usually in perspective, used to simulate an impression of a larger location.

Direct Advertising: Any printed advertising distributed directly to specific prospects by mail, by salespeople, or by dealers; not through paid media.

Direct-mail Advertising: That form of direct-response advertising sent through the mails.

Direct Marketing: The marketing of products and services when the producer or manufacturer does his/her own distribution to the consumer, and functions as his/her own retailer or dealer.

Director: The person who writes or rewrites, then casts and rehearses a TV or radio program and directs the actual air performance.

Direct Process: In two-, three-, and four-color process work, color separation and screen negative made simultaneously on the same photographic film.

Direct-response Advertising: Any form of advertising done in direct marketing. Uses all types of media: direct mail, TV, magazines, newspapers, radio. Term is used in mail-order advertising. Also see *Direct Marketing.*

Display: In visual merchandising, nonpersonal physical presentation of merchandise or ideas. Can be window, exterior, interior, or remote.

Display Advertising: Printed advertising that contains headlines, body copy, illustrations—some or all of these elements.

Display Type: Type used for headlines or other emphasized elements; also, any type larger than 14-point.

Dissolve (DS): In television or film production, a combination of fade-in and fade-out. A new scene gradually appears into focus while the preceding one vanishes. It is a transitional device used to indicate the lapse of time.

Dolly: The movable platform on which a camera is placed for TV productions when different angles or views will be needed.

Dolly Back: See *Dolly Out.*

Dolly In: Camera moving in for a closer look at subject. Other names for this video cue include: *move in, push in, go in.*

Dolly Out: Camera moves away from subject, creating a wider angle shot. Often used because the field of interest is broadened by the movement. Other names for this video cue include: *dolly back, pull out, pull back, come out.*

Double Spread: See *Spread.*

Double Truck: See *Spread.*

Down: Broadcast term meaning decrease the volume, make it quieter.

Down-and-under: A direction given to a musician or sound-effects person playing solo in a broadcast. It means: Quiet down from your present playing level to a volume less than that of the lines of dialogue that follow.

Drop-in: In broadcasting, a local commercial inserted in a nationally sponsored network program.

Drop-out Halftone: See *Halftone.*

Dry-brush Drawing: A sketch made with a brush and extra thick, dry ink, or paint.

DS: See *Dissolve.*

Dubbing: The combining of several sound tracks for recording on film.

Dubbing In: The addition of one TV film to another; e.g., adding the part containing the advertiser's commercial to the part that carries the straight entertainment.

Dubs: In television, duplicate tapes, made from a master print, sent to different stations for broadcast.

Dummy: (1) Blank sheets or paper cut and folded to the size of a proposed leaflet, folder, booklet, or book, to indicate weight, shape, size, and general appearance. On the pages of the dummy, the layouts can be drawn. Useful in designing direct-mail advertisements. A dummy may also be made from the *proof* furnished by the printer. (2) An empty package or carton used for display purposes.

Duograph: A two-color plate made from black-and-white art work. The second color is a flat color and carries no detail. Less expensive than a *duotone.*

Duotone: Two halftone plates, each printing in a different color and giving two-color reproductions from an original one-color plate.

Duplicate Plates: Photoengravings made from the same negative as an original plate or via DuPont Crona-press conversion.

E

ECU: See *Extreme Close-up.*

Editing: The second major stage of TV commercial production, following shooting, in which selected scenes are joined together with opticals, titles, and sound track into the finished commercial. Also known as *completion, finishing,* or *post-production.*

ELS: See *Extreme Long Shot.*

Em: The square of any type size; derived from the letter M, which is as wide as it is high. Unless specified otherwise, the *pica em* or 12-point em, is equal to 1/6 inch.

Embossing: Relief printing, using two dies to raise the printed surface above the rest of the sheet.

En: In printing, half of the width of an *em.*

Engraving: (1) A *photoengraving.* (2) A plate in which a design is etched for printing purposes.

Establishing Shot (ES): See *Long Shot (LS).*

ET: Electrical transcription. A recording of a radio program for later broadcast.

Extreme Close-up (ECU, XCU): A camera shot of a portion of the face or head. A "slice" of the face or head.

Extreme Long Shot (ELS, XLS): A very wide camera shot of a large area or setting.

F

Face: (1) The style or design of type *(typeface).* (2) The printing surface of a type character or engraving.

Fact Sheet: A rundown of information on a product. It is often provided to local radio announcers and disk jockeys as a guide in ad-libbing a commercial.

Factual Approach: Practical or rational presentation of appeals and selling points in advertising.

Fade: In television, *fading in* is the gradual appearance of the screen image, brightening to full visibility. In radio, to increase the volume of sound on a radio broadcast. *Fading out* is the opposite—a gradual disappearance.

Fade In Music: See *Sneak In Music.*

Fade Music and Pic: At the close of the program, the music (audio) and the picture (video) are faded out simultaneously.

Fade Out Music: See *Music Down and Out.*

Fading: Variation in intensity of a radio or TV signal received over a great distance.

Family of Type: *Typefaces* related in design, as Caslon Bold, Caslon Old Style, Caslon Bold Italics, Caslon Old Style Italics.

Finishing: See *Editing.*

Flat Color: Second or additional printing colors, using line or tints, but not process.

Flush: Type set to a uniform width so that the text block is even at both the left and right edges. *Flush left* means even on the left edge; *flush right,* even on the right edge.

Flyer: Circular or announcement; generally printed on one side.

Folder: Printed circular, folded and often used as a mailing piece.

Follow Shot: To follow by moving both dolly and camera with actor movement. It may be a shot in which the camera pulls back as the actor moves toward it, the distance between actor and camera remaining relatively constant in the movement. It may be the reverse of this, the actor walking ahead of the camera as it follows him from behind in whatever direction he is moving. Compare with *Pan (Panning).* Also see *Dolly; Truck Shot.*

Follow Style: Instruction to typesetter to set copy in accordance with a previous advertisement or proof.

Font: An assortment of type characters of one style and size, containing the essential 26 letters (both capitals and small letters) plus numerals, punctuation marks, etc. Also see *Wrong Font.*

Form: Groups of pages printed on a large single sheet; e.g., a book could be printed in 32s (32 pages to one sheet, or form).

Formal Balance: See *Balance, Formal.*

Format: (1) In print, the shape, style, size, and appearance of a publication. (2) In broadcast, the character of programming of a radio or television station: news, country music, rock, classical, talk, or ethnic programming.

Four-color Process: Procedure for reproducing color illustrations. This is done by a set of plates known as *process plates;* each prints one color; yellow, blue (cyan), red (magenta), black. The sequence varies, but together they produce full color printing. Also see *Process Plates.*

Free-form: A layout that arranges visual and verbal elements into irregular or superimposed relationships.

Free Lance: An independent artist, writer, TV or radio producer, or advertising person who takes individual assignments from different accounts but is not in their employ.

FS: See *Full-length Shot.*

Full-length Shot (FS): Generally a camera shot of a person from head to feet.

G

Galley Proofs: Sheets usually 15 to 20 inches long, on which the set type is reproduced for reading before it is made up into pages. Also see *Proof.*

Gaze Motion: The movement of a reader's eyes through an ad, directed by the layout of art and copy elements.

Ghost: An unwanted image appearing in a television picture; for example, as a result of signal reflection.

Glossy: Photograph with a shiny surface or finish, necessary for reproduction in print.

Go In: See *Dolly In.*

Grain: In machine-made paper, the direction of the fibers, making the paper stronger across the grain and easier to fold with the grain. In planning direct mail, it is important that the paper fold with the grain rather than against it.

Graphic Center: See *Optical Center.*

Graphics: Illustrations, art, diagrams, charts.

Gravure Printing: A process in which the printing image is etched (engraved) below the nonprinting area. It is the opposite of *letterpress,* printing from a raised surface. Instead of plates or forms, gravure printing usually employs a cylinder that is fully inked. The surface is then wiped clean, retaining ink only in the cups (sunken area). Tone variations are mainly achieved by etching cups to different depths. Method used for engraved announcements, documents, maps, and currency. Also see *Rotogravure.*

Greeking: A technique for copy comping which uses any portion of printed copy to represent copy that will appear in a finished ad. Also see *Copy Comping.*

Group Shot: A camera shot of more than three individuals.

Gutter: Normally, the vertical unprinted area between facing pages and beyond copy and illustration. Also see *Spread.*

H

Halftone: The reproduction of continuous tone artwork photographed through a glass (halftone) screen in the camera. Breaks up the reproduction of halftone art into dots (or screen), making possible the printing of shaded values, such as the light and dark tones of a photograph or wash illustration. Also see *Photoengraving.*

Hand Composition: Type set up by hand, as distinguished from type set up by machine. Compare with *Linotype Composition.*

Hand Lettering: Lettering drawn by hand, in contrast to that set in type.

Head: Display caption to summarize contents and get attention. *Center heads* are centered on type matter; *side heads,* at the beginning of a paragraph; *box heads,* enclosed by rules; *cut-in heads,* in an indentation of the text.

Headline: Major copy caption above text. The most important copy element in print advertising; usually, largest display type in ad.

Hi-fi Color: A method of printing full-color pages for newspapers by special printing plants, whereby the ad appears on one side, and the other side can be left blank for the newspaper's use. Designed with continuous design, like wallpaper, so that it may be cut at any point without destroying the ad.

Hit Theme, Music: Cue to audio engineer to bring in music at full peak or volume and hold until established. Also referred to as *roll theme, roll music.*

Hot Type: Metal printing type which when cooled is used for letterpress printing. Also see *Letterpress.*

House Brand: See *Private Brand.*

Hue: In color, the dimension that distinguishes one color from another, as red from yellow.

I

ID: A TV station break between programs or within a program, used for station identification. Usually 10 seconds, with 8 seconds for commercial.

Image: Real or imaginary impression by the public of a product brand, or the reputation of an organization.

Imaginary Line: In a TV interview situation, for example, the director may visualize an imaginary line joining two people conversing. The director must be cognizant of this line so that the mistake of positioning one of the cameras on the opposite side of the imaginary line will not be made. If one camera is positioned on the opposite side, then the cut to that camera will reverse the direction in which the subject is looking.

Imprint: The printing of additional copy on previously printed material. Also see *Dealer Imprint.*

In: Broadcast term meaning "begin" or "start."

Informal Balance: See *Balance, Informal.*

Insert (Freestanding): The loose inserts placed between the pages or sections of a newspaper. Usually used for distinctive color reproduction.

Insertion Order: Instructions from an advertiser authorizing a publisher to print an advertisement of specified size on a given date at an agreed rate; accompanied or followed by the copy for the advertisement.

Inserts (Magazine): A card or other printed piece inserted in a magazine opposite the advertiser's full-page advertisement. Insert is prepared by advertisers at extra cost. Inserts appear in many forms and shapes. Not sold separately.

Institutional Advertising: Advertising created primarily to build long-range goodwill or prestige for the advertiser rather than stimulating immediate product purchase. Sometimes referred to as *corporate advertising.*

Intaglio Printing: See *Gravure Printing.*

Italics: Versions of regular typefaces that have been slanted to the right.

J

Junior Unit: A unit of space that permits an advertiser to use the same plates for large and small-page magazines. Plates prepared for full-page space in the smaller magazine appear in the larger one with editorial material on two or more sides.

Justify Type: To arrange type so that letters are properly spaced and lines are of even length. Machine-set type is justified automatically. In printing, lines of copy are made equal in length by adding extra space between words or letters.

K

Key: Keying an advertisement by giving it a code number or letter so that when people respond, the source of the inquiry can be traced. The key may be a variation in the address, or a letter or number printed in the corner of a return coupon.

Keynote: The basic idea or main appeal of an advertisement or promotion.

Keynote Idea: The underlying theme for an advertising campaign.

Key Plate: In color-process printing, the plate with maximum detail to which other plates must be registered.

Kinescope: The recording on film of a live or videotape television commercial, electronically reproduced from the kinescope tube.

L

Layout: A working drawing that shows how an ad will look with the arrangement of creative elements in position. Headlines, copy blocks, illustrations, logotypes, and other items are indicated as a blueprint for the finished ad and a guide to those who work on copy, art, and production.

lc: See *Lower Case.*

Lead: In a news story or press release, the opening or introductory sentence(s). If no more than the lead were published, the essence of the story would be expressed. Contains the "5 W's": who, what, when, where, and why.

Leaded Matter: See *Matter.*

Leaders: A line of dots or dashes to guide the eye across the page, thus: ....

Lead-in: (1) In relation to audience flow, the program preceding an advertiser's program on the same station. (2) The first few words of a *copy block.*

Leading: (Pronounced led/ing). The insertion of metal strips (known as leads) between lines of type, causing greater space to appear between these lines. Leaded type requires more space than type that is set solid. The term is also used for additional line spacing in photocomposition, although no lead is used.

Legals: Copy that is required by law, such as trademarks or registrations. Also see *Mandatories.*

Legend: The title or description under an illustration. Sometimes called *cut-line* or *caption.*

Letterpress: Printing from a raised (or relief) surface. Ink comes in contact with raised elements and in direct contact with paper. Similar to a rubber stamp. Also see *Lithography; Gravure Printing.*

Letter Spacing: Spacing between type characters to extend them over a wider type measure.

Levels of Selling: Determined by who (which market level) is targeting the message to whom. Levels are: trade, national, retail.

lf: See *Lightface.*

Lifestyle: A distinctive pattern of activities, interests, and opinions of a market group which often cannot be deduced from demographic data.

Lightface (lf): A type design that has thin, light lines, in contrast to *boldface (bf).*

Linage: Any amount of advertising space measured in *agate lines.*

Line: A unit for measuring the depth of advertising space. Also see *Agate Line.*

Line Copy: Any copy suitable for reproduction by a line plate. Copy composed of lines or dots, distinguished from one composed of halftones. Also see *Line Cut.*

Line Cut: A photoengraving plate made without a screen; reproduces only solid lines or areas, without intermediate shades or tones. Also see *Line Copy.*

Line Drawing: Illustration made with pen, pencil, brush, or crayon for print advertising, composed of lines or crosshatch lines in imitation of shading or halftones. Variation in tone is indicated only by the width of the lines.

Linotype Composition: Mechanical typesetting, molding a line of type at a time. The Linotype machine is operated by a keyboard. Compare with *Hand Composition.* Widely replaced by *photocomposition.*

Lip-synchronization (lip-sync): In TV, recording voice as a performer speaks. Requires more rehearsal and equipment and costs more than narration.

Lithography: A printing process by which an image originally was formed on special stone by a greasy material, the design then being transferred to the printing paper. Nonprinting areas are treated to repel ink and to attract water. Today, the more frequently used process is *offset lithography,* in which a thin and flexible metal sheet replaces the stone. Ink and water are spread on the plate while the press runs. In this process, the

design is "offset" from the metal sheet to a rubber blanket, which then transfers the image to the printing paper.

Live: In television and radio, a program that originates at the moment it is produced, in contrast to a program previously taped, filmed, or recorded.

Live Matter: See *Matter.*

Local Advertising: See *Retail Advertising.*

Local Buy: A purchase of time for local broadcasting of radio or television commercials from a non-network station that initiates its own programming.

Local Spot: See *Spot Buy.*

Logo: See *Logotype.*

Logotype: Trademark, trade name, or signature of product or company embodied in a distinctive lettering or design. Example: The Prudential Life Insurance Company's "Rock of Gibraltar." Also referred to as *logo.*

Long Shot (LS): A camera shot of the full figure of the person or persons, in which much of the setting is seen behind and beside them. Also known as *establishing shot (ES).*

Loss Leader: A product offered at cost or below to attract store traffic.

Lower Case (lc): The small letters in the alphabet, such as those in which this is printed, as distinguished from UPPER CASE or CAPITAL LETTERS. Named from the lower case of the printer's type cabinet in which this type was formerly kept.

LS: See *Long Shot.*

Lucy: See *Camera Lucida.*

M

Machine Composition: Type set mechanically, or machine-set in contrast to hand-set.

Machine-finish Paper: See *Sized Paper.*

Mail-order Advertising: Method of selling in which entire transaction is handled by advertising and ordered by mail. No salesperson is involved. Can also be ordered by phone.

Makeready: In letterpress, adjusting the plates for the press to ensure uniform impression. The skill and care in this work serve to make a good printing job. Also see *Letterpress.*

Make-up: The general appearance of a page; the arrangement in which the editorial matter and advertising material are to appear.

Mandatories: Copy that is required by the client, such as company signature, logo, address. Also copy and/or information that is required by law to appear on such products as beer, liquor, cigarettes, saccharin, labels on foods and drugs. Also see *Legals.*

Market: A group of people who can be identified by some common characteristic, interest, or problem; use a certain product to advantage; afford to buy it; and be reached through some medium.

Marketing: Total research, development, design, production, planning, pricing, distribution, and promotional activities involved in moving goods and services from producer to seller to consumer. Total marketing requires integration of all these activities. The marketplace now is the orientation for what is produced by a manufacturer.

Marketing Strategy: The plan for marketing as adopted. Also see *Marketing.*

Market Profile: The demographic description of the people, households, or groups to be considered prospects for a product or group of products. Prospects may be segmented as to primary or secondary.

Market Segmentation: Dividing a total market of consumers into groups whose similarity makes them a market for products serving their special needs.

Market Share: A brand's percentage of total sales of a given product. The attempt to capture or regain even a one percent share of the market is a strong advertising goal.

Mass Medium: A medium that is not directed toward a specific audience, but widely accepted by all types of people as opposed to *class* or *selective medium*.

Mat: Mainly employed by newspapers to make press *stereotypes*. Use of mats is declining with the increasing use of offset lithography. Also called *matrix*.

Matched Color: A color that is not standard with a publication, but is matched to the advertiser's specifications.

Matrix: See *Mat*.

Mat Service: A commercial organization supplying advertisers, publications, and printers with ready-made mats and illustrations through a subscription service.

Matter: Composed type, often referred to as: *dead matter*—of no further use; *leaded matter*—having extra spacing between lines; *live matter*—to be used again; *solid matter*—lines set close to each other; *standing matter*—held for further use.

MCU: Medium close-up. Also see *Close-up Shot (CU)*.

Mechanical: All elements of an advertisement, proofs of type and illustrations, photos, etc., pasted in final arrangement (usually on artboard), ready for camera. Photography is then used to make printing plate. Also known as a *paste-up*.

Media: (1) The plural of *medium*, the vehicle that carries an advertisement, as newspapers, magazines, radio, television, direct mail, outdoor signs, and so on. (2) The methods or implements used by an artist to render layouts, sketches, and illustrations, as pencil, pen and ink, crayon, water colors, etc.

Media Mix: The plan of a promotion which segments for maximum effect, amount of space and/or time to be used in each medium. It apportions exposure to print (newspapers, magazines, mailings), radio, television.

Media Research: See *Media Study*.

Media Study: Analysis of audience and coverage of various media with objective of effective selection and economical buying for desired results. Also called *media research*.

Medium: See *Media*.

Medium Shot (MS): Generally a camera shot from the waist up, unless otherwise specified. Also called a *close shot*.

Metaphor: A figure of speech in which one thing is likened to another, in which a word or phrase ordinarily used for one thing is applied to another (e.g., "All the world's a stage.") Compare with *Simile*.

Mike Check: In broadcasting, director or technical director asks audio engineer to have all mikes (microphones) checked to make certain they are functioning properly before program hits the air. Usually an assistant on the studio floor does this with a "count down" technique.

Mike Level: In broadcasting, the mike (microphone) is opened and the talent speaks relative to the placement of the mike. The talent speaks lines exactly as he would were he on the air. Director often wishes to hear this level check.

Mini-cams: Hand-held video cameras with portable recorders.

Mixing: In broadcasting, mixing different audio effects, as music and voice, or leveling of volume from scene to scene.

MLS: Medium long shot. Also see *Long Shot (LS)*.

Mock-up: A facsimile of products or packages used in television.

Monotone: See *Black and White (B/W)*.

Montage: The superimposing of parts of many pictures into a single picture.

Mortise: An opening cut through a plate, block, or base to permit insertion of other matter, usually type.

Motivation: Similar to *motive*, but refers to the stimulus which initiates a motive.

Motivational Research: Psychological studies to probe basic conscious and unconscious reasons for buying habits. Respondents speak freely in this type of study. Questionnaires are not used. The method is unstructured.

Motive: Some inner drive, impulse, intention that causes a person to do something or to act in a certain way.

Move In: See *Dolly In*.

Moving Shot: In television, following the action with a camera.

MS: See *Medium Shot (MS)*.

Music Down and Out: Audio cue by which music is taken down and faded out completely, in audio taping, according to speed desired. Another name for this cue is *fade out music*.

Music In Full: In audio taping, music is brought up to normal peak set for the introduction of the program or at any other specified spot in the program.

Music Under: Audio taping cue by which volume of music is taken down under the dialogue or sound being used, usually for background purposes. Cue is sometimes worded: *take music under*.

Music Up: In audio taping, an increase in the volume of music. For transitional purposes, at the end of a scene, and usually at the end of the program. Another term for this audio cue is *bring music up*.

N

National Advertising: Advertising to the consumer by a primary producer or a secondary manufacturer as opposed to that of a local retailer. National advertising is not necessarily a matter of geography or national coverage.

National Brand: A brand distributed widely through many different outlets, in contrast to a *private brand*, or *private label*, owned by a distributor or retailer. Also see *Brand; Private Brand*.

National Plan: Advertising campaign tactics aimed at getting business nationwide, simultaneously.

Network: In broadcasting, a group of stations affiliated by contract and usually interconnected for simultaneous broadcast of the same programs.

Network Affiliate: One of the stations in a broadcasting network.

Network Buy: A purchase of time from a network of interconnecting stations for simultaneous broadcast of radio or television commercials.

Nielsen: Audience measurements for television programs taken and provided by the A. C. Nielsen Company. *NSI*—Nielsen Station Index for local television markets; *NTI*—Nielsen Television Index for network television.

NSI: Nielsen Station Index. Also see *Nielsen*.

NTI: Nielsen Television Index. Also see *Nielsen*.

O

Objective: The client's strategy or specific purpose for using advertising to send a message to an audience. Objectives are basically product or institutional for both immediate and long-range objectives.

Off Camera: A TV term for an actor whose voice is heard but who does not appear in the commercial. Less costly than being *on camera.*

Off Mike: In broadcasting, voice or sound away from microphone. Opposite of *on mike.*

Off-screen Announcer: An unseen speaker on a TV commercial.

Offset: (1) A lithographic printing process in which the image is first transferred to a rubber roller, or blanket, which in turn makes the impression on the paper. Also see *Lithography.* (2) The blotting of a wet or freshly printed sheet against an accompanying sheet. Can be prevented by slip-sheeting. Antique paper absorbs the ink and prevents offsetting.

Old English: A style of black-letter or text type, now little used except in logotypes of trade names or names of newspapers.

Omnibus: A layout that uses many visuals in a grid or graphically divided spaces.

On Camera: In television, action or sound within camera range and visible to the audience. Opposite of *off camera.* Affects the scale of compensation.

One Shot (1-shot): A camera shot of an individual. Also called *single shot.*

On Mike: Opposite of *off mike.*

Open End: A broadcast in which the commercial spots are added locally.

Open Mike: Cue to audio engineer to throw switch that controls the particular mike to be used.

Optical Center: A point, about three-fifths from the bottom of an advertisement, to which the eye seems naturally attracted and to which the designer tries to give a pivotal position. Also known as the *graphic center.*

Opticals: Visual effects that are put on television film in a laboratory, in contrast to those that are included as part of the original filming.

OS: See *Over-the-shoulder Shot.*

Out: Broadcast term meaning "end it"; take it out.

Outdoor Advertising: Signs and posters placed out of doors, on sides of building, on billboards, on roofs, along railroads.

Outline Halftone: A halftone with the background removed. Also called a *silhouette halftone.* Also see *Halftone.*

Overlay: See *Snipe.*

Over-the-shoulder Shot (OS): A camera shot of two persons taken over the shoulder of one of them. For example, in an interview situation involving two persons, we see one person over the shoulder of the other. Quite frequently, this type of shot comes in pairs, in which case the over-the-shoulder shots are matched. For example, we see Mary over the shoulder of Jane, and when the cut is made to the other camera, we see Jane over the shoulder of Mary.

P

Package: (1) The wrapper on a product or container. (2) In radio or television, a combination assortment of time units, sold as a single offering at a set price. (3) A special radio or television program or series of programs, bought by an advertiser (for a lump sum). Includes all components, ready to broadcast, with the addition of the advertiser's commercial.

Package Insert: Advertising material packed with a product, usually to advertise a different product or to provide instructions for use.

Page Proof: A proof of type and illustrations in page form as they will appear, usually pulled after *galley proofs* have been corrected. Also see *Proof.*

Pan (Panning): In television, to move the camera up and down or from left to right while keeping base, or dolly, stationary. Compare with *Follow Shot.*

Paste-up: See *Mechanical.*

Perspective: In layout, the relationship between objects and settings which involve distance from the eye. The visual illusion of distance created by making objects smaller as they "move away."

Photocomposition: A method of typesetting display letters and text by a photographic process onto film or paper for reproduction. Uses *cold type* (no metal). Also known as *phototypesetting.*

Photoengraving: (1) An etched, relief printing plate made by a photomechanical process, as a *halftone* or *line cut.* (2) The process of producing the photoengraved plate. This printing process is no longer widely used.

Photolettering: See *Photocomposition.*

Photo Offset: See *Offset.*

Photoplatemaking: Making plates (and the films preceding the plates) for any printing process by camera, in color or black-and-white.

Photoprint: The negative or positive copy of a photograph subject.

Photoscript: A series of photographs made at the time of shooting a TV commercial picture based on the original script or storyboard. Used for keeping record of commercial, also for sales promotion purposes.

Photostat: A very useful aid in making layouts or proposed advertisements. A rough photographic reproduction of a subject, inexpensive and quickly made.

Phototypesetting: See *Photocomposition.*

Phototypography: The entire field of composing, makeup, and processing phototypographically assembled letters, photodisplay, and phototext. Also see *Photocomposition.*

Pica: Also known as *pica em.* The unit for measuring width in printing. There are 6 picas to the inch. Derived from *pica,* the old name of 12-pt. type (1/6-inch high). A page of type 24 picas wide is 4 inches wide (24 ÷ 6 = 4).

Plate: A term loosely applied to any material used to make a printed impression, by letterpress, gravure, or lithography. Also called a *cut.* Also see *Photoengraving; Halftone.*

Plated Stock: Paper with a high gloss and a hard, smooth surface, secured by being pressed between polished metal sheets.

Playback: (1) The playing of a recording for audition purposes. (2) A viewer's or reader's report on what message he or she derived from a commercial or advertisement.

Point: (1) The unit of measurement of type, about 1/72 inch in depth. Abbreviated *pt.* Type is specified by its point size, as 8 pt., 12 pt., 24 pt., 48 pt. (2) The unit for measuring thickness of paper, one thousandth of an inch.

Point-of-Purchase Advertising (POP): Displays prepared for retailers by manufacturers to be used in stores where merchandise is sold. Often designed for customer self-service display units.

Position: (1) Advertiser's place in a publication or on the page. (2) A company's standing in the market.

Poster: Product sign for display outdoors or in a store window. Must be easily and quickly read at a distance.

Post-production: See *Editing.*

Preferred Position: Advertising space usually contracted for an extended period and at an increased cost. Sometimes granted to larger schedules as an inducement. Sometimes available on a rotation basis among advertisers. Top of page, next to reading matter, back page (of a newspaper), inside cover (of a magazine), or a special interest page, such as fashion, are examples. Also see *Position.*

Preprint: A reproduction of an advertisement prior to publication.

Press Proof: A proof made on the regular printing press before or during the actual *press run.*

Press Run: The printing of a specific job. Also, the number of copies printed.

Presstype: An art supply consisting of total alphabets on film sheets which can be used to transfer onto layouts for copy comping.

Primary Colors: In printing, red, yellow, and blue.

Private Brand: The trademark of a distributor of products sold by that distributor only, in contrast to manufacturers' brands, sold through many outlets. Also known as *private label, house brand,* or *store brand.*

Private Label: See *Private Brand.*

Process Plates: Printing plates for reproduction in full color. Can print the full range of the spectrum by using three plates, each bearing a primary color—red, yellow, blue—plus a black plate. Also referred to as *four-color plates.* Also see *Process Printing.*

Process Printing: Full-color printing that uses process plates. Also see *Four-color Process* and *Process Plates.*

Producer: One who originates and/or presents a TV or radio program.

Product Advertising: Designed to sell products with immediate results. Includes identification and description of merchandise and price, as opposed to *institutional advertising.*

Production: (1) In print advertising, the mechanical processes in preparation of an advertisement: layout, paste-up, typography, plates. (2) In broadcasting, the building, organization, and presentation of a TV or radio commercial, or program.

Production Department: The department responsible for mechanical production of an advertisement and dealing with printers and engravers or for the preparation of a TV or radio program.

Production Director: (1) Person in charge of a TV or radio program. (2) Head of department handling print production.

Professional Advertising: Directed at those in professions, such as medicine, law, or architecture, who are in a position to recommend use of a particular product or service to their clients.

Profile: See *Audience Profile.*

Progressive Proofs: A set of photoengraving proofs in color, in which the yellow plate is printed on one sheet and the red on another; the yellow and red are then combined; next, the blue is printed and a yellow-red-blue combination made. Then, the black alone is printed, and finally all colors are combined. The sequence varies. In this way, the printer matches up inks when printing color plates. Often called *progs.*

Progs: See *Progressive Proofs.*

Promotion: (1) Any nonpersonal activity used to influence the sale or acceptance of merchandise, services, or ideas. (2) More generally, the total of all personal and nonpersonal selling activities: advertising, display, publicity, special events. Also see *Sales Promotion.*

Promotion Mix: Assortment of activities designed to effect sales. The development of details and where emphasis is planned. Integrated activities.

Proof: Copy of an advertisement or typography before it is printed. Many proofs are made so that every person and department involved in the advertisement has the opportunity to check for accuracy before the ad is actually run. Corrections are made before the ad appears in print in a publication.

Proof File: Permanent record of all print advertising messages produced by a company.

Proportion: In layout, dealing with unusual sizes of elements to create visually exciting relationships.

Psychographics: A description of a market based on factors such as attitudes, opinions, interests, perceptions, and lifestyles of consumers comprising that market. Used in analysis and evaluation for market planning. Also see *Demographics.*

Pull Back: See *Dolly Out.*

Pull Out: See *Dolly Out.*

Pull Strategy: Marketing strategy in which the producer stimulates demand for a product by direct advertising to consumers, rather than to dealers, in order to attract or "pull" customers into retail outlets. Compare with *Push Strategy.*

Push In: See *Dolly In.*

Push Strategy: Marketing strategy in which the producer stimulates sales through retailers who, because of the potential for extra profits or because of some other beneficial arrangement with the manufacturer, will feature or "push" a product. Compare with *Pull Strategy.*

R

Ratiocination: A type of reasoning using formal logic.

Ready Audio: Standby cue to audio engineer.

Register: Perfect correspondence in printing; of facing pages when top lines are even; of color printing, when there is correct superimposition of each plate, so that the colors mix properly.

Registering a Trademark: In the U.S., the act of recording a trademark with the Commissioner of Patents, to substantiate claim of first use and to prevent imitation. Also see *Trademark.*

Register Marks: In engraving, cross lines placed on a copy to appear in the margin of all negatives as a guide to perfect register.

Remote Pickup: A broadcast originating outside the studio, as from a football field.

Reprint: A copy of an advertisement printed after its appearance in a publication.

Repro Proofs: Exceptionally clean and sharp proofs from type for use as copy for reproduction. Also called *reproduction proofs.*

Residual: A sum paid to certain talent on a TV or radio commercial every time the commercial is run after 13 weeks, for life of commercial.

Resizing: The production of an advertisement in various sizes for different units of space.

Retail Advertising: Advertising placed and paid for by the retailer or dealer, addressed to ultimate consumers, in contrast to national advertising from the producer or manufacturer to the consumer. Also called *local advertising.*

Retouching: The process of correcting or improving art work, especially photographs.

Reverse: White type against a dark background.

Reversed Plate: A line plate in which white comes out black, and vice versa.

Roll-fed Printing: See *Web Printing*.

Roll Theme, Music: See *Hit Theme, Music*.

Roman Type: (1) Originally, type of the Italian and Roman school of design, as distinguished from the black-face Old English style. Distinguished by variation in the weight of strokes and inclusion of *serifs*. Old style and modern are the two branches of the roman family. (2) Typefaces that are not italics are called *roman*. Also see *Italics*.

Rotogravure: High-speed gravure printing on rotary presses. Used for printing newspaper magazine supplements. Also see *Gravure Printing*.

Rough: In the production of layouts, a sketch to show the basic idea or arrangement of an advertisement. The first step in layout and advertising design. The *first roughs* are also called *thumbnails*.

Rough Cut: In a television commercial, the first assembly of the best takes of each scene to which the sound track is synchronized and special effects, title, and dissolves are added. Also called *work print*.

Rushes: See *Dailies*.

S

Sales Promotion: (1) Those promotion activities that supplement both personal selling and advertising, coordinate the two, and help to make them effective; for example, displays, publicity, special events. (2) More loosely, the combination of personal selling, advertising, and all supplementary nonpersonal selling activities. Also see *Promotion*.

Sans-serif: A typeface without little hair-line bars that finish the strokes. Compare with *Serif*.

sc: See *Small Caps*.

SC: Single column.

Scaling Down: Reducing illustrations to the size desired.

Scatter: A layout that incorporates many different movements into a seemingly undisciplined design. Actually is organized to provide interesting gaze motion for the message.

Schedule: Advertiser's plan for placement and timing of messages in a given period: week, month, or season.

Score: To crease cards or thick sheets of paper so that they can be folded.

Scotchprint: A reproduction proof pulled on plastic material from a letterpress plate or form. Normally used in conversion of color plate from letterpress to offset. Also see *Proof*.

Scratchboard: A clay-coated cardboard covered with black India ink on which a drawing is scratched with a stylus or knife to produce a drawing of extremely fine lines and details in white on a black background.

Screen: A fine cross-ruled sheet used in a photomechanical platemaking process to produce tone in advertisements, such as shades of gray present in a continuous tone photograph or halftone illustration. The size and number of dots on a screen deliver different gradations of shading. More dots or fewer to the square inch give different values of gray shadings. Also see *Halftone*.

Screen Printing: A printing process in which a stenciled design is applied to a textile (usually silk), or wire mesh screen. A squeegee forces paint or ink through the mesh of the screen to the paper directly beneath. Also called *silk screen printing*.

Script: (1) Copywriter's written form (or copy) for a broadcast commercial. Contains not only words, but also technical instructions for video or musical parts. (2) A face of type that resembles handwriting.

Segue: Broadcast term (pronounced seg-way) for a transition, usually musical; like a medley, music glides from one song to another, indicating change in time, place, or mood.

Self-mailer: A direct-mail piece that can be mailed without a wrapper or envelope. The address is printed directly on the mailer.

Serif: Short hair-like bars at the ends of the main stroke of each letter in certain roman typefaces.

Service Mark: A symbol or name used in the sale and advertising of services or products that are not individually packaged.

Set Solid: Lines of type set without *leading*.

SFX: See *Sound Effects*.

Shoulder of Type: The portions of a unit of type which extend above and below the type character, and which do not print.

Side Head: See *Head*.

Signature: (1) The name of an advertiser. Also see *Logotype*. (2) The musical number or sound effect that regularly identifies a TV or radio program.

Silhouette Halftone: See *Outline Halftone*.

Silhouetting: Eliminating the background of a photograph, e.g., showing the outline of a figure in a bathing suit against white space rather than against sea and sand.

Silk Screen Printing: See *Screen Printing*.

Simile: A figure of speech like a metaphor which uses the typical description of one object to describe a dissimilar object. Unlike a metaphor, the simile uses the word "like" or "as" to liken one thing to another (e.g., "Taste as fresh as the whole outdoors."). Compare with *Metaphor*.

Single Shot: See *One Shot (1-Shot)*.

Sized and Supercalendered Paper (s. and s.c.): Machine-finish book paper that has been given extra ironings to ensure a smooth surface. Takes halftones very well.

Sized Paper: Paper that has received a chemical bath to make it less porous. Paper sized once and ironed (calendered) is known as *machine-finish*. If it is again ironed, it becomes *sized and supercalendered (s. and s.c.)*.

Skin Pack: A packaging method whereby a plastic film is pulled tightly around a product on a card. Used for "card merchandising."

Slogan: A carefully polished group of words intended to be repeated by consumers verbatim and to be remembered by them with a favorable reaction.

Small Caps: Letters shaped like upper case (capitals), but about two-thirds their size—nearly the size of lowercase letters. Abbreviated *sc* or *sm. caps*. THIS SENTENCE IS SET WITH A REGULAR CAPITAL LETTER AT THE BEGINNING, THE REST IN SMALL CAPS.

Sneak In Music: An audio cue in which music is rolled with volume, either all the way down or very low. Then the volume is gradually increased until desired peak is reached. Generally used to bring music into background as a scene is progressing. Also called *fade in music*.

Sneak Out Music: An audio cue in which music is being used in background and director wants it to fade out completely. She may want it faded out slowly or rapidly according to effect that is desired to be conveyed.

Snipe: A copy strip added over a poster, advertisement; e.g., a dealer's name, special sale price, or another message. Also referred to as an *overlay*.

Solid Matter: See *Matter.*

Sound Effects (SFX): Various devices or recordings other than words or music, used in TV or radio to produce lifelike imitations of sound, such as footsteps, rain, ocean waves.

Spec: In typesetting, to specify or determine from samples shown in a type specimen sheet or book the typefaces and sizes to be used so that copy will fit in the space available.

Special Events: Specific devices, features, services, sales inducements, exhibits, demonstrations, attractions that influence the sale of merchandise or ideas. Often held for storewide attention.

Spot, Spot Buy: (1) In radio and TV, the purchase of time from an independent, non-network station. When purchased by a national advertiser, it is referred to as a *spot;* when purchased by a local advertiser (such as a retailer), it is a *local spot.* Also see *Local Buy.* (2) The term *spot* is also used to denote a short (ten second) commercial.

Spot Color: Usually a limited area of color without any screening; used for emphasis in print advertising, to attract attention.

Spread: Double-page advertisement on two facing pages. Also called *double spread* or *double-page spread.* When this occurs in the center pages of a publication, the print may extend into the *gutter.* This is called a *center spread* or *double truck.* This involves a higher cost for both plates and space. (2) Type matter set full measure across a page, not in columns. (3) In broadcasting, extending any part to fill the full allotted time of a program.

Stand By: Cue that a program is about to go on the air.

Stand By Music, Theme: Cue to audio engineer to stand by with turntable going and ready to slip cue record of theme or music being used in program.

Standing Matter: See *Matter.*

Statement Stuffer: An advertising leaflet that is mailed to charge-account customers along with their monthly statement.

Station Posters: Posters displayed in and on stations of subways, bus lines, and commuter railroads.

Stereotype: A duplicate plate for printing made by pouring molten metal into a *mat* or *matrix.*

Stock: Trade term that refers to the paper used in printing.

Stock Art: Inexpensive, ready-to-use art obtained from a company that maintains files of photographs or drawings illustrating a variety of subjects.

Stop Motion: A photographic technique for animating inanimate objects.

Store Brand: See *Private Brand.*

Storyboard: Series of drawings used to present the sequence of scenes for a proposed television commercial. Consists of illustrations of key action (video); scene-by-scene is accompanied by the audio part to go with it. Used for getting advertiser approval, also as a guide in production.

Storyboarding: The preparation of storyboards used for the development of television commercials or films generally. Presented to the client for approval after its use as a guide to production.

Straight-Radio Copy: Typewritten words only, to be read by whichever station announcer is on duty.

Subhead: Small type headline that follows larger type headline. Usually contains further information to reader.

Super: In television, the imposition of the *super* image from one camera over the image from another; emphasizes key points: the package, the keynote, the logo, the slogan. Also known as *superimposition.*

Superimpose: In print advertising, to lay out one element in a layout on top of another.

Superimposition: See *Super.*

Surprint: (1) Printing over the face of an advertisement already printed. (2) A photoengraving in which a line-plate effect appears over the face of a halftone, or vice versa.

Symbol: Something that represents something else by association, resemblance, or convention. Also see *Associative Symbolism; Analogous Symbolism.*

Synergism: An extra degree of energy produced as a result of uniting elements. The *creative connection* blends verbal and visual elements to produce a message that has more communicative power than the absolute sum of its parts (e.g., $5 + 5 = 11$).

T

Tag: In television, a local retailer's message at the end of a manufacturer's commercial. Usually 10 seconds of a 60-second commercial.

Take: In television or movies, the filming of an individual scene.

Take Music Under: See *Music Under.*

Talent: In broadcasting, actors, musicians, announcers, or other performers.

Tape: (1) In broadcasting, either audiotape or videotape used to record programs or commercials. (2) The process, "to tape."

Target Audience: Special group within an audience to which advertising is specifically aimed. Example would be an advertisement in a college publication addressed to skiers among the student readers.

Target Market: The defined segment of a whole market to which an advertiser directs merchandising, merchandise, and promotion. Can be identified by *demographics.*

TCU: See *Tight Close-up.*

Tear Sheet: Copy of a print advertisement after publication, torn from the actual publication. Positive proof of publication.

Telecast: A sound and pictorial image sent by television.

Theme: Main sales idea of an advertisement or of a campaign.

Three Shot (3-Shot): A camera shot of three individuals.

Thumbnail: The *first* rough layout, usually very small, which includes approximations of all the elements that must be incorporated into the design of an advertisement. Also see *Rough.*

Tight: A term describing illustrations, for items like furniture and machinery, which are drawn with great precision and detail.

Tight Close-up (TCU): A camera shot of only the head and face. Also called *big close-up (BCU).*

Tilt: A vertical movement of camera without any dolly movement. Either up or down. Some directors say *pan up* or *pan down* instead of using the word *tilt.* Also see *Dolly.*

Tint: A reproduction of a solid color.

Tissues: Full-size sketches of the best design for an advertisement drawn on textured white tracing paper.

Trade Advertising: Advertising aimed at retailers and wholesalers who buy products or services for resale, as opposed to the ultimate consumer.

Trade Character: An animate being or animated object designed to identify and personify a product or an advertiser.

Trademark: A pictorial device, number, letter, or other symbol used to identify a product or product family, usually registered and protected by law.

Trade Name: A commercial name adopted by a company (much as an actor or musician adopts a stage name that is more easily remembered by the public). Not to be confused with *trademark*.

Transit Advertising: Advertising on transit vehicles, such as buses, subways, taxis. Often also considered advertising in transit stations, depots, and terminals.

Transparency: See *Decalcomania*.

Travel Shot: See *Truck Shot*.

Truck Shot: Usually a lateral movement of the dolly and camera. A shot that is not toward or away from the moving subject. Camera movement that parallels the scene. Also see *Dolly*.

Two Shot (2-Shot): A camera shot of two individuals.

Typeface: The design and style of letters in type of a "family," such as Bodoni, Caslon. Usually named for the original designer.

Type Family: A group of type designs that are variations of one basic alphabet style. Usually comprising roman, italic or boldface, they can also vary in width (condensed or extended) and in weight (light to extra bold). Some families have dozens of versions.

Type Font: See *Font*.

Type Page: The area of a page that type can occupy; the total area of a page less the margins.

Typesetting: See *Composition*.

Typography: The setting of type for quantity printing. Also see *Composition*.

U

uc: See *Upper Case*.

Under: Broadcast term meaning hold sound or music in background.

Up: Broadcast term meaning increase the volume; make it louder.

Upper Case (uc): Capital letters.

V

Video: Loosely used as a synonym for television; more accurately, the visual portion of a television broadcast. Compare with *Audio*.

Videotape: In television, an electronic method of recording images and sound on tape. Most TV shows that appear live are done on videotape. Both sound and visual elements can be recorded and played back as often as desired, once recorded.

Videotape Recorder (VTR): A system that permits instantaneous playback of a simultaneous recording of sound and picture on a continuous strip of tape. Also see *Videotape*.

Vignette: A halftone in which the edges (or parts of them) are shaded off gradually to very light gray.

Visualization: The process of interpreting an idea in visual form. The purpose is to transmit the idea. It can be product alone; product in a setting; product in use. Also refers to the process of producing thumbnails and rough storyboards.

Visual Thinking: See *Vizthink*.

Vizthink (Visual Thinking): A coined word inspired by Paul Pinson's "Drawthinks" in *Advertising Age* (circa 1956). A thumbnail or rough that a copywriter "doodles" to reinforce verbal messages with visual graphics.

VO: See *Voice-over*.

Voice-over (VO): The voice of a TV commercial announcer or actor or singer recorded off-camera. Costs less than if delivered on-camera.

VTR: See *Videotape Recorder*.

W

Wash Drawing: A brushwork illustration, usually made with diluted India ink or watercolor. In addition to black and white, it has varying shades of gray, like a photograph. Halftones, not line plates, are made from wash drawings for reproduction.

Web Printing: In contrast to sheet-fed printing, paper is fed into the press from rolls. This method is used in rotogravure, newspapers, magazine presses, and increasingly in offset. Do not confuse with wet printing, though both may take place simultaneously. Also called *roll-fed printing*.

Weight of Type: The relative blackness of a particular typeface.

Wet Printing: Color printing on specially designed high-speed presses with one color following another in immediate succession before the ink from any plate or cylinder has time to dry.

wf: See *Wrong Font*.

White Space: Areas in an advertisement where no printing or illustration appear. Uninked areas.

Widow: In typography, applied to the last line of a paragraph when it has only one or two words.

Window Envelope: A mailing envelope with a transparent panel, permitting the address on the enclosure to serve as a mailing address as well.

Wipe: In television, a rapid transition shot replacing or pushing away one image on the screen and replacing it with another.

Work Print: See *Rough Cut*.

Wrong Font (wf): Letter from one series mixed with those from another series, or *font*. The **a** in this sentence is in the wrong font.

X

XCU: See *Extreme Close-up*.

x-height: The body of a letter that has no ascender or descender stroke. So named because it refers to the height of a lower-case *x*. Also see *Ascenders*.

XLS: See *Extreme Long Shot*.

X-ray Diagram: An illustration that portrays the cross-section or inside of a product.

Z

Zoom: In television, a rapid change of focus which makes the image grow larger (*zoom in*) or smaller (*zoom out*). Done with a special lens or rapid dollying. Also see *Dolly*.

Zoom In: A video cue whereby a zoom lens is changed from a wide-angle camera shot to a narrow-angle (telephoto) shot.

Zoom Out: A video cue whereby a zoom lens is changed from a narrow-angle (telephoto) camera shot to a wide-angle shot.

BIBLIOGRAPHY

Aaker, David A. and Myers, John G. *Advertising Management: Practical Perspectives.* Englewood Cliffs, N.J.: Prentice-Hall, 1975.

American Marketing Association. *Marketing Definitions: A Glossary of Marketing Terms.* Chicago: American Marketing Association. 1963.

Arnheim, Rudolf. *Visual Thinking.* Berkeley, Calif.: University of California Press, 1969.

Barban, A.M. and Sandage, C.H.: *Readings in Advertising and Promotion Strategy.* Homewood, Ill.: Richard D. Irwin, Inc., 1968.

Bay, Stuart and Thom, William. *Visual Persuasion.* New York: Harcourt Brace Jovanovich Inc., 1974.

Berryman, Gregg. *Notes on Graphic Design and Visual Communication.* Los Altos, Calif.: William Kaufman, Inc., 1979.

Book, Albert C. and Cary, Norman D. *The Television Commercial: Creativity and Craftsmanship.* Chicago: Crain Publications, Inc., 1970.

Burton, Phillip Ward. *Advertising Copywriting.* 4th ed. Columbus, Ohio: Grid Publishing, 1978.

Burton, Phillip Ward and Miller, Robert J. *Advertising Fundamentals.* Columbus, Ohio: Grid Publishing, 1976.

Caples, John. *Tested Advertising Methods.* Englewood Cliffs, N.J.: Prentice-Hall, 1974.

Dunn, S. Watson and Barban, Arnold M. *Advertising: Its Role in Modern Marketing.* Hinsdale, Ill.: Dryden Press., 1974.

Edwards, Betty. *Drawing on the Right Side of the Brain.* Los Angeles: J.P. Tarcher, Inc., 1979.

Ernst, Sandra. *The Creative Package.* Columbus, Ohio: Grid Publishing, 1979.

Hilliard, Robert L. *Writing for Television and Radio.* 3rd ed. New York: Hastings House, Publishers, 1976.

Jackson, Jim. *Seeing Yourself See.* New York: E.P. Dutton & Co., Inc., 1975.

Kleppner, Otto. *Advertising Procedure.* 7th ed. Englewood Cliffs, N.J.: Prentice-Hall, 1979.

Kotler, Philip. *Marketing Management Analysis, Planning , and Controls.* Englewood Cliffs, N.J.: Prentice-Hall, 1976.

Malickson, David L. and Nason, John W. *Advertising—How to Write the Kind that Works.* New York: Charles Scribner's Sons, 1977.

Mandell, Maurice I. *Advertising.* Englewood Cliffs, N.J.: Prentice-Hall, 1980.

Milton, Shirley F. *Advertising for Modern Retailers.* New York: Fairchild Publications, 1974.

Norins, Hanley. *The Complete Copywriter.* New York: McGraw-Hill, 1966.

Osborn, Alex. *Applied Imagination.* New York: Charles Scribner's Sons, 1963.

Politz, Alfred. "The Dilemma of Creative Advertising." *Strategic Advertising Decisions.* Ronald D. Michman and Donald W. Jugenheimer, eds. Columbus, Ohio: Grid Publishing, 1976.

Sandage, C. H. and Fryburger, Vernon. *Advertising Theory and Practice.* 9th ed. Homewood, Ill.: Richard D. Irwin, 1975.

Sissors, Jack Z. and Petray, E. Reynold. *Advertising Media and Planning.* Chicago: Crain Books, 1976.

Stanley, Richard E. *Promotion.* Englewood Cliffs, N.J.: Prentice-Hall, 1977.

Strunk, William, Jr. and White, E. B., *The Elements of Style.* 2nd ed. New York: Macmillan Co., 1972.

White, Gordon E. "Creativity: The X Factor in Advertising Theory." *Strategic Advertising Decisions.* Ronald D. Michman and Donald W. Jugenheimer, eds. Columbus, Ohio: Grid Publishing, 1976.

Winters, Arthur A. and Goodman, Stanley. *Fashion Advertising and Promotion.* New York: Fairchild Publications, 1978.

Winters, Arthur A.; Axelrod, Nathan; and Packard, Sidney. *Fashion Buying and Merchandising.* New York: Fairchild Publications, 1977.

Wright, John S.; Warner, Daniel S.; Winter, Willis L., Jr.; and Zeigler, Sherilyn K. *Advertising.* New York: McGraw-Hill, 1974.

Young, James Webb. *A Technique for Producing Ideas.* 3rd ed. Chicago: Crain Books, 1975.

INDEX

ABOUT THE
AUTHORS

SHIRLEY F. MILTON and ARTHUR A. WINTERS have a combined total of over fifty years experience in advertising: creative services, including copywriting; account supervision; and administration of their own agencies. Professor Milton went from her own agency in Los Angeles to a vice-presidency in a Madison Avenue agency. Dr. Winters has operated his advertising agency in New York under his own name. In these years and in these capacities, their experience has brought them into active participation in retail, industrial, and fashion advertising. From running sales meetings to handling copy, layout, graphics, and production; they have serviced clients in food and liquor accounts, heavy industrials, electronics, hotels, packaged goods, as well as a good share of fashion at every marketing level. Both are currently active as consultants in marketing communications.

Professor Milton is presently on the faculty of the Fashion Institute of Technology, State University of New York; has lectured on advertising copy, publicity, media, and sales promotion; and has written textbooks on advertising. She has an AB from Cornell University, an MA from New York University, and an MS from Fordham University. She is a member of Phi Beta Kappa and of Eta Mu Pi, honorary societies.

Dr. Winters is presently Chairman of the Advertising and Communications Department of the Fashion Institute of Technology. He has written several textbooks in these fields and has lectured and consulted in advertising, copy, layout and graphics, public relations, and promotion. He has a BA from Williams College, an MBA from Pace University, and a Doctorate in Education from Temple University. He is a member of Epsilon Delta Epsilon, honorary society of marketing educators.

JOSEPH GIANO is an art director and photographer who has developed original graphics and visual concepts for a large variety of print and broadcast media. He is a proponent of the "vizthinks process" which was developed in his longtime professional association with Dr. Winters.